Praise for *Beyon*

"Beyond Gold *will be a treasured resource for families of wealth. Thayer artfully combines stories, insightful commentary, thought-provoking questions, and practical action steps to guide the reader through a maze of thorny issues. She knows the territory well, and draws freely from her own experience and that of her clients.*"

— **Hartley Goldstone**, Founder, Navigating the Trustscape

"Thayer, in a veritable tome of best practices, shines a floodlight on how to promote wholeness and healthy change in families. She teaches beyond that which has been revealed before, by integrating family systems theory with what works with families of wealth. Her breadth of knowledge comingles with her practical approach and experience, to show us how to tap a family's inner resources for positive change. Beyond Gold *not only provides deep insight and education for those of us helping families, but is a riveting read to the end.*

— **Valerie Maxwell, PhD**, Founder, The Learning Gym

"Thayer gives us a book that speaks to the influence of wealth on the critical relationships in our lives. She brings a magnifying glass to the impact that wealth has on a variety of familial, personal, and professional relationships, while bringing practical exercises and insights on how to transform them."

"Whether you earned it, inherited or gained it in a settlement or windfall, Thayer's book provides life-changing insights to the influence of wealth on relationships. A must read for those who care deeply about the impact of wealth on relationships and how to make them generative."

— **Kirby Rosplock, PhD**, family business co-owner and director, GenSpring Family Offices

"There can be many pitfalls to being wealthy, but whether you are a wealthy person or an advisor to wealthy people, this book provides a life map for finding (and staying on) the bright side of wealth. Thayer Willis has shared exercises and experiences from her own practice in this book which brings her unique and compelling insights to a broader audience. She provides a balanced look at wealth: examining the financial and non financial assets that wealth can bring to a person or family. This is a must read book for anyone who is or will become wealthy, as well as advisors who work with wealthy people or families."

— **Karen Vinton, PhD**, Vinton Consulting Services

"I appreciate the effective approach Thayer has taken in this book by organizing the chapters by different relationships. In a succinct manner each of the chapters focuses on a specific relationship. She provides many ideas and solutions that are based on factual research and many years of real life experiences. Thayer is providing insights that WILL save or improve the relationships within the affluent and wealthy community."

— **Marvin J. Schmidt**, First Vice President, CIBC Wood Gundy; Senior Investment Advisor, The Schmidt Investment Group, Canada

Beyond Gold

Beyond Gold

True Wealth for Inheritors

Thayer Cheatham Willis

New Concord Press
Portland, Oregon

New Concord Press

Editors: Lionel Fisher; Ali McCart
Design: Martha Gannett
Composition: William H. Brunson Typography Services
Printing: Premier Press, Inc.

Printed in the United States of America

New Concord Press LLC
P. O. Box 3825
Portland, Oregon 97208-3825

Library of Congress Control Number 2012918358
ISBN 978-0-9725494-2-4

For all of my clients, past and present,
from whom I have learned so much.

Contents

Foreword

Know thyself.

—Delphic Inscription

Relationships. Do they help us meet the Greek admonition to know ourselves and the freedom of self and spirit that follows, or do they lead to conflict, anger, fear, and all the other illusions that cloud our ability to know ourselves, and the loss of freedom of self and spirit that follows? This is the deep question Thayer Willis asks us in the book you are about to read.

Some years ago, Thayer sought to bring into our consciousness the reality that financial wealth does not often bring with it happiness. Through exploring her own life experiences and those of her clients, she purposefully led us on a voyage through the shadow, or dark side, of financial wealth in the book *Navigating the Dark Side of Wealth.* Now, again using messages from her own life and those of her clients, she shows us the bright side of wealth; she takes us to the light.

I found this journey to be similar to that in Dante's great poem, *The Divine Comedy*. First we must understand our personal journey through the shadow of the Inferno. Then we can know the path to the light that begins with Purgatorio and ascends to Paradiso.

Thayer helps us, through a series of mindful questionnaires, to deconstruct our understanding of our core relationships, which can be especially complicated by substantial financial wealth. Then she guides us in reconstructing them to their potential for much higher functioning. Her process covers our relationships with our parents, siblings, extended families, friends, life partners, children, and professional relationships. She seeks to help us enhance each of these relationships with higher knowledge of ourselves, allowing us to be better partners in each relationship.

Thayer uses the concept that we and our families have four capitals to utilize toward our well-being: human, intellectual, financial, and social. She further asks us to acknowledge that we also have access to a fifth capital: spiritual. Her appreciation of how vast a family's capital is—far beyond its financial resources—represents a gift to those families who seek to thrive.

Her further insight that a family's human, intellectual, and spiritual capitals are its most valuable assets is deeply right. With Thayer's guidance, we gain the awareness not only that a family's true wealth lies within its members but also that the state of familial relationships can be a diagnostic tool for improving a family's well-being.

I know that the journey you are about to take will carry you, as you answer Thayer's questions, to much higher orders of relationship. Why? Because I have taken the same journey, and it has enhanced mine.

Thank you, Thayer.

Namaste.
James (Jay) E. Hughes Jr.
Aspen, Colorado, June 2012

Preface

TAKE A MOMENT RIGHT NOW TO VISUALIZE your family at its best, what you could have if relationships were strong and positive. It is possible . . . read on.

Beyond Gold: True Wealth for Inheritors, is a practical guide for handling relationships affected by the privileges and challenges of wealth. It is full of written exercises and activities, which will help you do much of the work of improving your life—on your own. My greatest purpose in writing this book is to give you hope. Hope, skills, and better relationships.

When I first thought of this focus for my work many years ago, I was inspired by my personal experiences. I had been reflecting on how I could have struggled so much in my life. It was clear that many outsiders assumed that because I grew up in a wealthy family, the founding family of Georgia-Pacific, my life must be easy and I certainly must be happy. However, financial wealth does not automatically equate to ease and happiness. I have been there, perplexed by this question.

Several of my peers from Dunthorpe, the beautiful, idyllic neighborhood in Portland where I grew up in the 1950s and 1960s, had tragically lost their lives to addictions and "accidents." Somehow, in 1985, when the young man next door to my family's home shot himself, it tipped the scale for me. This was the fifth such loss I was aware of in a neighborhood where I knew others saw nothing but privilege. I scoured the library and found *nothing* written about these challenges. So I deduced that it must be me who was supposed to figure out how to develop the expertise to help people like the kids I knew growing up. I needed relevant credentials, so I enrolled in Portland State University's Master's in Social Work program, studied family systems theory and practice, and secured a degree and then a license in clinical social work. I began to learn how to manage the wealth/happiness equation. Our relationships are at the center of it.

A very long time ago, in my twenties, I began to envision dreams for my life. The biggest and strongest by far was my dream of a loving relationship with a husband and children. This was a tough dream for me to realize, and I failed over and over in relationships, including three short marriages. I just could not get this dream out of the starting gate. Then, in my late thirties, I met the amazing man who would be the one—the one with whom I could have a real and loving marriage, and with whom I could have children. It is now twenty-five years later, and I am grateful daily for this dream come true. This is not to say that our marriage is perfect or even easy, but it is very good.

My other big dream was to do purposeful work. I helped people through eating disorders, and it was rewarding. But after ten years, I felt called to develop the work I do now: helping individuals and families create freedom beyond wealth. Since 1985, when I first thought of this focus, it has been an amazing journey. Though I started as a pioneer, feeling like I was inventing the field, I now have colleagues. As I have gotten to know others with a similar focus for their work, I understand that many of them felt they were pioneers too.

Nevertheless, when I wrote my first book, *Navigating the Dark Side of Wealth*, my goal was to organize everything I had learned about the challenges of wealth and write an inspiring guide to making life better. The book has served its purpose well and still attracts many readers, for which I am grateful.

Inheritance issues are the common denominator among my clients, and I have explored them in depth. Sometimes I work with successful entrepreneurs who were raised in very different circumstances than their children are now experiencing and they are concerned about the effects that financial wealth could have on their young family members. Other clients are fourth-, fifth-, or sixth-generation inheritors, well versed in the challenges of wealth. Some families have the added dimension of Christianity, Judaism, or another faith to draw them together, while others have found a variety of lifestyles and beliefs. Regardless of the many forms that family challenges can take, the ones I always scout for are those related to inheritance and its many facets.

My clients all have inner resources that they can tap for their own benefit and the benefit of their families. I'll share some of their stories with you. Their names and personal details have been fictionalized to afford them privacy, but they will help you gain perspective on your own situation. Sometimes emotions such as fear, anger, and pride get in the way of these inner resources. If so, these emotions must be addressed first. Then the work of building inner strength and constructing relationships begins.

I find it heartwarming to see cold, cutoff relationships heal as families begin to have the closeness they had only dreamed of. Almost all families can build better relationships. You may think yours is an exception, but I would challenge this. You'll be amazed at how a fresh approach can bring out strength and how tender feelings emerge when family members begin to have hope.

Introduction

What we believe becomes who we are.

—Catherine Pulsifer

Above all, I believe in family.

"There is no doubt," affirmed Winston Churchill, "that it is around the family and the home that all the greatest virtues, the most dominating virtues of human society, are created, strengthened, and maintained."

I, too, believe there is no greater social service we can provide to our country, to ourselves, to mankind as a whole, than to raise a family well.

Mother Teresa put it this way: "It is easy to love the people far away. It is not always easy to love those close to us. It is easier to give a cup of rice to relieve hunger than to relieve the loneliness and pain of someone unloved in our own home. Bring love into your home, for this is where our love for each other must start."

My Mission, Our Journey

In my workshops, presentations, and counseling, I reveal a bit about myself—who I am, what I stand for, my passion, and my mission in life—so that others have a preview of the journey I offer.

Inevitably, I bring to light my core principles, all twelve of which I describe here and present as lists in chapters one and twelve. For now, at the outset of our journey on the bright side of wealth, I'd like to introduce you to these core beliefs, since they guide me in all of my work.

First and foremost, I believe people in families want to get along. This will seem obvious to some, but many times in strained or cutoff relationships, family members work themselves into stand-offs in which they convince everyone, including themselves, that they don't care anymore or that reconciliation is impossible.

In these situations, pride usually enters the picture and holds family members captive in their stand-offs. This first principle is that these isolated family members would rather have some kind of a functioning relationship, regardless of how far-fetched or impossible that looks. I do not ask them about this or bring it up in any conscious way. I just know it, and I work for it quietly. You can too.

At their best, families want to nurture, cherish, and value one another. Families want to live in harmony, peace, and joy. We each want to take charge of our lives and experience the resulting freedom and happiness. Parents want their children to be happy.

Everyone's definition of happiness is highly personal. Your children's ideas of happiness are possibly so different from your own that you can barely fathom the treasures they hold dear. It's important, therefore, that we work hard to understand and acknowledge the things we can't change in order to focus on the things we can change, remembering at all times that the key to effecting change in others lies in our willingness to initiate change in ourselves.

Isolated family members do indeed suffer greatly. In truth, I firmly believe, they would rather have *some* sort of functioning relationship than total separation, regardless of how polite or tenuous the connection might be.

"Family," explain Doc Childre and Howard Martin, "provides necessary security and support, and acts as a buffer against external problems. A family made up of secure people generates a magnetic power that can get things done."

I also firmly believe that—barring the debilitating influence of addictions or abuse—family ties are important. When this vital cord is severed, it is at an impossibly high cost to everyone involved, adults and children alike, for when families come apart, like Humpty Dumpty they often can't be put together again.

It is important for each of us to consider the entire scope of our lives: our physical, intellectual, spiritual, and emotional realities, and take care of ourselves on all fronts. Financial assets certainly have a place in this equation, though it is a secondary place, and they are best viewed as a support to the less tangible assets.

Goals regarding our well-being, our families, and our relationships need to be expressed in a positive way, not negative. Anyone who has ever set goals with me knows that I will weed out any negativity and insist that the idea be expressed as a positive. Sometimes explorations veer into the dark side, the negative. They just need to be directed into the bright side at some point. Challenges need to be rewritten as opportunities. This is admittedly difficult at times, but it can be done.

Every accomplishment begins with the decision, the resolve, *to make better choices*—for negativity is primarily staying stuck, or worse. If a sibling clings to a conviction that he and his brother, for example, have irreconcilable differences—and he persists in attempting to prove his brother wrong on particular issues—I guide him in finding just one thing he and his sibling *do* agree on, regardless of how small or seemingly inconsequential that bit of common ground may be.

Therein lies the constructive start—the all-important shift from negative to positive at the very outset of the journey. This can turn challenges into opportunities.

Closely related to the first principle, that people in families *want* to get along, is that people want to be able to forgive. Forgiveness is the single most powerful tool any of us has. Failure to forgive can be the result of pride and crystallization of perspective.

For many, forgiveness is not possible as a starting point. There is sometimes a tremendous amount of work to be done before we can approach such a crossing without bringing out the heavy artillery. Forgiveness is for the one who forgives. It is the forgiver who benefits. Yet, usually, we have to work up to the courageous act of forgiveness, and rework it afterward as well.

The third principle is based on the idea that a deep commitment to your spiritual practice becomes security in life. I encourage everyone to give spiritual practice priority because this gives the greatest meaning to life and ultimately leads to security. Throughout this book, I refer to the Christian God, because this is my spiritual commitment. Your practice and the god you know are your private domain. What is important is the fact that you nurture your spirituality. Replace the language that I use with whatever speaks true to you.

Another powerful principle I strongly believe in is gratitude. "Gratitude unlocks the fullness of life," sums up Melody Beattie, counting the ways: "It turns what we have into enough, and more. . . . It turns denial into acceptance, chaos into order, confusion into clarity. It turns problems into gifts, failures into success, the unexpected into perfect timing, and mistakes into important events. Gratitude makes sense of our past, brings peace for today, and creates a vision for tomorrow."

Our gratitude is most powerful when it is shown, however. We need to display it—evidence it—if not in words, then in palpable actions and deeds. "Feeling gratitude and not expressing it is like wrapping a present and not giving it," agrees William Arthur Ward.

Still, for many of us, gratitude seems like a minor virtue—small, humble, insignificant. But therein lies the irony, for gratitude has the power to literally transform a life. Sometimes it still seems like such a stretch, even impossible, to express our thanks without experiencing contradictory feelings of resentment or depression.

Yet this is precisely when gratitude can buoy us immensely—when it can benefit us the most—for the harder the task, the greater the potential reward for shouldering it. We know what we need to do.

At the same time, uncertainty over how we actually feel in our personal relationships is a smokescreen. “I don’t know” is a response I find unacceptable when it comes to one’s attitudes or behaviors. The truth is we do know why we do what we do. We *do* know how we feel about the people we love. It may take digging deeply to find the answers, to understand our true feelings, but they are there to be found.

And when we identify and acknowledge our true feelings, we have something valuable to work with. With certainty in our hearts—like armor that safeguards, emboldens, and empowers us on our journey—the way forward seems surer, lighter, brighter.

I also believe that every single one of us needs meaningful work in our lives as much as we need the sun to rise every day. “Far and away the best prize that life offers is the chance to work hard at work worth doing” is how Teddy Roosevelt put it.

“I don’t pity any man who does hard work worth doing,” Roosevelt added. “I admire him. I pity the creature who doesn’t work, at whichever end of the social scale he may regard himself as being.”

The painful reality, however, is that many inheritors don’t understand that meaningful, self-affirming work is available to them, and many need help finding their way in this regard. We all have a deep, undeniable yearning for the grace that productive, worthwhile endeavors provide. And so I explore this path to self-fulfillment, whenever possible, with every client I work with, for I find fulfilling work is one of our greatest sources of happiness, bar none.

What’s more, when ennobling work is done in the service of others, the payback to self is immeasurably enhanced. As baseball immortal Jackie Robinson demonstrated with his unflinching work ethic against daunting resistance, “A life isn’t significant except for its impact on other lives.”

There’s a glorious secret about helping others, famously expressed by Flora Edwards. “In helping others,” assured the South Africa-born industrialist author, “we shall help ourselves, for whatever good we give out completes the circle and comes back to us.”

It took me many years to begin encouraging clients of the magnificent benefits of kindness and compassion to others, but I do it now wholeheartedly because I know, without a doubt, that by helping others, they will help themselves in immensely rewarding ways.

Above all, find your passion, follow your star. “Do what you love,” in the oft-quoted words of educator-author Marsha Sinetar, “the money will follow.”

For some, the money won’t matter at all.

Best of all, as Steve Jobs of Apple fame assured the Stanford graduates he addressed in his moving commencement speech of June 2005, doing what you love will get you through. “Sometimes life’s going to hit you in the head with a brick,” said Jobs of his firing by Apple, the very company he created. “Don’t lose faith,” he exhorted the Stanford graduates.

"I'm convinced that the only thing that kept me going was that I loved what I did. You've got to find what you love, and that is as true for work as it is for your lovers. Your work is going to fill a large part of your life, and the only way to be truly satisfied is to do what you believe is great work, and the only way to do great work is to love what you do," stressed Jobs.

"If you haven't found it yet, keep looking, and don't settle. As with all matters of the heart, you'll know when you find it, and like any great relationship, it just gets better and better as the years roll on. So keep looking. Don't settle."

Keep your dreams alive. Don't settle.

I've also found that people I call thirsty horses are those who are motivated to improve their lives and achieve happiness. The term *solution-focused* applies to thirsty horses, for it characterizes their keen drive to achieve the freedom and self-actualization they so passionately seek.

In achieving these personal goals, "nothing in this world can take the place of persistence," claimed Calvin Coolidge: "Talent will not; nothing is more common than unsuccessful [people] with talent. Genius will not; unrewarded genius is almost a proverb. Education will not; the world is full of educated derelicts. Persistence and determination alone are omnipotent. The slogan 'press on' has solved and always will solve the problems of the human race."

Keep in mind, however, that achieving goals isn't nearly as important as setting them to begin with. "It must be borne in mind that the tragedy of life doesn't lie in not reaching your goal," said Benjamin E. Mays. "The tragedy of life lies in having no goal to reach."

Each person has a unique story about everything that has happened in his or her life, and this story is to be respected. It can be delved into, challenged, possibly even reconsidered. But it is that person's story, and for that person, it is true. I accept that.

What's more, according to *Wealth in Families* author Charles W. Collier, family stories are essential to the well-being of a family: "They provide a view of the family's history and send a message to the children, in-laws, and grandchildren that they belong and that their family is unique." Through these stories, notes Collier, "The next generation gains a sense of the vital 'differences' of their family.

"Moreover, one reason for the proverb 'shirtsleeves-to-shirtsleeves in three generations' being true," adds Collier, "is that the individuals in the third and fourth generations often have no connection to the source of their family's financial wealth. They have no idea what it took to create the money they now must steward. Family stories keep that connection alive for many generations."

These, then, are the core principles and beliefs that form the backdrop of my work. They are the structure, the conviction, the strength derived from the experiences, wisdom, love, and grace bestowed on me by my family, and in more recent years, by my clients as well.

As I said at the very beginning, family is everything to me. For me, my family reflects the personal values, faith, insights, awareness, and beliefs that have clarified over many years of interacting with them. In gratitude, I would like to pass what I have learned along to you now.

Let's begin our journey on the bright side together.

Thayer Cheatham Willis

What Money Can't Buy
The Real Goal of Wealth

He is rich or poor according to what he is, not according to what he has.
—Henry Ward Beecher

Wealth is the ability to fully experience life.
—Henry David Thoreau

True wealth is of the heart, not of the purse.
—Pathros

WHAT IF YOU WALKED INTO A STORE that contained everything your heart desired?

What if you were then told, "Your money's no good here. What you yearn to possess is going to take more than your wealth to acquire."

"Unthinkable," might be your incredulous reply. "Name one thing my money can't buy."

Well, I can come up with a whole bunch of things money can't buy—not even great wealth if you possess it.

We all know, of course, about the things money can buy. What it can't buy is something else all together. That's what I'd like to talk to you about in this book—how to acquire those precious things your money can't buy.

First, let me ask you: What does wealth represent to you? It's a simple enough question, don't you think? Or is it? Okay, I'll put it another way: Exactly how do you define wealth?

Most people see their wealth strictly as financial capital or physical property and material possessions—nothing more, nothing less—even though we know intuitively that money is much more than that to most of us.

How much money, then, do people need to consider themselves wealthy? It's a question to which I have only one answer. This may sound evasive, but it's the best one I can come up with: it's all relative.

Some people define wealth as possessing more money than other specific individuals, say their brother-in-law. Or enough to keep ahead of the Joneses. Or enough money, period—enough in the truest sense of the word, meaning you really do have all you need and aren't concerned with getting any more. Well, maybe enough with a little left over.

In short, what represents a fortune to one person may be peanuts to another, and when you consider qualities of wealth beyond the financial, definitions can really go topsy-turvy. What is satisfactory to one may be woefully inadequate to another. Nowhere is it written just how much of anything qualifies as wealth.

As I said, it's all relative.

The Opportunity to Flourish

Jenna is the sole heir to a highly successful and popular resort chain. A child of divorce, minimal supervision, and maximum funds available for play, she didn't see any need for education beyond high school, and she had a wild streak a mile wide.

The CEO of the family business contacted me because he and the other officers in the company were deeply concerned about the future of the business. Jenna was only thirty-three but had been wreaking havoc in the business for several years. The board members were especially concerned because the way the succession planning in her family had been developed decades ago, Jenna had every right to take charge of the business on her thirty-fifth birthday. She made it clear that she intended to do so. Though she showed up for meetings at times and was capable of being well spoken, this was the exception for her rather than the norm.

Jenna had not mastered the responsibility that is included in the privilege of wealth. In fact, none of the company executives saw any sign that she was interested in mastering responsibility at all. Jenna preferred to devote her time to racing motorcycles in the far corners of the earth. For her, money was no object, and she spent it freely. She was attractive and had already had affairs within the business, which had destroyed families. She claimed this was not her fault. She took responsibility for very little, even a child she had as a result of one of her trysts.

Sadly, Jenna was pursuing happiness in all the wrong places. Clearly she felt it was her right to do what she felt like doing, but ironically, this practice would backfire on her. She was yet to learn what money can't buy. The definition of wealth for Jenna, when I met her team of executives, would no doubt have been a quick, breezy answer about money. And asking her to answer the question, What does wealth represent to you? would certainly require her to explore uncharted territory.

As it turned out, Jenna wasn't ready to work with me, but I was in her boardroom because those who managed her company saw a train wreck ahead, already being set up by Jenna. Her executives have worked with me to manage their relationships with her and with each other. Stability and perspective are always possible in relationships, even if just in small amounts.

A Question for Inheritors

This is our opening question: What does wealth represent to you? Again, it's all relative. When I ask this question of my clients and presentation audiences, I hear almost as many different answers as there are people in the room, but there are some common threads, especially when it comes to acknowledging that wealth consists of more than tangible assets. Among the qualities I hear most are power, control, responsibility, security, love, freedom, and family.

People have given widely varying views on true wealth over the centuries. "The real measure of your wealth is how much you'd be worth if you lost all of your money," writes an unknown author.

In a Boston College survey of the nation's so-called super-rich, a total of 165 households with an average net worth of $78 million responded to fifteen questions ranging from "How would you describe your current overall goals regarding your wealth?" to "How does your wealth get in the way?" to "Describe the biggest mistake you have made with your wealth so far."[1]

Among the evocative responses on the survey was this comment on envying wealth: "If we can get people just a little bit more informed, so they know that getting the $20 million or $200 million won't necessarily bring them all that they'd hoped for, then maybe they'd concentrate instead on things that could make the world a better place and would help to make them truly happy." One respondent had this caution for other inheritors: "Financial freedom can produce anxiety and hesitancy. In my own life, I have been intimidated about my abilities because I inherited money." On money buying happiness, another remarked, "You just don't get as much happiness per dollar."

In other words, you really can't buy happiness. Nor can your money get you a first-class ticket on the next jet to the bright side of wealth. Your passage from the dark side of wealth to the bright has nothing to do with your wallet and everything to do with your mind, heart, and spirit and how freely you're willing to open them to cross over.

To possess true wealth and not just a financial fortune, we have to be spiritually and morally strong, loyal and true in relationships, passionate for constructive work we enjoy, resolved to ride out tough times, tenacious to achieve difficult goals, and willing to recover from inevitable setbacks. *This* is true wealth.

Challenges Inheritors Face

Whether you have acquired your financial wealth by inheriting it, settling a legal dispute, winning the state lottery, or earning it through work, you are susceptible to inherent temptations such as arrogance, ingratitude, and greed, capable of luring you into dark attitudes and negative, destructive behaviors.

I know a man, Douglas, who, solely because of his father's wealth, views himself as better than others. He is such a snob that he has severely limited his world. It's too bad. If he had worked and made his own mark in life, he would have interacted with a wider range of people and would have no doubt broadened his own outlook. Instead he spends most of his time thinking about his money and living in a world that is essentially very small.

And then there is Jenna, whom you met at the beginning of this chapter. She has fallen prey to many dark attitudes and behaviors. In her chase after the next big thrill, she was destroying friends, family, and the amazingly successful business that her family worked so hard to build. She was leaving a wake of destruction, and who knew if she would ever gain any perspective. She may have thought of herself as free to do whatever she pleased, but to those around her, it looked like the abuse of freedom. Just about everyone she knew was afraid for themselves and for her.

Can Money Buy Freedom?

Most of us are keenly aware of the cornucopia of possessions our money can buy. Constant reminders of this indisputable fact confront us everywhere we turn—enticing ads for luxury cars, exotic vacations, and clothes, always more clothes. The assault by advertisers, media stories, and our own desire to keep up with the Joneses screams, "It is never enough!"—making this reality inescapable. Often, however, we want to believe our money also purchases freedom from worry and fear. We are tempted to think our wealth should assure us peace of mind. Sadly, this is not so, for no amount of money can purchase this kind of freedom. Even though the house you buy—the yacht, the Italian sports car, the corporate jet—may represent ultimate freedom of choice to the non-wealthy, there is more to liberty than simply money.

The more possessions we accumulate, the more accustomed we become to our material acquisitions, the more convinced we are of their indispensability. We come to feel we simply cannot get along without these possessions. We come to believe it would be no less than tragic if we were forced to sacrifice our possessions, and soon we begin to worry about losing them.

What began as sweet freedom's march ends in a prison built with the bricks of worry and fear. In short, if we refuse to take life's complex offerings, if we are not grateful for its myriad gifts, and if we never learn to enjoy our bountiful circumstances, we are not truly free. We all need some amount of money to function in society, but that amount is strictly relative. Freedom, therefore, is in many ways a state of mind. It is an attitude, a choice.

What's more, freedom always has a cost. Janis Joplin sang, "Freedom's just another word for nothin' left to lose." What she was saying is that whether we're forced into letting go of our perceived needs or we choose to let them go, it is the letting go that releases us from our self-generated worry and fear. Letting go rescues us.

Therefore, it is not money that buys our freedom. Our attitude toward money liberates us. And with that freedom, we have access to strong relationships and happiness.

Looking on the Bright Side

With a healthy attitude surrounding wealth, we have access to the many privileges that make up the bright side of wealth: freedom, choices, confidence, a sense of indebtedness and service, love, power, gratitude, a wide doorway to competence, the acceptance of all circumstances with humility and grace, respect for the rules of life, generosity, and most of all, kindness.

Jenna, the wild young woman set to inherit her family's hugely successful business when she turns thirty-five, does have a chance to make it out of the negative behaviors she's been indulging in. This will most likely happen when she hits bottom or loses something very dear to her. Sometimes such losses open the door to a positive, constructive turning point, such as finding religion. She is young, so despite a rough adult journey so far, she can still certainly acquire healthy attitudes toward wealth and people. It's possible; there is hope.

Another family I worked with had developed a truly eclectic mix of members, partly because different branches of the family grew up on different continents, and fierce individuality was a family trait. That same fierce individuality had been an essential factor in the family's wealth creation three generations back. Texas oil was an arena where fortunes were built and lost quickly, and where following a hunch, sometimes against the advice of everyone, could lead to success. By the time I met this extended family, many of them had some very good reasons to want to work together, but skills for this process were thin and some old offenses stood in the way. As a result of clarifying values, exploring identity, hearing and telling family stories, teamwork exercises, and fanning the spark of hope in this family, most relationships took on new depth, renewed closeness, and reinvigorated interest in being a family. The bright side of family became visible to them again after its long absence. Often it takes only one family member to initiate this effort.

Privilege Includes Responsibility

The bright side of financial wealth is the responsibility we know we must accept to gain the empowering value of our freedom. It is the willingness to define freedom beyond wealth. It is the realization that the greatest asset parents can provide young inheritors is a solid foundation for maturity and growth. It is the recognition that reaching adulthood with a solid foundation, however we accomplish this, is essential to taking charge of our lives and building a meaningful life for ourselves. It is the conviction that at this point in our lives, at this juncture in our journey to happiness, it is simply up to us to build the character, integrity, and strengths we value on our own.

Most inheritors have the luxury of time to explore talents and abilities. Ours is the choice to travel, study, find mentors, champion causes, and ultimately discover the best possible ways to help others. With our financial wealth, we can pursue a passion as intensely and as far as we wish, using the pursuit itself to learn many of life's lessons. We can develop insightful vision through our endeavors, using our wealth to energize and enrich our lives. If desired, we can channel our insights into purposeful work and a meaningful career through the privilege of exploration unbounded by the burden to earn.

When we cultivate this healthy attitude to the optimum advantage in all our endeavors, it also reaps the fullest benefit for our families. This book will help you do that.

Core Principles

As we prepare to venture onto this journey into the bright side, I would like to share with you the core principles that form the backdrop for my work advocating for inheritors. I rely on these principles in guiding families toward stronger relationships, in coaching clients as they pursue personal integrity and legacy, and in presenting a new paradigm for happiness to rooms full of seminar attendees. Gathered through insight, awareness, and observation over many years, these principles are based on what I have learned about family members and the dynamics of family relationships—for family is the heart of my life and work. These principles provide the guideposts along our journey toward purpose and spiritual well-being.

1. People in families want to get along.

While this may seem obvious to some, in many strained relationships, family members work themselves into stand-offs in which they convince everyone, including themselves, that they don't care anymore or that reconciliation is impossible. Pride enters the picture. The principle is that these isolated family members would rather have some kind of a functioning relationship, regardless of how impossible that looks. And in my experience working with families, it is often possible to restore these relationships to at least a polite, pleasant relationship.

2. People want to be able to forgive.

Forgiveness is the single most powerful tool any of us has. Failure to forgive can be the result of pride and crystallization of perspective. For many, forgiveness is not possible as a starting point. There is sometimes a tremendous amount of work to be done before forgiveness is possible, but the freedom it offers is worth it. We can't know the freedom forgiveness brings until we begin to forgive others.

3. People want to take charge of their lives and have access to the resulting happiness and freedom.

Each person defines happiness and freedom in a unique way, and it is only possible to help someone take charge by discovering and honoring her unique values and perspective.

4. People want their children to be happy.

Because everyone's definition of happiness is highly personal, our children's definitions of happiness may be so different from our own that we can hardly fathom the treasures they hold dear. It is helpful to acknowledge and understand the things we cannot change—other people—and to then focus on the things we can change. Often a big candidate for change is our own attitude.

5. Positive expression is more effective than negative.

Thoughts, especially goals, are most effective when they are expressed in a positive way. Sometimes explorations veer into the dark side, the negative, and it is possible to direct them into the bright side. Challenges can be rewritten as opportunities. This is admittedly difficult at times, but it can be done. What do you see? "Opportunityisnowhere." Think about it.

6. We know why we do what we do.

When we are questioned about our attitudes and behaviors in relationships, "I don't know" is rarely an acceptable answer. The truth is, we do know why we do what we do. Go after the answer. Then we have something to work with.

7. Gratitude is a powerful attitude.

To some, gratitude seems humble, small, and insignificant, but the irony is that it has the power to transform lives. It is always a stretch to force ourselves to express gratitude where we don't want to do it, but we can turbo charge it by visualizing the gratitude at the same time we utter the words.

8. Wellness is essential.

Physical exercise, nutrition, intellectual stimulation, spiritual development, and financial well-being are just as important as psychological and emotional health in pursuing happiness. Sense of purpose, spiritual practice, relationships, and work are essential components of true wealth. Financial assets can certainly belong in the wealth equation, as long as they do not take on inflated importance.

9. People love meaningful work.

Many people need help even believing that meaningful work is possible. Learning to do meaningful work seems even more out of reach. But it is possible. Explore the options, always thinking, *How can we move this forward?*

10. Helping others is the greatest source of happiness.

One of life's major ironies is that giving—helping others—is far more fulfilling than receiving. Most of us go through a period of thinking that accumulating possessions will make us happy only to find that it isn't as fulfilling as we expected. If we are fortunate, we discover that helping others brings surprising delights. For some people, the value of helping others takes years to learn. For others, this easily becomes part of their spiritual practice.

11. A deep commitment to your spiritual practice becomes security in life.

I encourage everyone to give spiritual practice priority because this gives the greatest meaning to life, and ultimately leads to security. Throughout this book, I refer to the Christian God, because this is my spiritual commitment. Your practice and the god you know are your private domain. What is important is the fact that you nurture your spirituality. Replace the language that I use with whatever speaks true to you.

12. Each person has a unique story about everything in life.

Every person's story is to be respected. It can be delved into, challenged, possibly even reconsidered, but it is his story and for him it is true. Life is more manageable when we accept this about each other.

13. People have to want change.

"Thirsty horses" are those people who are willing to drink from the spring of change to welcome happiness into their lives. I have always liked the term *solution-focused*, and have found that, for a thirsty horse, solutions are not elusive. To gain the most from reading this book or working with me, people must be thirsty horses.

By incorporating these core principles into the work we approach in this book and in our relationships, we supply ourselves with the inspiration, insights, tools, and positive outlooks that will allow us to reshape our attitudes to achieve freedom, happiness, and all the assets promised to us on the bright side of wealth.

Overcoming Your Own Resistance

You may be skeptical, thinking the techniques in this book might work for others but not for you and your family. Many—if not most—people think this way, figuring that an outsider can't possibly fathom the difficulties in their family. The truth is, in the vast majority of cases, people are dead wrong on the assumption that their dysfunctions are too far gone for any redemption. Your difficulties may seem insurmountable, but with the right approach, they can usually be conquered.

Families are a lot like a good breakfast granola: mostly sweet with a few nuts—and every family has them.

"Yes, but . . . you don't know my family," many clients and workshop attendees persist in their doubts. They point out reasons why their family members would not respond positively to the tried-and-true techniques I offer in this book. Some of the most common reasons are the death of someone whom family members have not properly or constructively grieved (sometimes this person was the family "glue"), tough divorces, family secrets, health problems, poor family governance, lack of trust, poor financial literacy, fallout from an economic downturn, and the list goes on.

Most families grapple with these liabilities in messy ways and naturally regroup as well as possible, though there are often lingering hurts. The litmus test of how well your family has developed its human and intellectual capital is how well its members withstand crises when they hit.

You may not be able to heal all wounds or transform every toxic relationship into one of harmony, and you certainly will not fix all the difficult behaviors you see in others, but this book can help you better understand many of the problems plaguing your family. It can help you bring your best self to your interactions with people around you, better align your behavior with your values, and improve your all-important communication skills.

Believing in these healthier ways of relating to others and working to incorporate them into your daily life *will* have a positive effect on family members (including further ripple effect), heal many hurts, and dissolve long-lingering resentments. You have my solemn assurance on this.

"Your family and your love must be cultivated like a garden," confirms Jim Rohn, American entrepreneur, author, and motivational speaker. "Time, effort, and imagination must be summoned constantly to keep any relationship flourishing and growing." After all, the rewards of making this effort are huge—at the very least, you will have the peace of mind that you have done the right thing.

Taking Stock of Ourselves
Defining Our Resource

For a man to conquer himself is the first and noblest of all victories.
—Plato

Never grow a wishbone, daughter, where your backbone ought to be.
—Clementine Paddleford

Knowing yourself is the beginning of all wisdom.
—Aristotle

"Know thyself? If I knew myself, I would run away," Johann Wolfgang von Goethe is said to have remarked upon viewing the Greek maxim inscribed over the entrance to the ancient temple at Delphi. Most of us *would* run away.

For to face ourselves is not only frightening, but it also presents us with a mandate for growth and change. It's a challenge many of us aren't up to and would prefer to avoid at all costs. Yet Socrates so subscribed to the Delphic inscription that he referred to it often in his classic dialogues. Certainly, this timeless rallying cry for self-knowledge has become an essential prologue to personal fulfillment.

Most of us know we're running away from ourselves, but we have no idea how to go about finding a suitable replacement. No matter. The truth is, each of us has received the only clay God will ever give us to fashion the paragon of virtue and success we hope to become. The only person we'll ever get to work with is the one staring back at us in the mirror, so we may as well get busy.

There's a tongue-in-cheek prayer that pleads, "God, let me be the person my dog thinks I am." A commendable goal, but it isn't enough. "Don't accept your dog's admiration as conclusive evidence that you're wonderful," cautions advice columnist Ann Landers. You have to know it yourself.

Carl Jung ardently agrees: "Your vision will become clear only when you can look into your own heart. Who looks outside, dreams; who looks inside, awakes."

True Sources of Success

Laura came to me focused on her relationship with her boyfriend of the past three years and convinced that this relationship was where she needed serious help. As we began, it became evident to me that her relationships with her ten-year-old son, her ex-husband, her employees, and her parents were all troubled too—virtually all of her relationships. So it was easy to see that her therapy work needed to be deeper and more fundamental than a focus on one particular relationship would imply.

In Laura's divorce, she had received a substantial legal settlement, over $300 million. And though she had worked in an arena where financial wealth is common—she had been responsible for large sums of money in her work—until five years before, she had never had this kind of wealth of her own. She liked to think of herself as the same young woman who had grown up middle class with good parents and a normal brother, Ken, but the rest of the world didn't see her this way.

She was pursued by development professionals looking for funding, she was envied by friends and acquaintances, and she often found herself exalted on a pedestal. All of this resulted in a pervasive feeling of awkwardness for Laura. Despite having established a charitable foundation and being inspired by work she found meaningful, she really didn't know where she fit in the world. Mostly she just felt awkward.

So our work needed to begin with Laura's awareness of herself, her identification of values, and her acceptance of her identity as a wealthy person. Though she hesitated when she realized the enormity of the work, she bravely chose to head into it. We took it in manageable steps, and her life has taken shape in interesting and substantial ways. As Laura became more centered in who she is, all of her relationships improved, some without much effort.

Taking Stock

Therapists have found that until a client can name a problem or issue, he cannot work to change it. One of the dynamics that leads people like Laura into therapy is the nagging feeling that there is something wrong and, along with it, the inability to see it clearly. They only catch glimpses. One of the most basic functions of the therapist is to create a focus in which the client can explore the issue and find out exactly what about it is troubling. Once the issue is articulated, then there is something to work with. There are several tools in this chapter to help you identify the problem or issue where you need to work, and this, as always, is the place to start.

The journey of transforming wealth into an asset in your many relationships—rather than the liability it can sometimes feel like—begins by getting to know yourself better and clarifying your relationship with wealth. Let's start by taking stock of ourselves. The material in this chapter will help you identify your nonfinancial assets and liabilities along with the assumptions, beliefs, prejudices, and values that compose your private persona and public identity. What's more, you'll have begun the ambitious task of defining your true sources of success and happiness.

In every relationship, we encounter many obstacles, not the least of which is our inability to see ourselves and our situations objectively. For many people, denial is a powerful obstacle, "a common tactic," in Charles Tremper's words, "that substitutes deliberate ignorance for thoughtful planning." This chapter provides tools to slice through the jungle of self-delusion that prevents us from navigating the dark attitudes and behaviors that often erode relationships, self-esteem, and happiness—which, by the way, tempt us all. From this awareness, we can make our way to positive attitudes and healthy relationships.

When I begin my work with each client, I give her an assessment of the attitudes she is bringing to her work with me. It's a good place for you to start as well. The Wealth Attitude Assessment in Exercise 2.1 will help you assess your assumptions about yourself and your money.

---

e
2.1

EXERCISE 2.1

Wealth Attitude Assessment I

Today's date ______________________

Please rate, on a scale of 1 to 5, how true each belief is to you at this moment.

1: *Never/Disagree* **2:** *Rarely* **3:** *Sometimes* **4:** *Usually* **5:** *Always/Agree*

_____ 1. When I think about my wealth, I feel guilty.

_____ 2. It's hard to have a sense of my own identity because I feel like I'm living in someone else's shadow.

_____ 3. I feel alienated or isolated from the relationships I would like to have.

continued on next page

_____ 4. I have not yet taken charge of my life or my wealth.

_____ 5. The abundance of choices I have in my life feels like *too* many choices.

_____ 6. It would be hard for me to think of something I did this past week in which I really feel a sense of accomplishment.

_____ 7. I am not happy with my spending practices and habits.

_____ 8. I don't enjoy doing many of the things I feel I should do.

_____ 9. I know that just about anyone would say I have plenty of wealth, but I have trouble achieving a healthy perspective on this.

_____ 10. I am never satisfied with the amount of my wealth.

_____ 11. I know that others envy me, but they can't possibly imagine how troubling, exhausting, overwhelming, and frightening my life feels at times.

_____ 12. Charity is a social or moral obligation to me, something I have not figured out how to enjoy.

_____ 13. Without my inherited wealth, I would be scared and would feel I had lost an important part of my identity.

_____ 14. I am afraid to ask for help for fear of embarrassing my family..

_____ 15. I long to have something of value other than my wealth.

_____ 16. I wish I could live a normal life with a normal job and a normal amount of money so I would not have to deal with my wealth.

_____ **Total Score**

A high total score, 45 and above, on this assessment indicates that you need help with your attitudes and behaviors. A medium score, ranging from 29 to 44, indicates that you can use help though you have worked out some of these important concerns. A low score, 28 and below, is the range of healthy wealth attitudes and behaviors. If you have a low score, congratulations! The work in this book will be much easier for you. Continue reading to gain insight on your life journey and those of your family members and friends.

At the end of the book, I will ask you to reassess your wealth attitudes to see how the discussions and exercises here have caused you to shift your beliefs in these areas. You may be surprised at how your assumptions shift over time when you consider new perspectives.

Your Psychology in Financial Terms

When my daughter was only eight years old, in my eagerness to begin nurturing her financial literacy, I asked an investment manager friend, Michelle Rand, to teach her some basic concepts and help her choose a small investment. Michelle began by talking about the most basic definitions of financial terms. As she described them in terms for a child, they were clear and easy to grasp.

She began with capital, defining it as wealth in the form of cash or cash equivalents. Though capital can be a cash instrument like a bond, it is usually liquid and available to invest or spend. She told her about assets, which are similar to capital in that they have value in the marketplace. Assets are more commonly in some form other than cash, such as stocks, bonds, or real estate. Michelle also told her that equity is what you actually own in any context. So if you own shares of a company in the form of stock, though there are a lot of shareholders, the shares that *you* own are your equity. In another example, if you have a mortgage on a house, the part of your house that is paid for is your equity. The part of the total value of the house that you still owe is your debt, or liability. Any debt you are responsible for is a liability for you.

These financial terms can also be used to describe capital in our lives in a broader psychological sense, and this kind of capital may be a new concept in your family. Beyond financial capital, other assets on the bright side of the wealth ledger include human, intellectual, and social capital:

- ***Human capital*** encompasses our talents, which are enhanced by education, parenting, values, and spirituality.

- ***Intellectual capital***, which is also enhanced by education, reflects how family members learn and communicate as well as how families make decisions together, create family governance, support family members in seeking and/or giving mentorship, and make career choices.

- ***Social capital***—how family members interact with the community or communities that they are a part of—includes community service, philanthropy, and foundation work.

- ***Financial capital*** is the property of the family, all the financial assets and instruments of the family, including partnerships and trusts.[1]

All four forms of capital are important, of course, and many families have elements of each type. Say you have a family business and someone decides to work somewhere else.

When he returns, he brings back skills and knowledge that he has learned in the outside world, adding to the family's human capital. When other family members become professionals or experts, they are enhancing the family's intellectual capital. When your relatives interact with the community or are philanthropic, they build the family's social capital. We all have equity, capital, and assets in our families. It is affirming to specifically identify these qualities and thus build our awareness of them.

We all have liabilities in our families too. These threaten to take away the equity, capital, and assets. Some common liabilities are death, divorce, secrets, inability to maintain health, poor trust relationships, inflation, taxes, and poor financial education.

It's important to look at how we can cultivate and harness the assets we have in our work and in our families. Such nurturing leads to the sweetest prize of financial wealth—strength—and helps ward off the liabilities that threaten to take that wealth away.

While financial professionals use percentages, graphs, and charts to discuss measurements of capital, we measure family capital slightly differently. These measures are qualitative and revealed in the answers to questions such as: Did my daughter and her husband work out their differences and stay married? Are my sisters speaking to each other again after their perceived unequal treatment by our parents? Has my son taken charge of his life? Is my wife successfully pursuing happiness? Do I understand how the bright side attitudes and behaviors in Figure 2.2 reflect and reinforce the best of my family values, relationships, and ideals? Do I see how my dark side attitudes and behaviors might well erode my positive values, relationships, and ideals?

The following chart lists some attributes that can be found on the dark and bright sides of wealth and how they manifest in our attitudes, behaviors, and relationships. On the bright side, think "assets," and on the dark side, think "liabilities."

2.2 Figure 2.2

Comparing the Dark and Bright Sides of Wealth

The Dark Side of Wealth	The Bright Side of Wealth
	Attitudes
Low self-esteem, insecurity, self-doubt	Confidence, competence
Entrapment	Freedom
Arrogance	Humility
Entitlement	Acceptance of all circumstances with grace
Thinking the rules are for others	Respecting the rules

Ingratitude	Gratitude
Greed	Generosity
Anger	Kindness

Behaviors

Denial	Taking charge
Spending heedlessly	Spending appropriately
Avoiding a saving plan	Following a saving plan
Gambling	Investing competently
Compulsive giving	Purpose-driven philanthropy
Debt accrual	Staying out of debt

Liabilities	***Assets***
Neglect of human, intellectual, financial, and social capital	Strong human, intellectual, financial, and social capital
Poor family governance	Effective family governance
Poor health maintenance	Physical health
No mission statement	Personal mission statements written by each family member Family mission statement
Lack of financial education	Financial education
Poor communication	Strong communication skills
Unhealthy trust relationships	Strong trust relationships
Inflation	Team of excellent professionals to work with
Taxes	
Death	
Divorce	
Secrets	

Shareholder Equity Evaluation Questions[2]

Have individual family members taken charge of their lives?

Are individual family members successfully pursuing happiness?

Are family strengths evident?

Is human, intellectual, and social capital increasing?

Is the family's capital stronger than its liabilities?

Nonfinancial assets and liabilities can affect our relationship with ourselves as well as those with our family members and friends. Likewise, the various forms of capital—human, intellectual, social, and financial—play a large part in our personal and family happiness.

When evaluating your family's shareholder equity, remember to focus on the strengths as well as the weaknesses in each type of capital. Who in your family has taken charge of his own life and exemplifies his values consistently? What can other family members learn from this example of human capital? Do you have a particular family member who is a good communicator and adds intellectual capital by facilitating joint decision making? How does your social capital include philanthropy? Does your family have a foundation, or do you do community service together?

When Laura, whom you met at the beginning of this chapter, gathered the courage to do the work of finding out who she was, she found that she had allowed her once-healthy character to become buried during a marriage that challenged her financial identity. As she explored her relationships with her parents and brother, Ken, she found that they had all grown and matured and that her father, in particular, was now a source of wisdom she had not realized. He not only understood her marriage and divorce, he helped her gain perspective on it and be kinder and more forgiving toward herself and her ex. Ken had matured in his profession, law, and was a resource for the entire family in understanding how different legal choices could play out. He sometimes brought up concerns no one had thought of, and the ensuing discussions revived closeness in the family. Laura, her family of origin, and her son all benefited from these connections. Though Laura emerged into the bright side gradually, she found that life was full of resources and promise after all. This was her reward for working through troubling attitudes and emotions.

When you write the answers on the following chart, you may be surprised to see the many types of capital your family possesses. They can all increase the family's strength, build its positive reputation in the community, and even inspire others to achieve more.

2.3 Exercise 2.3

Your Family's Human, Intellectual, Social, and Financial Capital

Regardless of whether you get along with individuals in your family or even like them, take a few moments to write down and appreciate the different types of capital you see in your family.

Human Capital (parenting, values, spirituality):

____

____

____

Intellectual Capital (mentoring, decision making, family governance, career choices):

____

____

____

Social Capital (community service, foundations, philanthropy):

____

____

____

Financial Capital (assets, equity, trusts, partnerships, financial investments):

____

____

____

____

While simply listing these types of capital in your family may not heal or even improve any of your relationships, it will help you define and appreciate the family assets with which you travel this journey. It will help you create freedom beyond financial wealth.

Nonfinancial Assets and Liabilities

Focus on the nonfinancial assets and liabilities that you inherited from your parents. Every family has liabilities. Some of them are unavoidable: death, some instances of poor health, and taxes, to name a few. These liabilities can erode your strengths: your family's human, intellectual, social, and financial capital. The extent to which we strengthen ourselves before the liabilities hit is very much to our advantage. As we build awareness and strength, usually the by-product is readiness for the liabilities that will inevitably come. Readiness reduces risk.

2.4 EXERCISE 2.4

Identify Your Family's Assets and Liabilities

Turn back to Figure 2.2, Comparing the Dark and Bright Sides of Wealth, to complete this exercise.

1. **Circle** all the dark and bright attitudes and behaviors that you honestly believe describe you. Did you find more on the bright side or the dark side?
2. **Underline** dark and bright attitudes others have told you that you have, even if you disagree. Consider for a moment the possibility that you do tend to exhibit some of these negative attitudes and behaviors. How might you begin to transform yourself or your life to turn these negatives into positives? How might you embrace or even strengthen the positives?
3. Looking at your family as a group, **draw a box** around the assets and liabilities that are most prominent in your family. For example, does your family have more than the national average of divorces (50 percent)? Or do you see that most family members take good care of themselves?

Just as in a business, family shareholder equity can be measured. Exercise 2.5 will help you do that.

2.5 EXERCISE 2.5

Family Shareholder Equity Assessment

On a continuum from zero to one hundred, where would you place individual family members for the first three elements—A, B, and C—of shareholder equity? For instance, place an A on the scale below to mark the degree to which individual family members have taken charge of their life (A1 for you, A2 for your mother, A3 for your father, A4 for a sibling, and so on), and a B to mark how well family members successfully pursue happiness, and on to C, D, and E. You may wish to use the legend to keep track of who your marks represent.

0	25	50	75	100

A. To what extent have individual family members taken charge of their lives?

B. To what extent are individual family members successfully pursuing happiness?

C. How evident are each family member's strengths?

D. To what degree are human, intellectual, financial, and social capital increasing as a result of each family member?

E. To what extent would each family member represent family assets that are stronger than liabilities?

Legend

1. ________
2. ________
3. ________
4. ________
5. ________
6. ________

Some relatives who have not taken charge of their lives may belong near zero while others who manage their lives well would fit closer to one hundred. Many will be somewhere in between. Consider initiating a discussion in your family about how people have taken charge of their lives. When you think about those people who are up near one hundred, what are their characteristics?

When I ask people in my workshops or at family meetings to respond to this, they often make comments like, "They are industrious, competent, self-starters, and motivated." Sometimes they say take-charge people are bright, but intelligence is not a prerequisite for taking charge of one's life. If we were to name an overarching quality of taking charge, perhaps *character* would be it.

The shareholder equity questions will help you assess your family's strengths and weaknesses. Ask each question of yourself—you do know these answers—and find out how well your family is doing.

Especially focus on your family's strengths. In my family, my father's father died when my dad was seven. The death of a parent when children are young typically creates considerable intensity in surviving family members. Among my father and his three brothers, their intensity proved to be a strength in starting from scratch and building a business empire.

I've often wondered how our family history would have been different if my grandfather had lived into old age. Though my father's mother had eight children, her parents lived with her, helping her take care of her children, and she worked as a schoolteacher. Education was a very high value for her. She felt it was no less than a ticket to a better life. In our family, my father's oldest brother paid for the education of all three of his younger brothers.

The result is a family strength that is quite evident in my father's family and a value that continues to this day.

Though you can trace your own values, beliefs, and behaviors to your family, you may have decided to do the opposite of what you experienced in your family. Some of my clients or workshop attendees point out that they have acquired their attitudes or values in opposition to behaviors of other family members.

One client clearly insisted that the reason he made his financial fortune is that he came from poverty. In a memorable statement, a woman told me she focused on having a successful, healthy family to break her family history of alcoholism. It strikes me that this is simply human nature: to go after what we feel we missed. And I certainly see this among my clients. Sometimes their efforts are amplified because of their financial wealth.

Knowing where your attitudes and behaviors—about money, wealth, and other qualities—come from is important. Examining the source may feel difficult and threatening, but you are bound to find both positives and negatives. Some positive family rituals, values, or stories might surface, which you may wish to reinstate for your family.

Once you think about how you benefited from certain relationships when you were young, you may also consider reviving those that were cutoff for some reason. The Intergenerational Questionnaire in Exercise 2.6 presents an opportunity for you to explore your memories, the values in your family, and tough issues you might prefer to forget but you may learn from. You will also revisit qualities such as generosity, kindness, and a sense of humor that you or your family may have let slip away. Your awareness, then, of your own values, where they came from, and the values of family members who preceded you is a big step in our journey together.

2.6 Exercise 2.6

Intergenerational Questionnaire

As you write your answers to these questions, dig deep and be as honest as you possibly can. Share these with someone close to you if you desire. You may certainly keep your answers entirely private if you wish. This exercise is for you to know yourself better.

1. Was money discussed openly in your family when you were a child? Yes ____ No ____
2. Was wealth discussed openly in your family when you were a child? Yes ____ No ____
3. Did your family make any distinction between wealth and money? Yes ____ No ____
4. Were you involved in either wealth or money discussions when you were a child? Yes ____ No ____

5. What messages, direct or indirect, did you receive from your mother regarding money?

6. What stories did she tell you about her childhood (about anything, not just money)?

7. What do you have that's special from your mother?

8. What messages, direct or indirect, did you receive from your grandmothers regarding money?

9. What stories did they tell you about their childhoods (about anything)?

10. What do you have that's special from your grandmothers?

11. What messages, direct or indirect, did you receive from your father regarding money?

12. What stories did he tell you about his childhood (about anything)?

continued on next page

13. What do you have that's special from your father?

____

____

14. What messages, direct or indirect, did you receive from your grandfathers regarding money?

____

____

15. What stories did they tell you about their childhood (about anything)?

____

____

16. What do you have that's special from your grandfathers?

____

____

17. What is your family's greatest strength? What strength can you see through the generations?

____

____

18. Who, among the family members you have known, best exemplifies originality?

____

____

19a. Did you have an allowance when you were a child? Yes ____ No ____

19b. If yes, were you allowed to spend your allowance? Yes ____ No ____

19c. If yes, were you given any guidance on this, and what was the guidance?

____

____

20a. Were you encouraged to give time, talent, or treasure to make the world a better place? Yes ____ No ____

20b. If yes, how were you encouraged?

____

____

21. Who in your family has shown you the value of generosity?

____

____

22. Were you encouraged to save money? Yes ____ No ____

23. Was the message you received about rich people positive ____ or negative ____ ?

24a. Were you allowed to earn money before the age of eighteen? Yes ____ No ____

24b. If yes, were you encouraged to do so? Yes ____ No ____

25. What did you learn from earning money when you were young?

____

____

26. Did you ever have the experience of earning a reward (like a trip or a privilege)? Yes ____ No ____

27. Was your family stoic and self-sufficient, never needing to see a counselor or a consultant? Yes ____ No ____

28a. Was it difficult in your family to ask for help in general? Yes ____ No ____

28b. Financial help? Yes ____ No ____

28c. Emotional help? Yes ____ No ____

29. From whom in your family did you learn kindness?

____

____

30. Did your family talk about emotions? Yes ____ No ____

31. Who in your family has shown you what a great sense of humor is?

____

____

continued on next page

32. Who in your family have you seen exemplify optimism?

____

____

33. Were you raised in a spiritual environment? Yes ____ No ____

34a. Were there any conflicts between your spiritual environment and the money values in your home? Yes ____ No ____

34b. What message did you receive from your parents about this?

____

____

35. Was the attitude of entitlement allowed in your home? Yes ____ No ____

36a. Were you taught gratitude by your parents? Yes ____ No ____

36b. If yes, how?

____

____

37. What has been your greatest joy?

____

____

38. Does your parents' legacy to you include financial assets? Yes ____ No ____

39. What kinds of nonfinancial assets define your parents' legacy to you?

____

____

40. What is the legacy you are creating? For what will you be remembered?

____

____

When you have your answers as complete as possible, you may wish to take a few days to reflect on these questions, as many people find that they remember more over time. You may also wish to discuss your answers with someone close to you, though this is essary. At the very least, your answers and your reactions to these questions will i how you came to be the way you are.

Another way to use this Intergenerational Questionnaire is with your family, one question at a time. At your next family gathering, consider asking everyone question 17: "What is our family's greatest strength? What strength can you see through the generations?" Suggest going around the table or the room so everyone, including children, can answer this question. Another meaningful one to ask is question 37: "What has been your greatest joy?" We think we know what people would say, but we don't. Everyone will be surprised by some of the answers that others come up with. Rarely do families think or talk about these kinds of things. Yet some of these questions are powerful and can build family capital. This questionnaire is a tool to enter the inner world of your family members and bring everyone closer.

If, as you have read so far, you have found that your knowledge of yourself is what is slimmest, then you already have a clear place to focus as you work through this book. Time spent getting to know yourself is tremendously valuable in your journey to the bright side of wealth, and it is the essential first step in building strong, positive relationships.

Perhaps you feel you know yourself well and need to focus on a different relationship. Maybe you have one terribly troubled relationship, you understand a lot about it, and you are ready to do the work necessary to make it better. Bring that relationship to mind before reading on.

Remember, families want to get along, even if relationships have gotten so bad that no one is willing to say so. Recall the power of forgiveness. You may feel entitled to an apology from others, but in reality, to build the kind of relationships you want, you may be the one who needs to apologize. If you're ready to do the work to improve your relationships, you need to also be prepared to do things you don't want to do. Do you really want the kind of relationship legacy you have built? Is it time to be more honest and brave and heal these relationships?

As you read on, I will provide tools for approaching each kind of relationship people typically have—parents, siblings, extended family, friends, spouses, children, and professionals—but first, a look at our relationship with ourselves.

The Journey of Discovery
Who Am I?

You have to leave the city of your comfort and go into the wilderness of your intuition. What you'll discover will be wonderful. What you'll discover is yourself.

—Alan Alda

To the question of your life you are the answer,
and to the problems of your life you are the solution.

—Joe Cordare

Courage is being scared to death—and saddling up anyway.

— John Wayne

First in this journey to the bright side must come the essential voyage of self-discovery—that inner journey to the undiscovered country we call our *self.* Before we can begin to explore our issues and problems with family, friends, colleagues, and everyone else with whom we would like to live and work in peace and harmony, each of us must explore the depths of who we are. We must find, understand, and accept the person who no one but us can truly know in our hearts.

It is a journey we all must take—each in our own time, each in our own way—and for most of us, that time has come, that time is now. It is a journey we can only make alone, despite the guidance and caring of others.

And it's a journey you will know is yours when it comes. "You will recognize your own path when you come upon it," *Moneylove Club* writer Jerry Gillies assures us, "because you will suddenly have all the energy and imagination you will ever need."

But each of us must start by acknowledging that we all have inherited a unique set of personal assets. For some, this includes great intelligence. Some people are given exceptional good looks; others, amazing athletic ability. Some people's assets include substantial financial resources. Every person is unique in the type and quality of the gifts bestowed on him or her. And while some seem to have received more than others—a few much more than their fair share—we all inherit some kind of assets.

In our pursuit of self-realization and happiness, the time has come for us to acknowledge our personal traits and qualities—our precious, if hard-earned, mental, physical, spiritual, and emotional resources.

A Tentative, Tenacious Journey

Patricia is an amazing woman whom I have worked with for many years. She comes from an abusive background, one that few would envision in the beautiful, stately ranch house they might have seen from afar. Patricia's family had business prominence, which resulted in a tremendous amount of name recognition. She was an only child, so she was left alone to develop coping strategies for family behaviors that, as a child, she couldn't understand.

When Patricia and I had our first phone conversation, she was so shy that she didn't interact with people at all. Her goals were to live in a community and to establish friendships. Significantly, she had what it took to do her work, that spark of determination to build a good life.

We devoted years to understanding the deeply troubled family system that was Patricia's heritage. This unwieldy step was essential for her to gather the courage to move forward and begin to interact with others. There were entire months when she disappeared. Without immediate family members relying on her, she would just take off. She called it "travel mode." There was no stopping her, and I came to understand that this was part of her processing. It was a kind of restlessness and impatience with our work. She would always return ready to work again.

Slowly but surely, she accomplished her goal of moving into a community and building friendships. One of her gifts is a wonderful, sharp sense of humor, and we have joked many times about the fact that her pace is so slow. What does it matter? She has moved steadily toward her goal and now has lovely friendships.

The real cost of the childhood abuse was that it caused Patricia to doubt herself so deeply. For years she simply couldn't find *anything* of value within. In her case, her wealth was isolating, and she was well aware that if she hadn't inherited wealth, her life would have been very different. It is a testament to her strong intelligence, and ultimately to her character, that she's specifically discovered her true, confident self despite the effects of the abuse. I have felt privileged to be the one beside her, supporting her, brainstorming with her, and cheering her on.

For each of us, before we can begin to explore our issues with family, friends, colleagues, and everyone else with whom we would like to live and work in harmony, we must explore our relationship with ourselves. We must find, understand, and accept the person no one but us can truly know. Ultimately the voyage of self-discovery is made alone, and it helps to have a guide for direction. If you will allow me to guide you in the pages ahead, I'm confident you will come to know yourself better.

Elements of Healthy Relationships

Acknowledging what you have received from your parents is a sign of maturity. It is common to think about financial assets as our inheritance, yet there is so much more. For example, kindness, generosity, patience, and discipline are qualities we are most likely to inherit from our parents. For some people the negative, difficult memories will dominate, but for most of us, it is possible to also acknowledge positive values, attitudes, and behaviors. The one trait no one inherits, however, is a meaningful life. And strong, healthy relationships make up an enormous part of building a meaningful life.

I believe there are seven elements that help us strengthen our relationships and achieve a meaningful life. These elements are:

- Identity
- Values
- Respect
- Competence
- Trust
- Communication
- Generosity

The challenge with financial wealth, however, is that it tends to complicate our efforts to incorporate these elements into our relationships. Often our attitudes about wealth distort relationships as well as our identity, values, and priorities. I call this the "velvet-cushioned trap." Let's look at each of these elements in the context of our many relationships and consider how wealth may be impeding our connections with people and our happiness.

Then we'll work on overcoming these obstacles, first with ourselves and then in our other relationships, throughout the book.

Identity

Before any of us explores our relationships with others, it is important to know who we are and what's working, what's not. In other words, each of us benefits from clarifying our identity: what we stand for, what people can count on us for, knowing our reality, our world view, and *liking* it. Furthermore, those of us who are wealthy need to know how financial largesse fits into our identity.

How Wealth Masks Identity

Fortune, whatever its size, means something to each of us and impacts our identity. It's important to get your bearings on your identity before you can like who you are. Katie was a client who was confused and adrift in life because she had always hated rich people. She received an unexpected inheritance upon her father's death and now found herself "one of *them*." She was practically immobilized by the dramatic shift in her circumstances. It had turned her world upside down. I helped her explore her new identity and find ways to make it work for her.

In another instance, Todd was a songwriter who drew on his anguish from lacking enough income to support his creative endeavors. After inheriting a sizable amount of money, he struggled to stay in touch with his muse. He hated to give up songwriting, but he no longer had the intensity of need he'd possessed before receiving his inheritance. His challenge was to find other sources of creativity that were rooted in aspects of his identity and values independent of wealth or poverty. He wound up transitioning to a focus on lost love, another area of intensity in his life. For me, his was a great and inspiring success story.

Many people stumble along for a few years, trying to redefine their identity after a major liquidity event. Sometimes they muddle through, and they and their affairs turn out okay. Sometimes they don't. Some people can address this challenge by journaling. Others meditate. Perhaps working through this book will help you better understand your identity: who you, at your best, can be. You may also benefit by working through this and other issues with a therapist, especially one who has experience working with people in similar circumstances to yours.

Knowing our identity is most important in our relationship with ourselves, and it constantly shapes our relationships with others too.

Values

Values are what we live our lives by, what we care most about, our strongly held beliefs. They are basic and defining, yet sometimes difficult to identify because we are not consciously aware of them. We must first explore our own values, and with that foundation, we can later consider how they shape our relationships with others.

One way to identify values is to use an assessment. The assessments I find to be most useful are DISC assessments, a powerful series of behavioral strength and attitude evaluation tools offered by TTI Performance Systems. DISCs are based on four aspects of human behavior: dominance, influence, steadiness, and conscientiousness. Because our behavior is based on our values, these assessments are an effective way to access individual values. Often used in the workplace, these assessments bring to light employees' and employers' personality types, strengths, and weaknesses in an effort to strengthen individual and team performance, morale, and company culture. They are equally as useful with families for the same reasons.

DISC assessments must be administered and interpreted by professionals. You and your family can benefit from the DISC assessment process, but in the meantime, consider a less formal values exercise that you can do now.

Exercise 3.1 **e 3.1**

Values Identification and Clarification

This is a very useful exercise to bring your values into sharp focus. Read through the instructions below and then use the following list of values to identify your answers.

1. **Circle** the strongest values in your life. Do not be overly analytical. Just mark the values that resonate with you intuitively. As much as possible, employ your heart more than your mind as you choose the values that are most meaningful to you. You may add to the list if there are important words you do not find there.
2. Next, **star your top ten values**, the ones that are so important that you would be dissatisfied if you did not have them. If you wish to analyze further, prioritize your top ten.
3. Finally, **underline** the values you have not yet fully developed but *aspire* to have. These words describe the person you want to become. Some of these may be values you have already identified as the ones you have in your life. They may already be circled and starred. You may add an underline as well. It is possible to have a value *and* to aspire to it. An example of this is integrity. You may have it already in much that you do, yet you may still aspire to it in a few more areas of your life.

continued on next page

Abundance
Acceptance
Accomplishment
Adventure
Affection
Athleticism
Authenticity
Beauty
Being outdoors
Belonging
Candor
Challenging work
Charity
Communication
Community
Compassion
Competence
Competition
Contributing
Control
Courage
Creativity
Dedication
Dependability
Enjoyment
Equality
Ethics
Excellence
Expertise
Faith
Family
Financial wealth
Forgiveness
Fortitude
Freedom
Friendliness
Generosity
Gentleness
God
Grace
Gratitude
Health
Healthy lifestyle
Helping others
Honesty
Honor
Hope
Humility
Humor
Impeccability
Inclusivity
Independence
Integrity
Intelligence
Joy
Justice
Kindness
Knowledge
Laughter
Leadership
Learning
Love
Loyalty
Mercy
Moderation
Morals
Objectivity
Open-mindedness
Originality
Passion
Patience
Peacefulness
Perfection
Personal growth
Philanthropy
Power
Rationality
Relaxation
Religion
Resilience
Respect
Responsibility
Risk
Safety
Security
Self-discipline
Self-reliance
Sense of purpose
Sensitivity
Sensuality
Significance
Spirituality
Spontaneity
Stability
Status
Success
Support
Surrender
Taking charge
Tenacity
Tradition
Trust
Truthfulness
Unselfishness
Vulnerability
Wisdom
Working alone
Working with others
Youthfulness
____
____
____

Take some time to look over the groups you came up with. You may be surprised at your observations.

You can take off some of the pressure to commit to the lists you are creating by realizing that this is merely a snapshot of you today. If you were to do this exercise again tomorrow or in a year, the values you identify may be somewhat different. However, you would find the majority of the same values show up for you time after time. A few will change as you evolve and grow, but many of your values will not change, especially your top three. Certain others will always show up in your top ten.

Respect

The attitude and practice of respect can be foreign if we haven't seen it modeled well. For those of us who grew up with parents who exemplified respect for themselves and others, we have been given a great gift. For everyone else, learning to be respectful is one of the most important lessons for any relationship.

The ability to respect others is founded on character—especially honor, empathy, consideration, appreciation, and humility. When a person has poor character, it can be difficult to recognize good character in others, even when the situation warrants it. Yet respect is a building block of strong, positive relationships, and we can all cultivate it.

Some of the most striking experiences of respect are the ones that we don't expect. Parents take a leap of faith to respect their children in choices that are not necessarily the parents' choices for them. That leap forms the commitment to care for family members even if it isn't convenient.

Some young members of wealthy families are allowed to grow up without behaving respectfully. We see all kinds of assaults on others within families, including bullying, discounting, and neglect, in the absence of respect. Coming from those who have been given great resources in our society, this kind of behavior is even more offensive.

When wealthy people are respectful to others, likewise this carries an impact. Some people expect poor behavior from the wealthy, and the refreshing quality of respect can be significant. The skill and practice of respect is a relationship builder in any context.

Competence

Competence can be elusive for inheritors. Financial wealth makes it so easy to quit when the going gets tough because we have the means to find more comfortable environments. However, if you commit to persevering through difficult situations, you can develop competence. You'll build confidence, have a stronger potential for personal happiness, and be able to recognize and support other people's competence too. Remember that one of the bright sides of wealth is that you can afford to hire an educator or a therapist or coach who can help you through the tough times. What matters most is that you not give up.

Competence is indeed a worthy goal, the very best way to create a meaningful life. Competence will not be given to anyone on a silver platter—or even a paper plate—but once it is achieved, it cannot be taken away. In addition to being a goal in and of itself, achieving competence can also be a means to an end.

I watched my own mother develop competence in this way. The end she had in mind was serving others in community affairs. She worked her way up to president of the parent-teacher council of our school and continued in her community work to become vice president of the Oregon Symphony board, chair of the Portland Opera board, and chair of the Doernbecher Children's Hospital board.

With her competence, my mother learned how to find and fill needs on community boards. Often, if a particular skill was needed, she would learn it herself. She learned how to network and enlist the generosity of donors. She is an excellent speaker, and this has helped her accomplish many of her community goals. Her focus was simply enriching our city and state. She took charge of her life. She did not give up in difficult situations. Consequently, she learned, became competent in the matter at hand, gained confidence, and then made things happen. This was a powerful message for me.

Trust

Trust is the basis of every healthy relationship. It takes time to build, and there is no way around the necessity and importance of it. No relationship can progress very far without it. Trust creates the foundation for effective communication, respect, attraction, motivation, and a sense of safety.

First and foremost, we need to be able to extend trust to ourselves. Unfortunately, some people just are not able to do this without a lot of work. It may be helpful to look at your past to see if issues of mistrust stem from there.

In developmental psychologist Erik Erikson's stages of development, the first stage, infancy, is Basic Trust vs. Mistrust.[1] If we don't resolve the conflict between them and learn hope at this young age, we will always struggle with trust. It is possible to work through this stage as an adult, though it is difficult and time consuming. If we can be receptive and open to trust, we can build strong, positive relationships with other people.

Communication

Just as identity, values, success, competence, and trust are crucial to explore and define in our relationships—with ourselves and with others—communication is a necessity. While we typically consider communication to be necessary between two or more people, it's important to be able to communicate well with yourself too.

Most of us have varying levels of honesty in our own thoughts. Sometimes it is necessary to push yourself to be open to the deeper truth within. Though it may seem counterintuitive at first, it is actually good stress management to identify and clarify even the truths that we wish were otherwise. For instance, if I find myself blaming others frequently for my problems, it might be useful to consider how I am responsible for what happens in my life. It could be a life-changing shift in attitude. Then, with another shot of courage, we can begin to work with the truth, get help, and redesign or do whatever it takes to move forward in a more balanced manner.

As we begin to define and clarify our awareness of who we are in the world, we need to consider how we interact with others. By tuning up our communication skills, we strengthen our relationships.

Generosity

Generosity is our highest calling. The happiest people I know build relationships with themselves, other people, and God by serving others. Once we discover the joy of giving in this way, there is no need to explain the experience.

Service underscores generosity. However, when promoting service to my clients, as I have done at times with the intention of offering a path of constructive and rewarding endeavors, I have sometimes been met with resistance. Some people see service as giving away something of value, usually their time and talent. This is viewed as a loss, and they think, *Why would I ever do that?* The answer is because service taps in to our higher calling and connects us with something that is bigger than our individual ego. There is only so much self-centered behavior any of us can stand without becoming egocentric and, even worse, narcissistic. Giving, service, and sacrifice help us to understand and remember what is really going on here on Earth. We are all in this together, and in the ways that we can, it is important for us to be supportive to others. These are the kinds of endeavors that give our lives meaning and joy.

When you identified your own values earlier in this chapter, was generosity, service, or sacrifice among them? I have found that service and sacrifice are two of the values that are most conducive to having a meaningful life.

Success

Just as strengthening the seven elements of successful relationships—identity, values, respect, competence, trust, communication, and generosity—can improve your ability to develop and take good care of a relationship, so can clarifying your concept of success. Often our parents and our children have very different ideas about what constitutes success than we do. Is it how much money we have? How we acquired that money? Is it a title, a diploma, or the extent to which we control our life or others' lives? Do we achieve success when we have taken charge of our life? When we are happy?

One way to discover success in your life is to think about problems, obstacles, and challenges you have faced and how you overcame them. For isn't success, when all is said and done, simply the ability to learn important lessons through challenges and find solutions?

Learning important lessons through mistakes is a perennial human challenge. One day, I found a little pamphlet that had been distributed in honor of my Uncle Owen at his retirement party in 1968. In it he talked about the challenges and blessings he had faced with the help of his executive team, which included my father, in building Georgia-Pacific Corporation. He quoted his daughters' headmistress, Miss Madeira: "Function in disaster and finish in style."

At every crossroad, it takes courage and character to function in disaster. Often we develop courage when life crashes around us, and we find ourselves in more pain than we think we can handle. That pain motivates us to find the strength to overcome obstacles to our success and happiness. Finding and cultivating strength in yourself and your family despite such instances is a major route to success.

Feeling successful ultimately comes from making your own way in life. One of the best things that ever happened to me is when I realized that my inheritance and future financial security were in jeopardy, and I believed that I would be forced to earn a living. Until I was in the middle of this crossroad, I had not begun to develop real, hard-won competence.

Two significant events occurred in my life at almost the same time. It was 2001, and my husband had reached the end of the road in a job he loved. Though his income had been excellent, suddenly it was zero. He was incredibly upset with himself, feeling he had made a series of very poor work-related decisions. I wasn't sure when he would be able to work again, as he now questioned core competencies upon which he had always relied. At the same time, my family of origin became quite concerned about how our investments were performing—it looked like the wealth my father had created could be lost.

I remember waking up to the fact that the two places I had been counting on for income seemed suddenly very unreliable. I realized that if I was going to have financial security, I'd better get busy and create it myself. I sat down and wrote my first book, and my business took off from there. Happily, both of the financial liabilities I experienced were resolved. My husband found his way into an even better job, and the finances in my family of origin straightened out. This story shows, though, that in tough circumstances, our resilience, resourcefulness, and attitudes are tested and honed. Meeting these challenges resolutely is what leads us to success.

How you define success is immensely important in fostering your relationship with yourself. More than that, success is important to keep in mind in your relationships with others. How do you define a successful relationship? How would the other person define it? In what ways can both individuals involved help each other to pursue their own definitions of success?

Moving Toward the Bright Side

Now let's apply the seven elements of relationships to your relationship with yourself. In this section, you will have the opportunity to explore your relationship with yourself and your identity as a wealthy person. You will find several exercises and activities to help you in this discovery process. As you learn more about what is important to you, you will be able to see more clearly how you can improve your life. Make no mistake, though: it is up to you to take charge of this and do your work. The exercises and activities here will provide valuable guideposts and inspiration—in the end it is you who commands the energy and the resolve to improve.

Patricia, whom you met at the beginning of this chapter, became an expert at gathering her courage to face her fears in the relationships she longed to develop. She learned to let her sense of humor show, and she was encouraged by its welcome reception with new friends. She identified interests that she was likely to share with others, and she taught herself how to connect within these commonalities. One of her talents and interests was painting, and one day when she found herself talking with two acquaintances who also liked to paint, they decided to start a painting group and meet regularly for lunch. They would paint on their own and bring their art to show and critique. This group, which grew to five participants, gave Patricia a sense of belonging and connection. It had all started with Patricia identifying aspects of herself that she liked and cultivating her willingness to share them with others.

Exercise 3.2 **e 3.2**

Personal Mission Statement

Writing a personal mission statement is a great way to visualize what you would like your relationship with yourself—and those with other people—to look like. Wealth expert and attorney Jay E. Hughes Jr. suggests following these five steps for writing your personal mission statement.[2]

continued on next page

1. Write the ten values you consider most crucial to your success.
2. Write what you would, at the very end of your life, tell your immediate family had been most important to you in life.
3. Write a description of yourself twenty years from now.
4. Write a brief history of your life until now (only a paragraph!).
5. Write your personal mission statement (based on your answers to questions one through four).

Hughes also advises people to be bold when writing a personal mission statement. All too often, he explains, people don't realize how strong they are and how much they can accomplish. Also, it's important to think about the value of mentoring, both being mentored and mentoring another, and to understand the value of teamwork. Success is rarely created alone.

Don't worry if your mission statement isn't perfect. This is just the first draft. A few sentences should be plenty. Do the best you can, but don't overdo it. Remember to have fun! If humor occurs to you, don't hesitate to add it to your statement.

Sample Personal Mission Statement

> My relationship with God guides my life, and I strive to walk with Him daily. My highest priorities are loving my family members, making a difference in their lives, and, as much as possible, making a difference in the lives of everyone I know. It is important to me to be kind, to have integrity, and to be a lifelong learner. I will never lose the desire to laugh and to bring laughter to others. Above all, I want to be remembered for making the most of my time here on Earth in the service of my Lord and Savior, Jesus Christ.

Remember, this is just a sample. Your own personal mission statement may be longer or shorter, and what you say is highly personal. Let it take shape in whatever form feels right to you. You may be surprised at the clarity of your statement.

Gratitude

Our relationship with ourselves—even extended to our happiness—is greatly affected by the presence or absence of gratitude in our lives. Experts have found links between gratitude and happiness. My colleague Jeffrey Schwartz, coauthor of the bestseller *The Mind and the Brain*, has told me that our minds can indeed transform our brains for the achievement of our dearest aspirations and the betterment of our lives. I have heard Daniel Amen, psychiatrist and bestselling author of *Change Your Brain, Change Your Life*, say that focusing on the things for which we are grateful makes our brain feel good, and it rewards us in kind.

One way to nurture your own sense of gratitude is to consciously practice it daily. In a broad sense, you can take a few moments every day to mentally note five things you are grateful for. When my children were young, my husband and I resolved to teach our children that joy does *not* depend on money or material items; joy is proactive and comes from deep within. So beginning early in their childhood, at the end of their bedtime prayers, we each named five things we were grateful for that day.

At the end of one particularly stressful day, the main thing I felt thankful for was that our puppy had waited that morning for someone to let him out to do his dog business. There had been a long lag between the time he woke up and the time he was finally let out, and I searched the house nervously looking for an accident, only to find none had occurred, to my great relief. It seems silly, but I was grateful all day, filled with a simple joy over our pup's gift to me.

If you commit to this practice of gratitude for just one month, you will be happily surprised at the results. If you prefer, make it a morning ritual. Or do it any other time of the day, though I recommend a regular time so you nurture it as a habit. Make it a prayer if you like, or a meditation, or a gratitude journal. You can even do it while you brush your teeth. Whatever form your personal reflections take, the important thing is that you practice them regularly and build new habits.

---

e 3.3

Exercise 3.3

Gratitude

The gratitude practice can also be applied directly to each relationship in your life. Let's start with your relationship with yourself. What are five elements of this relationship that you are grateful for?

____

____

____

____

3.4 Exercise 3.4

Action Plan

Every goal you set—whether pertaining to your relationships or other areas of your life—requires an action plan to help you achieve it. Make each goal specific, something you want as opposed to what you "should" want, and small enough that you are very likely to accomplish it successfully. Use the following form to set an action plan for improving your relationship with yourself.

Today's date: ______________________

Today, the goal I set for myself to know myself better is:

____

____

____

____

In order to accomplish this goal, I will perform the following activities:

____

____

____

____

Support people who might assist me are:

____

____

____

____

I realize I may sabotage my plan by:

____

____

____

____

So I will avoid this by:

____

____

____

____

I will complete this goal by ________________________ (date).

(Recommendation: three to six months)

Knowing who you are and what you stand for is the best investment you can make in your relationships. We all know how disappointing it is to find that a new friend is not really who we thought they were. It is respectful, kind, and efficient when each of us is exactly who we appear to be and able to behave in a consistent manner. As we develop bright side attitudes and behaviors, we find that life becomes more fulfilling and meaningful. Knowing what we value helps us choose a mate and friends. The best relationships are based on shared values. In order to be responsive, it is tremendously valuable to identify and clarify your own values first. As you take charge of your life in this way, all your relationships will become stronger.

Throughout this book, we will talk more about enhancing your relationships with specific family members, friends, and professionals. Let's start with your relationship with your parents.

Your Parents, Your Foundation
Building from the Ground Up

I talk and talk and talk, and I haven't taught people in fifty years what my father taught by example in one week.
—Mario Cuomo

It is easier to build strong children than to repair broken men.
—Frederick Douglass

You are the bows from which your children as living arrows are sent forth.
—Khalil Gibran

| Relationship Elements: | **Competence** | **Trust** | **Respect** |

YOUR PARENTS ARE YOUR FOUNDATION. They are the strength, resilience, hope, and promise of the precious structure that is built upon it—the rock-solid, though sometimes teetering, edifice that is *you*. The durability or weakness of both the foundation and the structure—mirror images of each other—are a fancier way, I suppose, of stating the obvious: the fruit seldom falls far from the tree.

"Just as no worthy building can be erected on a weak foundation," echoes American author R. C. Samsel, "so no lasting reputation worthy of respect can be built on a weak character."

It follows, then, that it takes tremendous effort on our part as the children of our parents to identify—even more, to *fix*—those areas where we think our parents fell short in molding us. All the while, we can reconcile and forgive those deficiencies, if necessary. And of course these are deficiencies, which are based entirely and subjectively on our perceptions and needs. Our awareness of our own foundation is the necessary starting point in the strength, resilience, promise, and hope that we, in turn, pass along to our own children.

Becoming Who You Were Meant to Be

Nancy's story is a case in point. She came to me for help managing her relationship with her elderly mother, Elaine. While she was growing up, Nancy had become locked in a destructive dynamic with her mother and, in the process, had given Elaine almost total control over their relationship. Nancy had actually let her mother take control over her entire life. Nancy had never married because no man was good enough for her mother, and she had never had children.

As a result, Nancy was miserable and, at age fifty-two, she behaved in some ways like a sullen child. Her four brothers each had very different relationships with their mother, but none of them were healthy, so they couldn't help Nancy with her struggles.

A substantial inheritance was at stake, and Elaine never hesitated to use this as leverage. Soon after we began working together, one of the first steps Nancy made to improve her life was to get a job so she could have financial independence. She had never had a job because none was ever good enough for her society-conscious mother. It was difficult for her to take such an independent step, but Nancy reaped rewards almost immediately—she gained confidence and felt the relief of knowing she could take care of herself if her mother did indeed cut her off. Nancy began to blossom into the person she had only dreamed of before.

As she grew in confidence and competence, her relationship with her mother began to shift as well. Nancy's growing independence turned out to be more of an asset than she had anticipated. Much to her surprise, this was linked to her successful employment, and she felt less controlled by the whims and threats of her mother. At first Nancy's mother pressured her to return to the relationship dynamic they had had for so long. After a while her mother gave in and established a more adult relationship with her daughter.

Nancy stopped hiding, lying, and giving mere outward compliance. Instead she began to express who she is and what she believes in, in small, subtle ways. It didn't take long before Nancy's presence shifted in a positive direction. In a few short months, she was becoming a strong, positive woman. All of her relationships improved. She had inherited the tenacious strength of her mother's character, and as she became able to put it to use for herself instead of allowing it to be used against her, she was able to flourish. It was a joy to watch her step into being the person she wanted to be in so many ways. The sullen quality I saw in her at the beginning of our work was replaced by enthusiasm and optimism.

Nancy could have spent the rest of her life locked into a negative relationship with her mother, but she knew this wasn't the best use of her time. She was in enough pain when I met her to take on the tough work of strengthening herself so that she could manage all of her family relationships better. She could have made excuses to stay angry at her mother and brothers, but instead she chose to examine where she came from so she could strengthen her relationships—including the one with herself.

As we work to improve our relationships with our parents, we bring into play the seven elements of strong relationships: identity, values, competence, trust, respect, communication, and generosity. The most important of these elements in most relationships with most parents are competence, trust, and respect. Though no parent is perfect, most do their best to be competent leadership examples. Parents also work to encourage the competence of their offspring through education, experience, and training. Trust and respect are fundamental to any positive relationship. Without them, relationships are painfully limited.

In this chapter we will take a close look at attitudes and behaviors you have learned from your parents. Then we will work to tune them up so you can work with attitudes and behaviors you have consciously chosen. By the time we reach adulthood, and certainly once we become parents, it's important to do our best to work through and let go of the negative attitudes and behaviors we carry from our childhood. This is no easy task, but it can be accomplished. If it seems impossible, you may benefit from the help of a therapist to resolve wealth-related or other problems you may have learned in relationship with your parents.

Financial Knowledge

Ideally we learn our foundation of financial knowledge from the lessons our parents taught us and the behavior they modeled. One basic lesson we should all have learned by early adulthood is how to set up and keep to a budget. This includes planning for all monthly expenses, making sure the total is less than the expected monthly income, and tracking all money that's spent. Likewise, shopping wisely and using a credit card responsibly are very important. Sticking to our shopping list, comparing prices, and resisting impulse purchases most of the time are elements of shopping wisely that we don't often learn on our own. The same goes for retaining credit card receipts, tracking how much we charge, and paying off our credit card bill.

And, of course, there's saving, investing, and donating. Ideally, we should decide how much of our monthly income to set aside and do it before we spend money on anything else, including bills. We should keep three to six months' worth of expenses in a liquid account for emergencies. To invest wisely, we need to understand the basic principles and types of securities, determine our risk tolerance and asset allocation, and work comfortably with financial advisors. Donating wisely requires us to not only determine how much we want to give but also to identify the causes we care most about. We should also research organizations that support those causes to ensure they are responsibly managed. No more than 25 percent of any nonprofit organization's funds should go toward administrative, public relations, or marketing expenses, and the rest should go directly toward the cause.

All people, no matter how well they were raised, have some gaps in their knowledge about the world. It can be difficult to identify our own gaps, but it may be easier in the tangible realm of money than in other more nebulous areas. Exercise 4.1 lists some common knowledge gaps among wealthy adults who were not taught to responsibly handle money. Which of these gaps apply to you?

e

4.1 EXERCISE 4.1

Gaps in Financial Knowledge

I know how to set up and keep to a budget. Yes ____ No ____

I am able to use a credit card responsibly. Yes ____ No ____

I shop smartly. Yes ____ No ____

I know how to save. Yes ____ No ____

I understand how to invest. Yes ____ No ____

I am able to give money away wisely. Yes ____ No ____

If your parents didn't teach you some of the financial basics listed in Exercise 4.1, it's time to get yourself on track. It's time to stop blaming them, using that as an excuse for your own financial gaps and messes. Until we reach age eighteen or twenty-one, many people do not expect us to function in ways our parents did not teach us. But when we become young adults, it is time to start taking charge by learning how to be financially responsible and changing behaviors that are not working well.

To help us understand where our parents were coming from, we'll explore parenting styles and how they typically shape children in wealthy households. Then we'll take a look at ways to overcome any challenges we feel stem from our parents.

Formative Parenting Styles

Understanding the parenting style prevalent in our home when we were growing up is a useful starting point for examining our own behaviors. To build this awareness, many of us need to take time to understand both the positives and negatives of our experience. There are three main parenting styles: authoritative, authoritarian, and permissive.

Authoritative Parents

Authoritative parents give their children a voice. These parents are willing to listen, consider their kids' input, and be influenced by it at times. Sometimes the parents' actions or policies can change when their kids make a good case for what they believe is a better approach.

Their children feel free to develop a case and present it well. Children of authoritative parents often grow up with many useful skills for adulthood, including looking at issues from more than one point of view, negotiating, and working as part of a team. This is important for children who grow up in wealthy families because they need to develop independence and the inner resources to build meaningful lives for themselves.

Children of authoritative parents are typically financial literate. These children know what is expected of them, and they are given the latitude to develop work experiences that are a good fit for them. These are the kids who benefit most by having summer jobs because parents give them a lot of space to get the job, manage it, and handle the money they earn. They are given guidance in how to develop and use a budget as well as how to be responsible with their money, and they are often allowed experiences in philanthropy on age-appropriate levels.

Authoritarian Parents

Authoritarian parents often decide what their children will do with most aspects of their lives. Children do not win autonomy easily; it is more typical for them to receive money specifically for what their parents want them to develop. The main financial problem inherent in growing up with authoritarian parents is that the children gain little to no experience using money and don't develop insight into how decisions are made and play out.

If one or both of your parents exhibited this parenting style, you may find yourself dependent on your trustee, advisors, or spouse. You might also be prey to people who see you as naïve and don't have your best interests at heart.

Permissive Parents

Permissive parents might hand out money to their kids without restrictions. In one family I know, the patriarch is in his late sixties and addresses every problem with money. For example, when his cousin complained about not having enough access to the family jet, he gave that cousin $1 million and told him to buy some rights to another jet. If your parents threw money at problems to fix them, you were most likely to learn this approach to problem solving.

By the same token, children of permissive parents are unlikely to learn effective problem-solving strategies. Perhaps they did not acquire tolerance for hearing the words *no* or *later*. This sets them up to lock horns with teachers, friends, colleagues, and bosses. Children of permissive parents usually do not have the tools or tolerance to follow a budget.

It's difficult for children of permissive parents to live within their means. They may unconsciously try to buy friendships. They don't have many boundaries around money and often lack the discipline to handle money that comes to them, whether it is income or a gift. They might overspend, lose track of money, or get into trouble with debt. It may be easy for people to take money from them if they're not keeping track of it. They often run to Mom and Dad when they run out of money, evidence of having not financially grown up.

Other Parent Challenges

In every family, parents make an effort to parent as well as they can. Parents face challenges, though—sometimes stemming from the way their parents raised them. There are some families in which the challenges are much more difficult. We'll take a look at a few more parenting considerations to think about when evaluating your relationship with your parents and how they raised you in regard to your wealth.

Narcissistic Parents

Narcissism can give rise to a vicious cycle of goals, standards, and evaluative pressures. Consider one example of goal setting: playing an instrument. The child achieves one set of the parent's standards—say, playing at a piano recital. Then the parent, eager to continue nurturing excellence, sets a whole new row of hurdles—bigger and better recital venues—foreclosing on that child's right to celebrate. In lieu of celebrating small successes, the parent points to larger goals.

When strong children are forced to comply with incessant hurdles, they smolder with resentment toward parental attitudes that discount their ability to contribute to the family.

More sensitive children simply collapse into discouragement and low self-esteem. In any case, the children withdraw for protection from further painful experiences. At some point in childhood, many of these children turn away from the truth within and construct a false self, the product of the parent's desire.

This process of hurdle setting can be a healthy part of growing up, as parents are always seeking to cultivate children's capacity to master appropriate developmental tasks. In healthy families, accomplishments are always celebrated before new hurdles are erected. What distinguishes the narcissistic parent from the healthy parent is the absence of celebration of accomplishments and the *emotional attachment to uniquely favorable outcomes*, and therein lies the damage.

Wealth has the ability to amplify the stakes in the entire familial picture: the height of expectations, the depth of disappointments, and the breadth of opportunity to acquire or deny resources. Over time, this cycle of striving linked to emotional satisfaction builds a toxic relationship.

Gifts and Money, Love and Attention

Many children who grow up in privileged homes feel their parents tried to express their love through buying them gifts, or that parents compensated for not spending enough time with them or giving them enough attention by lavishing them with gifts or money.

If you grew up this way, you may actually feel deprived because your parents essentially neglected you. Children who have not worked through this may harbor resentment that can show up in many ways. Some teens could try to compensate by shoplifting, or young adults might give everything away.

The "bling ring" case in the news in early 2010 is a perfect, if unfortunate, example. Six teens from wealthy homes robbed more than $3 million from the homes of celebrities such as Paris Hilton, Lindsay Lohan, and Orlando Bloom. These teens, from very affluent families, shared an obsession with celebrity culture and partied in their victims' homes, leaving their fingerprints everywhere and flaunting themselves before security cameras. It seems as though they were begging to be caught. One wonders, what was going on with these kids? It was a mix of entitlement, disrespect, and little fear of consequences. Inevitably, this stemmed from neglect in their own homes. Each of us needs to feel significant, and if our parents don't give us recognition that moves us to feel special, we seek it elsewhere. Young family members, lacking maturity and discernment, may look for it in destructive ways.

Sometimes when young adults feel they were deprived of love and attention as children, they develop a kind of logic to justify unhealthy behaviors. If you grew up in this kind of environment, unconsciously you may feel the world owes you something. You may justify taking from others because you feel you were ripped off. Or as an adult, you may go to great lengths to squeeze every penny out of someone with whom you are negotiating a transaction. And you may never feel that a transaction was fair enough.

In relationships, you may have trouble expressing love and resort to doing what your parents did: showing people you care in the form of overly generous gifts. Some people feel embittered; others talk about it in a detached, matter-of-fact way and seem emotionally distant and cold. Some people lose trust in those whom they might look to for affection because those expectations went unfulfilled in childhood. It is not uncommon for people to feel so starved for attention that they build walls around themselves. This can specifically affect relationships with the people whom we feel neglected us, but the broader problem is that it can affect all of our relationships. It can have the unintended effect of isolating us.

Awareness is crucial to healing the wounds of neglect. Once you recognize how you feel and why you feel the way you do, you can talk to people you care about in your life and tell them that you want to learn to express love differently. You can ask them to please be patient while you work at shifting your attitudes and behaviors.

Parental Polar Opposites

When parents are at opposite ends of the spectrum in their financial habits and values, the mixed messages are almost like raising children in two religions. It can be confusing to the kids. Differences in financial habits and values are likely to cause heated arguments between the parents. Even if the parents do not argue about money in front of the children, the parents' conflicting spending and saving patterns can cause children to feel insecure.

If you grew up with parents who were polar opposites, you may have developed some destructive behaviors. Some children from this environment may even become manipulative, pitting one parent against the other in order to get whatever they want. If one parent denies a request, the kids simply ask the other. Once these children become adults, they usually do not know how to handle finances harmoniously with their spouse because they didn't see this modeled at home and likely haven't learned it anywhere else.

If your parents handled money in incompatible ways, they probably did not provide you with much financial literacy because they were not able to find common ground on which to provide that kind of education. They probably were not able to agree on giving you an allowance, keeping a budget, or following any basic financial principles.

Paradoxically, if your parents disagreed about money but divorced, you may find family financial issues easier to comprehend than when your parents lived together. Children in this scenario can more easily understand, "This is the way we do things in this parent's household. There may be different rules in my other parent's home, but these are the rules in this house."

Financially Irresponsible Parents

Whether or not your parents agreed about money, if one or both of them were irresponsible about family finances, that may have been very damaging to you while you were growing up.

Financial irresponsibility takes many shapes. There is the shop-to-relieve-stress approach to life, which ignores the financial consequences. Many shoppers plunge into debt with this method. There is the never-talk-about-it approach in which children learn by example that there is always money. You just ask for it, and it is given to you without accountability. There is the abuse of family members by one who uses their position of leadership and authority to steal or lose family money. Offspring are often caught up in this process and very much affected by it. There is the carrot-and-stick model in which offspring are subtly or openly controlled by money. The one holding the carrot and the stick makes all the rules, and their only objective is that everyone complies with their priorities. In this practice kids only learn reactive personal finance.

You may find that your relationship with one or both of your parents is strained. It takes only one person in the relationship to initiate healing and personal growth. You have nothing to lose by tuning up your attitudes and behaviors. You may think it is the other person who needs to change, but the truth is, there is always room for improvement in our own behaviors.

EXERCISE 4.2 **e 4.2**

Parental Practices Assessment

Consider the financial lessons you've learned from your parents. Keep in mind that you may have learned some behaviors through lessons your parents actually taught you and others simply through observation of their behaviors.

1. Did your parents teach you about personal finance? Yes ____ No ____
2. Did your parents teach you financial values? Yes ____ No ____
3. Did you get an allowance? Yes ____ No ____
4. If yes, was it independent of grades, chores, or behavior? Yes ____ No ____
5. Did your parents express love in ways other than giving you money or things?
   Yes ____ No ____

continued on next page

6. Were your parents' independent relationships with money compatible with each other? Yes ____ No ____
7. Were your parents responsible about handling money? Yes ____ No ____
8. Were any gaps in your financial knowledge small enough that they didn't cause problems in your life? Yes ____ No ____
9. Do you feel your parents treated you and your siblings fairly and equally? Yes ____ No ____
10. Do you know what you will inherit and when? Yes ____ No ____
11. Are you comfortable asking your parents about your future inheritance? Yes ____ No ____
12. Did your grandparents and parents agree with each other when it came to giving you and your siblings gifts or cash? Yes ____ No ____

If you answered yes to ten to twelve of these questions, you probably don't have many potentially troubling parental practices surrounding wealth, or you may have worked through them already. If you answered yes to six to nine questions, you likely feel confused about money and find that wealth interferes with your relationship with your parents. This may have seeped into relationships with other family members, friends, or romantic partners. If you answered yes to five or fewer questions, the way money was handled in your family has probably caused significant difficulties in your understanding of financial issues, distorted your attitudes about money, and caused money to derail important relationships.

Learning Financial Values

Whether or not your parents taught you anything about money, even if they never talked with you about it, you learned a lot from them just by observing the way they handled money. These are financial values, and the most important values in life are caught, not taught.

Did your parents carry impressive amounts of cash around in their wallets? Were they generous tippers? Would you say they liked to flaunt their wealth, be quietly generous, or hide their resources altogether? Did they often make large purchases on a whim? Or were they careful about spending and saving, perhaps to the point of being stingy? Did they seem to judge people according to how much money they had?

e
4.3

EXERCISE 4.3

Financial Values You Caught

Write one or two positive financial values your parents modeled.

____

____

____

How has this affected your own attitudes, values, or behaviors concerning money?

____

____

____

____

Although my parents were very conservative in the information they gave to my siblings and me, I am grateful that they did not provide us with closets full of fancy clothes and other material possessions. I was not that big a spender. I remember that my closet had few enough clothes that nothing was squished together. I didn't think anything of it; I didn't feel deprived. A few years ago, I received a message from a nanny, Majella Blanas, we had when I was young. She wrote:

> Do you remember the poodle skirt I bought for you when I got North's Davey Crockett outfit? I was surprised at how few clothes you had in your closet, which was probably another important lesson your mother was teaching you about what is really important and what is superficial. But I didn't realize at the time the values you were learning. I simply did not understand, considering the family's wealth, why you and your brother and sister had fewer material things than perhaps even the average child. But it sounds like you profited from the lessons, much to your parents' credit.

Later, those values kicked in more. I'm very careful with spending money now. Most important, I've never felt that my full sense of well-being comes from money. I believe my son and daughter consider me to be careful with finances. My husband and I discuss money much more openly than my parents did with me, so I also believe they feel the topic is not forbidden. When our kids are present, we only talk about age-appropriate facts and practices, and we are very conservative with our definition of this. We encourage our children to ask us whatever they wish, but we may not give them all the information they are asking for if it's not appropriate for their age.

The financial values that your parents consciously or unconsciously imparted to you are most likely reflected in your behavior to this day.

Allowance

Allowance is another important factor to consider in evaluating how your parents taught you about money. Financial parenting experts often talk about the importance of allowance, and there is a lot to this practice. Even some parents who give their kids an allowance fail to do so in a meaningfully constructive way that teaches positive values and money-handling skills. At one end of the spectrum, some parents give allowance haphazardly, forgetting to pay it at all some weeks or arbitrarily giving different amounts from week to week. That could possibly do more harm than good, sending mixed messages about financial responsibility and accountability.

If you received an allowance, was it tied to performing household chores, school grades, or other behaviors? There may have been some learning opportunities associated with that, but tying allowance to these behaviors can also create unnecessary parent-child struggles. What if you didn't perform the expected chores or achieve the expected grades? If your parents caved in and gave you an allowance anyway, that probably encouraged you to think there were no consequences to your actions.

Many wealthy parents give huge amounts of allowance with no rules or expectations about spending, saving, or giving to charity. This, too, can do more harm than good. While a few kids will think of saving, investing, and giving money away, most will not. If they don't learn these lessons in the early years, they are less likely to learn them on their own later. Furthermore, these kids are the ones who don't know the value of a dollar, who often spend as if money is bottomless. Additionally, they become easy prey for others to manipulate them into bad decisions about money.

For your own financial well-being, let's consider in Exercise 4.4 what allowance looked like in your childhood.

e 4.3

Exercise 4.4

Allowance Analysis

Were you given an allowance? Yes ____ No ____

If so, was it tied to chores, and if so, what chores?

____

____

Did your parents enforce your chore obligation? Yes ____ No ____

Looking back, does the amount of allowance you received seem appropriate (not too high or too low)? Yes ____ No ____

Did you receive allowance regularly? Yes ____ No ____

Were you expected to pay for certain wants and needs with allowance? Yes ____ No ____

Were you required to divide your allowance into categories for spending, saving, and donating? If so, what did you learn from this? Yes ____ No ____

____

____

Has the way you were given allowance affected your own attitudes, values, or behaviors concerning money today? If so, how? Yes ____ No ____

____

____

____

If you did not receive allowance—or if you received it in a way that was not constructive—you may have difficulty keeping to a budget. Not everyone has to have a written-out black-and-white budget, but we do need to have at least a general idea about what we have and make our expenses fit into this amount. People who have never had an allowance, or whose allowance was not structured in a constructive or consistent way, often fail to build a sense of parameters. They don't acquire the confidence you get when you know how to work your personal finances, you have your needs covered, and you have money left over to choose to use for some of your wants. Be careful to remember that this is important in all families, wealthy and non-wealthy alike.

Moving Toward the Bright Side

Until you feel comfortable, confident, and competent in your personal finances, you will remain dependent and insecure. You will not be able to make wise choices about money, and you will likely continue pointing fingers at your parents for having failed to educate you in these important life lessons.

It is crucial, however, to stop blaming them. They did their best. You cannot turn back the clock and change how you were raised. Besides, filling your gaps in financial knowledge is actually quite simple, and there's no excuse for keeping yourself in the dark!

Remember Nancy from the beginning of the chapter. When I met her, she was focused on handling her relationship with her mother better, and this was certainly a worthwhile focus. Through her steps to become independent from her mother, Nancy gained confidence in her job, finding that she could support herself if she ever needed to. She financially grew up. This was just as valuable a treasure as her improved relationship with her mother was.

Scrutinizing Your Choices

A good way to begin replacing any negative attitudes and behaviors you learned from your parents is to keep track of your inflow and outflow of money for several months. Even this first step may feel like a monumental task, but it should not take long for you to begin to see your habits. Once you identify them, you can make choices about them, cultivate the ones you like, and outgrow the ones that don't serve you anymore. When you tackle setting a budget, you begin to take charge of your personal financial life.

4.5 EXERCISE 4.5

Easy Tips to Get Started

Everyone, wealthy and non-wealthy alike, starts in the same place for learning to budget and building financial values. Start here.

1. Make sure you reduce the debt in your life to zero.

2. Keep a ledger for a month to track your spending.
3. Use this ledger to build a budget for future months. Use it for one year, and longer if you find it useful.
4. Continue to use the ledger to monitor your spending, saving, and giving.

These steps will be the basis for a deeper look at how your personal financial practices are working for you in chapter ten.

Personal Finance Lessons

If your parents did not teach you how to balance a checkbook or how to budget, save, invest, and use credit cards responsibly, there are many websites, books, and other resources that will get you up to speed. You don't need a PhD in finance to fill in these types of gaps. See the resources section and my website, www.thayerwillis.com, for recommendations.

If your eyes glaze over or your hands get clammy at the thought of learning the financial ABCs, perhaps you have a friend, mentor, advisor, or relative who is financially savvy, whom you can ask to walk you through the basic nuts and bolts. Asking for help is a sign of strength, not weakness.

Communicate about Inheritance

Communication is vital to every healthy relationship, but especially within your family when it comes to inheritance. The wills and trusts that your parents have established can trigger family discord. In many cases, the problem stems from real or perceived inequity in how assets have been or will be distributed.

Other problems arise when parents keep their children in the dark about their plans. In such cases, parents often feel it's best not to let their children know how or when they may inherit substantial wealth, for fear this information would rob their children of the motivation to make their own way in life. These fears may or may not be founded, but lack of communication can lead to lack of preparation and ultimately resentment.

If you were raised in a wealthy home assuming you would inherit lots of money and your parents instead have decided to donate most of their assets to charitable causes, you may experience disappointment and resentment toward your parents if they failed to communicate this. Your incorrect assumptions may have led you to make education and career choices that you may not have made had you known you'd need to support yourself. You may not have learned how to live within a more modest budget, how to save, how to spend wisely, or how to invest.

In another scenario, my client Sam had no clue about the extent of his parents' wealth and was shocked when he inherited a vast fortune when he was in his fifties. He had spent thirty years at a job he hated, sacrificing his work life to make a lot of money. If he'd known he was going to inherit so much, he would have made very different career choices. He resents his parents for setting him up this way.

There are other dangers that arise from keeping kids in the dark. When offspring receive a sudden and surprising windfall, they are often unprepared to deal responsibly with that liquidity event. Sudden wealth can be confusing and can destabilize their identity and relationships.

It's hard for parents to know the right course of action. For one son or daughter, full disclosure might be better; for another, it would be more supportive not to disclose any inheritance information.

If you are in the dark about your parents' intentions about their estate plan, it is probably very difficult to raise the subject with them. You may feel they'd think you are greedy or that you're just waiting for them to die so you can inherit their fortune. Especially if you suspect that your parents consider it crass or inappropriate to discuss money, you may not know how to approach the subject with them.

One constructive way to bring up the topic is to ask your parents when they will be available for a discussion. In this way, you are making space for a discussion. Then, when they give you that opportunity, sit with them for a quiet, relaxed, and private conversation. Tell them that you are working on your estate plan and that it would be very helpful to know what you might be receiving eventually so you can factor that into your own plans. You can use the accompanying exercise to guide you.

Even though this is a reasonable request, some parents may not feel comfortable disclosing this information to you. That just may be the way it is. If so, let it go and carry on without the information. Make your plans as if there will be no inheritance. It's important to accept the culture of your family and your relationship with your parents. You have the right to ask about anything that is going to affect you, just as they have the right not to tell you.

Exercise 4.6 **4.6**

Opening the Door to Discussion

1. Ask, "Are you available? If not now, when?" Make a date for your discussion.
2. At the beginning of the discussion, say, "I'm working on my estate plan, and it would be very helpful for me to know if your plan is for me to receive anything, what that is, and when, so I can factor this into my plan." Then be quiet—literally bite your tongue if necessary—and let them respond.
3. Ask, "Would you tell me how you reached that decision?"
4. Ask, "What are you expecting from me in response?"
5. Whatever they say, do your best to accept it. Your job at this point is to understand what your parents' hopes and dreams are for you, financially and otherwise.

In any case, it's wise to prepare yourself for the entire range of possibilities: from inheriting significant wealth to inheriting nothing. It is better for young adults in their teens, twenties, and thirties to assume there may be no inheritance so the task is to make their own way in life. Even if your parents intend to give you a substantial fortune, their intentions may not play out for you. The stock market could take a serious hit. There are many potential variables: you and/or your parents can lose precious jobs, manage wealth poorly, or fall victim to a disreputable investment scheme. Prepare for your adult life as if you need to take care of yourself financially.

As we enter adulthood and continue to grow and mature, our relationships with our parents will at best transition into friendships, gently shedding the parent-child dynamics. This is the ideal. As you take responsibility for your financial life, you open wonderful new doors in your relationships with your parents.

4.7 EXERCISE 4.7

Gratitude

What are five elements of your relationship with your parents for which you are grateful?

____

____

____

4.8 EXERCISE 4.8

Action Plan

Now develop an action plan for filling a significant gap in your financial knowledge and thus improving your relationship with your parents.

Today's date ______________

The goal I set for my relationship with my parents is:

____

____

____

____

In order to accomplish this goal, I will perform the following activities:

____

____

____

____

Support people who might assist me include:

____

____

____

____

I realize I may sabotage my plan by:

____

____

____

____

So I will avoid this by:

____

____

____

____

I will complete this goal by ________________________ (date)

(Recommendation: three to six months)

As an adult, no matter how difficult your upbringing may have been, it's crucial that you acknowledge the tremendous role your parents have played in your life—both positive and negative. You may find it difficult to make this assessment accurately, but you can do it. Until you do, the attitudes and behaviors you hold on to can weigh you down and erode other relationships in your life.

This is as true for your relationship with your siblings as it is with your parents, as we will see in the next chapter.

Your Siblings
Friends, Rivals, and Everything Between

Siblings are the people we practice on, the people who teach us about fairness and cooperation and kindness and caring, quite often the hard way.

—Pamela Dugdale

Like branches on a tree we grow in different directions, yet our roots remain as one. Each of our lives will always be a special part of the other.

—Unknown

If thy brother wrongs thee, remember not so much his wrong-doing, but more than ever that he is thy brother.

—Epictetus

| Relationship Elements: | **Respect** | **Communication** | **Identity** |

Among Aesop's many wise fables, a longtime favorite of mine leads us directly into the heart of this important chapter's advice on how to maximize the myriad opportunities to improve relationships with all members of our family. Here is Aesop's pithy fable on the importance of remaining united:

> A farmer who had a quarrelsome family called his sons and told them to lay a bunch of sticks before him. Then, after laying the sticks parallel to one another and binding them, he challenged his sons, one after another, to pick up the bundle and break it. They all tried, but in vain. Then, untying the bundle, he gave them the sticks to break one by one. This they did with the greatest ease. Then said the father, "Thus, my sons, as long as you remain united, you are a match for anything, but differ and separate, and you are undone."

Together, we thrive and grow.

Children who grow up bonded to brothers and sisters do not have to make the journey to adulthood alone. They can share a blend of love, camaraderie, and genuine friendship that can linger and sustain them for a lifetime. They are our siblings—and they can be the best friends God ever gave us. As Erica E. Goode wrote in a 1994 *U.S. News & World Report* article, "Sibling relationships—and 80 percent of Americans have at least one—outlast marriages, survive the death of parents, resurface after quarrels that would sink any friendship. They flourish in a thousand incarnations of closeness and distance, warmth, loyalty and distrust."

And so, as we skip and stumble through our early years, despite parental inattention, competition for fleeting affection, or other inhibiting factors, some siblings who are inheritors grow up to remain close throughout their lives. Other inheritors, unfortunately, grow up distant from one another, continuing to maintain minimal contact through the years. Still other sibling relationships become fraught with anger, hurt feelings, and resentment, eventually progressing to the point of estrangement. If parents value sibling closeness among their children, they need to exemplify it with their own siblings and actively encourage it among their children.

At best, "To the outside world, we all grow old, but not to brothers and sisters," observes writer Clara Ortega. "We know each other as we always were. We know each other's hearts. We share private family jokes. We remember family feuds and secrets, family griefs and joys. We live outside the touch of time."

"Being in a family is like being in a play," points out Jane Nelson, marriage, family, and child therapist. "Each birth order position is like a different part in a play, with distinct and separate characteristics for each part. Therefore, if one sibling has already filled a part, such as the good child, other siblings may feel they have other parts to play, such as rebellious child, academic child, athletic child, social child, and so on."

Author and researcher Ellen Galinski puts it this way: "In families, children tend to take on stock roles, as if there were hats hung up in some secret place, visible only to the children. Each succeeding child selects a hat and takes on that role: the good child, the black sheep, the clown, and so forth." Often these roles are predictable and some people love to conjecture, as in, "Let me guess, you're the baby in your family…" However, sometimes siblings take on roles that defy the stereotypes.

Stepping Up to Lead

Kathy was the baby of the family, and her older brother and sisters could have been her best friends. But in her family, this was not to be. Her father, Bill, was a successful businessman, lucrative beyond his own wildest imagination. He had opened his first burger joint in the late 1940s, and with his focus on service and hard work, along with some luck, within twenty years he had built his business into a multimillion-dollar complex of drive-ins. His timing was right, his instincts were right, and he recognized what he had. There was a formula, and all of his burger joints upheld the successful formula to the letter. Though the food was inexpensive, it was delicious, and the profits were impressive.

Bill figured out the business as he needed to and taught parts of it to his five children, though not very systematically or thoroughly. They all worked in the business, learning it from the ground up. At first it looked like Bill had all of the necessary facets of leadership covered by his up-and-coming offspring. But disagreements emerged, offenses were given and taken, and the children didn't live up to the potential he had hoped for. His eldest son, Nick, chose to pursue life as a musician, joined a band, and left the business. One of the daughters, Libby, loved having an executive position in the company with a nice salary, but she spent most of her time showing horses. Another daughter, Caroline, chose to marry and become a full-time mom. She had little interest in the family business except as a source of income.

Then Bill had a heart attack at the young age of sixty and didn't survive. Because his wife had been uninterested in the business and had not learned its management, the kids took over. One of Kathy's other sisters, Shelley, decided she was the one to become president and run the business. Many people, both in the company and outside of it, watched with a great deal of interest to see if she could do it. Questions about her ethics and business practices began to emerge, but over time, she surrounded herself with aggressive officers, and no one could get enough information to prove that she was doing anything wrong.

However, Kathy suspected foul play and deceit. She had become a CPA so she would be familiar with the world of business and money management. She repeatedly offered her skills to help with the business, but Shelley always turned her down. This in itself caused Kathy to be suspicious. For years she couldn't prove anything, and she was unable to rally her siblings to confront Shelley. Each sibling was receiving a stream of income from the business, and no one wanted to rock the boat and risk shutting off the money faucet.

Eventually, the business began to falter, and when it did, it imploded quickly. Shelley had hidden so much information that the business had become a house of cards. Kathy was able to prove Shelley's wrongdoings as she gained access to documents. Kathy and her siblings argued over which transgressions were whose fault and who was entitled to what money. Outsiders who had known the family for decades shook their heads in disappointment. Bill had been so well liked and had seemed to manage his success well, but the truth was, without his strong leadership and moral compass, his offspring wrecked his business legacy. As tragic as the loss of the family business was, the destruction of the business family was more tragic.

Sibling roles became confused and disputed. Kathy developed a higher degree of competence than might have been predicted due to the choices her siblings made, especially Shelley. Kathy still was unwelcome in the leadership of the company, and eventually it came to light that Shelley's dishonest business practices were the cause for her secrecy. All of the siblings' natural roles were challenged and redefined in adulthood.

Birth Order or Disorder?

To some extent, sibling relationships can be traced to each individual's personality traits and proclivities—a mix of genetic makeup, education, training, environment, and wealth. Considering the fact that our siblings inherit from the same DNA, it's amazing how different we can be from each other in terms of personality, intelligence, competence, talent, and attitudes about family, money, success, and just about anything else.

Some of what molds who and what we become can also be traced to our birth order and the unique tendencies that sometimes, but certainly not always, accompany being born first, last, or in the middle of the pack—or being an only child. When wealth is added to the mix, we find additional, interesting twists on how birth order plays out among inheritors.

Many studies show that our birth order extends a predictable power over who we become and how we feel and behave. It isn't easy to change traits in ourselves that stem from our birth order, but this knowledge can be insightful as to why we feel or act the way we do.

You also may benefit by understanding how the birth order of your siblings can impact them, which can lead to softening your heart or forgiving them for differences, disagreements, or emotional distancing that may have resulted in part from birth order. Let's look at some of these influencing factors.

Oldest Children

The firstborn child tends to be competent, obedient, and diligent. Researchers have found a slightly higher IQ in eldest children compared with their younger siblings. Firstborns had an average IQ of 103, middle children 100, and the youngest 99.[1]

Firstborns are also disproportionately represented in high-paying jobs. A survey conducted among employees of the CEO organization Vistage found that more firstborns occupy more executive suites (43 percent) than middle children (33 percent) or youngest children (23 percent).[2] In addition, more eldest children become surgeons or acquire MBAs than their younger siblings, according to Robert Zajonc, a Stanford University psychologist.[3]

The reasons for these advantages over younger siblings are many. Nervous new parents tend to fawn over their first child, even to the point of paying constant attention, pampering, and overly protecting them. Sometimes, this may actually encourage development and growth, noted Petter Kristensen and Tor Bjerkedal in "Explaining the Relation Between Birth Order and Intelligence."[4] Before other children come along, parents typically devote to the first child 100 percent of whatever amount of child attention they make available, the article reveals.

Unsurprisingly, therefore, oldest children often feel responsible for their younger brothers and sisters. When they help teach their younger siblings—reading to them when they're young, teaching them how to tie their shoes or play a game—they are reinforcing what they have learned as firstborns. This may contribute to their slightly higher IQs. In addition, firstborns are often strivers and achievers, regardless of natural IQ, which is already in place.

On the flip side of the coin, firstborns can be quite pampered, at least until the next child comes along. At that point, the eldest child will often attempt to win back the parents' attention. This is, of course, a futile campaign. Firstborn children often encounter emotional problems later in life. If their experience of acquiring a sibling and the resulting loss of parental attention is one of broken trust, this can create lifelong trust problems. If firstborns develop difficulty trusting, this will affect all their relationships.

Firstborns, especially males, often automatically receive the benefits and burdens of assuming the role of leader (of the family, its wealth, and a business, if one exists). This tradition is not as strong as it once was, but it is certainly still the norm. Leadership can be very rewarding, both emotionally and financially, although most parents today, at least in this country, make an effort to equalize their estate. They often do their best to find ways to distribute equally or to find assets of equal value to bequeath to all the children.

A firstborn's leadership, however, can also create resentment and discord among younger siblings—especially if the oldest is not the most competent, or is not competent at all. Some parents who see how their offspring behave as they reach adulthood may shift responsibilities and benefits to the most competent sibling. Others, however, follow the tradition of passing leadership roles on to the oldest child. This can seem unfair to younger siblings, who then may develop resentment issues.

Dominating Shadows

Often, the eldest son or daughter of a successful parent struggles with the huge shadow cast by the older generation's success. Such offspring tend to have a hard time making their own mark on the world. With such a huge example to live up to, they may assume they are expected to create an equal measure of success, when in fact, such achievements are rare. Often the older generation's success stemmed as much from luck as it did from talent and tenacity, but the luck factor may be discounted by the next generation, which unintentionally piles the stress on itself.

Successful parents don't intend for their children to struggle in their shadow. Most are busy building their business or financial empire and don't see their efforts at being successful as a liability. It is usually a big accomplishment for the next generation to build success of any kind, and many parents recognize this. If working in the family business isn't a great fit for the children of these parents, they need to make their own way somewhere else. A Native American proverb describes the dilemma this can become: "If you want a place in the sun, you must leave the shade of the family tree." It is imperative, therefore, for some young family members to get out in the world and make their own place in the sun. A useful question for these young adults to ask is: I am the first generation of . . . what?

If you feel that you're stuck in the shadow of your parent, the key is to find your passion, your mission, your ministry; build your life around it; and find your place in the world. It is important to avoid trying to adopt the success of your parents as your own. Their success is not your success! Each of us must achieve our own success. If your parents have a rigid definition of success, they may question yours. Nevertheless, it is important to follow your dream and build the life you envision—eventually most parents relent. Hopefully, yours will recognize your success and celebrate it. Even if they don't, you will have been true to yourself, and this is the only way you can create real success.

Middle Children

Middle children are difficult to categorize, especially when there are more than three children. They can be both competitive and cooperative. They can also be social, laid-back peacemakers yet rebellious risk takers. The key to understanding middle children is to study the behaviors and characteristics of the sibling just ahead of them.

Middle children observe their big brothers or sisters and strive to differentiate. If the older sibling is competent and conforming, the next sibling is likely to be rebellious and risk taking. This formula also works in large families with two or more middle children—each middle child looks to the next oldest child and then strives to differentiate. However, older siblings may still influence younger middle children. So the scope of choices the middle child may make is wide and varied.

"Unfortunately, life may sometimes seem unfair to middle children, some of whom feel like an afterthought to a brilliant older sibling and unable to captivate the family's attention like the darling baby," notes pediatrician-professor-author Marianne E. Neifert.[5] "Yet the middle position offers great training for the real world of lowered expectations, negotiation, and compromise. Middle children who often must break the mold set by an older sibling may thereby learn to challenge family values and seek their own identity."

What's more, middle children sometimes feel passed over. They often are not acknowledged for the leadership qualities they have, even when an older sibling might be less competent or less of a natural leader. Likewise, sometimes the power is passed by gender, not birth order. Males can be favored simply on the basis of being male, and greater competence in a sister may be discredited due simply to gender.

In the Chapman business family, Wendy is one of the middle children, and Peter and Paul are her older twin brothers. When their father wanted to pass the business leadership on to Peter, Peter chose to abdicate and go out on his own. This left the less dominant twin, Paul, as the next in line by birth. Their father insisted that Paul be designated company president despite Wendy's clearly demonstrated competence and leadership. Wendy felt rejected and unacknowledged.

The situation was resolved, however, when their dad died at a young age and Wendy was promoted to family business leader on the basis of merit. Wendy claims, "If my father had lived, I believe that I would have left the business to make my own way rather than live with the frustration of never being recognized." While they were all heartbroken to lose their father, this loss shook up the leadership in the next generation significantly. Wendy remains close to her brothers, and Paul still works in the business, which she has successfully led for the past thirty years.

Fortunately, most middle children do not have to face such extreme situations as these. The lucky ones are able to enjoy the blessings of being both the little sister or brother to their older siblings and the older sibling to their younger brothers or sisters. Sometimes middle children perceive fewer expectations placed on them and are able to make their own way more easily than the older and younger siblings are.

Walking in Your Siblings' Shoes

When middle children reach adulthood, the decisions they made as children need to be examined and possibly challenged. Perhaps these decisions—specifically their reactions to the sibling who came before them—took them away from, rather than toward, the best choices for a fulfilling life.

It's important for adult children who feel they may have been passed over for leadership roles to put themselves in their siblings' shoes and imagine the stress they live with. Their siblings' stress may be the result of leadership and responsibility that does not fit them well. They may be defensive and arrogant, feeling pressured to do a job they were not prepared for. Sometimes compassion can yield flexibility and role shifting to more prepared siblings. Though this is certainly not the norm, it can be an option worth exploring.

Middle children—and their younger siblings—may suffer when the firstborn child is put in charge of their financial or legal affairs and makes bad decisions. If you recognize that your older sibling is not able to manage the financial or legal responsibilities, you can do your best to offer constructive advice about how the wealth can be protected and enhanced. But it's futile to interfere to the point of frustration—yours and theirs. Ultimately, you may be powerless. You certainly have a right to speak up, but that might be the only right you have. It is important to remember that all siblings, regardless of birth order, can be challenged in fulfilling roles they are expected to fill. Be careful to find out the reality before judging them.

Youngest Children

Youngest children, unsurprising to me, are often the comedians of their families. A major reason, I believe, is because by the time they are born, their parents are much more relaxed about parenting. They are more lax about dispensing discipline and tend to pamper the baby of the family. Because these children are younger, they sometimes feel inferior and jealous of their big brothers and sisters, who have more freedom and power in the family. This can cause younger children to become somewhat manipulative.

Elena was clearly used to getting her way. The first day I met her, it was easy to see that she had learned to use her family members' weaknesses to get them to go along with what she wanted. The interesting part of this equation was that, though she was the youngest of the three siblings, Elena was the most business minded and had a natural ability to learn money management. She had even been investing as well as living off of the trust distributions she had been receiving since she'd turned twenty-one. To her it was fun to build her own account and watch it grow. By age thirty-five, she had built an account on her own of over $3 million. Even so, her family saw her as the manipulative child she had been, and they did not instill any trust in her abilities. She always felt they didn't give her a chance. Then the opportunity arose.

Elena's challenge was to rescue the family wealth from her older brother, Perry, who seemed to think he was a good money manager but wasn't, and to keep her middle sister, Anna, from stepping in to divert more money to herself (Anna was a big spender). Elena intended to work with professional money managers for the benefit of the family. Their father, an inheritor himself, saw her skills in growing investments. She was clearly the best one in the family to take on the financial responsibility. She viewed her task as a game in a sense, though a serious game. As she succeeded in talking everyone into letting her direct the investing of the vast family fortune, it was clear that, when the time came for distribution of the principal, she intended to see the wealth divided equally among the three siblings. Once her family members acknowledged Elena's skills, her need to manipulate faded. As her keen abilities benefited her parents and siblings, she found her family members, even Perry, to be cooperative with her money-management decisions. In all of this, though, there was a noticeable negative. Perry really lost his bearings and felt that his position as eldest was usurped. He appreciated Elena's ability to manage wealth well, but he felt resentful. Everyone in the family knew it, and it was a sore spot that only healed roughly.

In some cases, youngest children are so much younger than their siblings that they are almost like an older or only child, and they can develop corresponding birth order traits. Family-of-origin life can be frustrating for the youngest child who is skilled and has leadership qualities but whom the family disregards when it comes to the tradition of passing on wealth responsibilities. This kind of mismatch of skills and position can create a drain on the family fortune and become a liability for all family members. Many times youngest children are so used to being taken care of, they do not become hard workers or educate themselves in financial matters. Often charming, funny, and relaxed, youngest siblings can be good at choosing a mate who will take care of them and pamper them the way they were pampered by their parents and siblings.

Only Children

Single children often are unfairly characterized. In recent years, we have seen many myths and stereotypes about only children dispelled, such as the assumptions that they are selfish, socially inept, dependent on others, anxious, and spoiled brats. Or that they are prone to feeling lonely. Or that their lack of siblings as playmates makes them more outgoing in order to acquire friends. Or that they may not work well in groups, given their lack of experience living with other children. While none of these stereotypes can be fairly applied to all children without siblings, there are still some characteristics that tend to apply to only children. They are often high achievers in school; they tend to forge strong, positive friendships; and they typically have good relationships with both parents, rather than just one, as is more common among children who have siblings.

Only children do not have to vie with siblings for parental attention, so they do not have to contend with the rivalries and competition that children with siblings do. The lack of siblings can allow for a wide range of personality types among only children. In my work, I have found only children to be good to work with. Perhaps because they haven't had sibling experiences, they are typically open and willing to interact with me. My only-child clients have been motivated and responsible.

Clearly, single children do not have to share their inheritance with siblings. This is not necessarily an advantage. Sole inheritors may have more responsibility on their shoulders in managing the inheritance. Also, they don't get to share part of their life with a true peer. I have often thought that in families where there are two or more children, it's a plus to have these other people on the journey through life forever. We might not like our siblings, but there can be a profound benefit in sharing history and experience.

Whatever their birth order, many siblings don't get along, especially those from wealthy families. Sometimes it's because there is more room in big houses for family members to isolate themselves; sometimes it's because the stakes are higher and arguments blow up bigger than in families where there are more modest resources.

Blended Families

If your parents divorce, remarry, and have children with a new spouse, you will perhaps have step-, half-, or new siblings. These new members are bound to create family challenges. Aside from the emotional havoc that is likely to ensue, there will be financial issues, especially if the new stepparent or half- and stepsiblings are included in your parent's wills. You probably will have strong feelings about this—feelings you will need to resolve for your own stress management and peace of mind.

Blended families are challenging for everyone involved. If you add wealth into the equation, it doesn't take a rocket scientist to see that the stakes become much higher, which can make the potential problems even hotter and more volatile. Use the seven elements of healthy relationships and the tools you find in this book to help you manage these relationships.

Difficult Siblings

We can choose our friends, but we cannot pick our family members. Some people wonder, *How did I get in this family?* Unfortunately, it is common that siblings are not friends—sometimes they even feel like enemies. Sometimes it's because of how the siblings behave or the choices they make as adults. Perhaps a sister is dishonest, mean, or unethical in the way she handles money or business. Or a brother may be uncaring, self-centered, and selfish.

One common problem in wealthy families is narcissism. Wealthy families have more than the average number of narcissists. This may be because wealthy people are often pandered to and miss the reality checks that most other people receive as they go through life. These reality checks help us all develop qualities that we can use well when relating to others. In fact, an excellent—but discouraged—way to build narcissistic behavior in a child is to "spoil them rotten" and not deny them anything.

It is extremely difficult to deal with narcissistic siblings—or parents, for that matter, or anyone else wholly self-absorbed. It helps if you understand that narcissists are unable to empathize with you and cannot view your concerns as important (though they may pretend to do this). You really can't expect caring and reciprocity. If you can recognize early on that you're dealing with a narcissist in your family and accept these uncontrollable factors, you will have an easier time coping.

It's also important to realize that you can't reach them. Narcissists have their own agenda. They don't care about you, your life, or your well-being—financially or otherwise. Remember, though, they don't mean to be negative; they just have a grandiose sense of their own importance. They view everything as being about them. This sounds negative, but it's really more about being self-centered. Predictably, narcissists usually have at least one narcissistic parent.

There are excellent books that can help you learn to cope with narcissistic family members. See the resources section of this book for some suggestions, and be sure to visit www.thayerwillis.com for more. There is no rule that you must like your siblings. How you behave is much more important than how you feel about other people.

Walk Away from Your Wealth?

I have seen many deeply frustrated clients who have struggled with incompetent or dishonest older siblings who have been placed in charge of trusts for the other siblings. One client, Sarah, has been repeatedly impacted negatively by the way her brother, Tim, runs the family's finances in the four years since their father's death.

Sarah and her husband live modestly on income they earn in their respective professions, preferring not to touch her substantial inheritance. This is unusual, but it has worked well for them. Tim is flamboyant, spends wantonly, and wants everyone to know what he has—and actually wants people to think he has even more than he does. Fortunately for Sarah, Tim lives in another state, but not quietly. Not only does it upset Sarah that Tim squanders the family fortune and that some of his poor investments impact her future inheritance, she also fears his behavior will expose her as a wealthy person in the small town where she lives. The stress has caused her to develop a heart condition and a troubling skin condition, neither of which she had before Tim took his place as the financial head of the family.

Another client, Anne, has been immersed in several lawsuits for many years. At first, she wanted to right wrongs she found in the family finances, and she has now devoted a large part of her life to this. A middle child, she had already received a substantial inheritance and could have made a comfortable life with it. However, the destruction Anne saw among the family members who were running the family business was more than she was willing to tolerate. Her older sibling had been involved in illegal activities and had tried to hide this under layers of deceit. She came to me asking how she could best acquire peace of mind and how much stress the inheritance was worth.

Eventually, after proving the misdeeds of her family and extended family, Anne was able to take over the family business. As a young adult, she wouldn't have predicted this path for herself, but this was where her journey took her. She has devoted herself to running the business and has somewhat restored the family's good name. She is still working on it.

It is important for these people to consider the question: What would you think of walking away from the financial wealth as a way of letting go of the problem? Some people feel that the resulting freedom would be alluring. Others decide the financial wealth is more important and to persevere in the fight, but it's worth considering the choice.

Psychological Stages of Development

All human beings, regardless of their birth order, experience specific psychological stages as they mature. Inheritors often develop late in a world cushioned by wealth, largely the result of not having to make their own way in life, having too much insulation from the kinds of experiences that help us mature, or not having the skills to manage interactions well with other young adults.

Where there is a lack of skills to communicate and relate, and where financial stakes are high, some family members' behaviors can become extreme. For example, it is not uncommon in wealthy families for nuclear family members to stop speaking to each other or even to sue each other. Sometimes we find people acting like children well into adulthood when developmentally we expect them to have outgrown childish behaviors. Understanding the stages of development and that inheritors may move through them more slowly can help us especially in strengthening our relationships with our siblings.

Psychologist Erik Erikson identified eight stages during which people must come to grips with conflicts between opposing concepts in order to develop a positive resolution, or virtue. Failure to resolve both extremes of a given life-stage challenge will make it difficult for people to maintain healthy relationships and to be able to negotiate the world successfully. This causes people to become stuck at their current emotional level, failing to progress to future stages.

Figure 5.1 lists Erikson's eight life stages. In each stage there are conflicts. These conflicts can linger and defy resolution, or they can cause people to develop certain virtues. People develop virtues inherent in each stage only if they successfully grapple with the conflicts

that arise from that stage. Obviously, most people can't remember whe
and whether their parents picked them up, fed them, or changed their dia
cried. But people who feel distrustful or lack a general sense of hope likely faile
the conflict of basic trust vs. mistrust during the infancy stage.

One stage in which wealthy children might become stuck is during early elementa
school years. Often, privileged children have nannies and maids to dress them and clean up after them. Many parents in wealthy families do not expect their children to take on responsibilities, such as chores. Later these people can find it elusive to develop a sense of purpose or competence.

5.1

Figure 5.1:

Erikson's Eight Ages of Man[6]

Stage	Conflict	Virtue	Challenge
Infancy	Basic Trust vs. Mistrust	Hope	To believe your caregivers were reliable. Did they pick you up when you cried? Feed you when you were hungry?
Toddler	Autonomy vs. Shame and Doubt	Will	To learn to explore the world without feeling smothered or neglected by parents.
Kindergarten	Initiative vs. Guilt	Purpose	To be able to plan or do things (such as dress yourself) on your own.
Age six through Puberty	Industry vs. Inferiority	Competence	To recognize differences in your abilities compared with others, such as classmates.
Teenager	Identity vs. Role Confusion	Fidelity	To question yourself, figure out where you fit in; to feel free to explore.
Young Adult	Intimacy vs. Isolation	Love	To discover whom you want to be with or date, what you want to do with your life.

continued on next page

	Virtue	Challenge
[illegible]nation	Caring	To measure your accomplishments and failures, to help the younger generation.
[illegible]spair	Wisdom	To reflect on the past and feel satisfied with your accomplishments or become bitter and unhappy.

If you identify any traits [illegible]e stages that you feel you have not developed, you can work to develop them now. Certainly, it is more difficult to do so after the natural age for that stage has passed, but with motivation and professional guidance, it is usually possible. Also consider areas where your siblings may have become stuck. This will help you understand the motives for some of their behaviors.

As you do this, you will also discover areas of strength—both your own and your siblings'. When you think of your family as a whole, there are key questions you can ask yourself to identify family shareholder equity. Imagine for a few moments that you are with your family of origin for a Sunday dinner. In your mind's eye, look around the table and consider each person:

- Have you and your siblings each taken charge of your lives?
- Are individual family members defining, pursuing, and experiencing happiness?
- Are family strengths evident?
- Are human, intellectual, and social capital increasing?
- Is family capital stronger than family liabilities?

You may find that your family is stronger than you previously thought. Do your best to remember these strengths in times of difficulty.

Sibling Rivalry

Most commonly, relationships that are formed when we are children remain as they are established in those early years. If you experienced sibling rivalry as a kid, unless you make a huge effort to change this, the rivalry will carry on. Furthermore, you will most likely pass this pattern down to your children.

Anna had rarely spent time with her Uncle Stuart, her father's brother, while she was growing up. As an adult, she enjoyed speaking with him at a wedding and realized she didn't even know her first cousins from her Uncle Stuart's family. She found out from her mother that her father hadn't spoken to Stuart in decades. She also realized she had unconsciously picked up that cutoff attitude with her Uncle Stuart and his family. It occurred to her that she didn't know them well enough to even have an opinion about them, so she called her uncle and asked to visit him. She was delighted that two of his children were also in town when she visited, and she discovered that she very much likes them.

Anna began thinking about her own cutoff relationship with her sister. It suddenly occurred to her that she had unintentionally picked up that behavior from her father. She decided it was time to break this pattern and heal. Luckily, there were no deep problems between the sisters; they were just unconsciously reenacting the cutoff behavior they had acquired from their father. Anna's first step was to pick up the phone. She felt nervous about breaking the silence, and she had no grand goal. She simply called to say hello and do her best to start to have some contact. The conversation was a little awkward, though it went well enough, so she suggested they meet for lunch. She shared with her sister her experience of getting to know their Uncle Stuart and discussed how their father's behavior toward him may have influenced their own distant relationship.

The sisters have not become best friends, but they are polite and kind to each other, they keep in touch, and they provide opportunities for their children to know each other. They have decided not to allow the negative patterns they learned from their father to be passed down to yet another generation.

It's not always as easy to heal rifts with siblings as it was for Anna. The first step is awareness and choice. If you are a forgiving person and if you're able to shift your perspective, it is possible to heal rifts. Like Anna, it's important not to set the bar too high by expecting to become best friends with your previously estranged sibling. Simply thawing out a tense, icy relationship may be enough—or at least a good place to start. Then let the relationship progress over time to reach a comfortable, sustainable level of respect and kindness. Even this modest goal requires some deep thinking first and solid communication skills.

Communicating Effectively

Communication skills are crucial to every healthy relationship, but we are often challenged the most in communicating with our siblings. The basic communication guidelines are to be kind, stay positive, and be respectful. These guidelines sound deceptively simple. To put them into action, develop the following skills:

Attending is being fully present for the family member with whom you are communicating. Being fully present means staying in the present and striving to understand what is important to the other person's point of view, not simply waiting to talk or planning what you will say next.

Listening is a poorly practiced skill in our culture in general, but we all know how powerful it is to be really listened to. Think of that rare person in a crowded room who draws you into conversation and makes you feel like you are the only person there. I often have clients practice the skill of listening, and nearly everyone is surprised at how difficult it is to listen well enough to report to our group what they heard.

Empathy is the fertile ground of communication. If we can empathize with a family member, we can become close. If we cannot empathize, we cannot improve the relationship.

Curiosity is the way to move forward. Even if you are bored with family members or think you know everything that goes on in their reality, the truth is you don't know. Be curious, just like you might be curious about someone you just met. Be kind and ask questions.

I would even add a bonus communication skill: ***Improvisation***.

"Improv is about dealing with what is, not with what you wish it was," comments talented improv artist Shelley Darcy. Improv, she claims, motivates us to reach for whatever truth we can find in the moment. In improv—acting in the spur of the moment without a script or cues—we have to let go and think outside the box in order to participate. Improv entices us out of familiar territory, and we find ourselves bravely opening mental doors, some of which are covered with cobwebs. Its key components are:

1. Teamwork.
2. The scenario—a snapshot of life—taking place in the present.
3. A scenario that has value. The vital component could be comedy, intrigue, personal meaning, education, or just fun. This wonderful piece, the scenario, is created out of the collaborative and cooperative skills each participant contributes.

Watching an improv scenario on stage or television, audience members see what seems like rampant chaos and an anything-goes environment. However, this is not the case at all. There are a few stated rules in improv and several implicit guidelines. "Yes, and . . ." is the improviser's mantra. This requires participants to accept their scene partner's offer and build on it. Just as in a family discussion, actors in an improv scene can reject, or block, what others introduce to the scene. If they do, the action "dies." On the other hand, if they accept another's offer with the *yes* part of the mantra and build on it with *and*, the discussion is constructive and positive.

Actually, all of this requires considerable discipline and—getting back to my point—teamwork. Improv shows your true character. In this highly revealing place, it's impossible to hide who you really are. Furthermore, your co-improvisers will not tolerate much negativity, if that is what you bring to the group. According to Daryl Olson, improv artist extraordinaire, "Improv is 100 percent commitment to being in the moment and letting go of your own agenda. There is a misconception that improvisers just get up and go without a plan. Improvisers do have a plan; but, to succeed, they have to be able to be changed and switch directions in an instant. Improvisation is fun; but it is also a discipline. The best improvisers have learned to find balance between the discipline and the fun. Improvisers spend their lives maneuvering through an unknown landscape. Good improvisers don't ignore that they feel doubt and uncertainty; however, they don't run away from it. They face doubt and uncertainty with confidence."

What if we all applied this practice to our everyday lives? What if we used our improv skills to live in the moment, to see our reality as it really is, and to effectively communicate with those who are close to us?

When family members learn communication skills and use them well, they feel safer and more open with each other. Figure 5.2 outlines specific techniques for sending and receiving messages effectively.

Figure 5.2 5.2

Sending and Receiving Messages Effectively

Sending Messages Effectively

Clearly own your messages by using "I" language. For example, say, "I feel afraid of you," instead of "You scare me."

Make your messages complete and specific.

Match your nonverbal messages with your verbal.

Be repetitive.

Ask for feedback concerning the way your messages are being received.

Make the message appropriate to the receiver's frame of reference.

continued on next page

Describe your feelings by name, action, or figure of speech. For instance, "I feel afraid of you, intimidated, skittish" is specific feedback that adds useful information.

Describe the other person's behavior without evaluating, interpreting, or judging.

Acknowledge how the other person is feeling.

Make sure that your body language communicates your attentiveness to the discussion by looking at the person you are speaking with and keeping a focused body posture.

Receiving Messages Effectively

Paraphrase the content of the message accurately and nonjudgmentally.

Describe what you perceive to be the sender's feelings.

State your interpretation of the sender's message and negotiate with the sender until there is agreement about the message's meaning.

When striving to implement safe communication in families, we can learn and practice specific tools. Communication tools in wealthy families include listening, assertiveness, empathy, honesty, openness, cultivating and acknowledging gratitude, forgiveness, body language, mentoring, philanthropy, and governance. These tools work best when all family members identify and clarify their values, write personal mission statements, and work together to write a family mission statement.

Sometimes it's not possible to reverse lingering sibling resentments and rivalries. When this is true, I help some clients, for their own health and sanity, to distance themselves. If your sister abused you in a way that you have so far been unable to recover from, it's best to stand back, get an arms-length perspective, and tell yourself, "I see this. I know it's hurtful, frustrating, and wrong. But I'm not going to let it dominate my life." Acknowledge the situation, accept that it is out of your control, and focus on the positive points you do have. It's important to remember that you still have a lot—identify what you have and clarify it by exploring its value.

Letting Go, Moving Forward

As I've stressed already, it is important to live your life on your own terms in order to build your own relationships, successes, and failures. A lot of people let perceived injustices dominate their lives. Regardless of how much truth lies in the injustice, be careful to not waste your own life in this negative preoccupation. When people get stuck in this trap, they lose more than anyone else does.

Caroline remained furious for years about her perceived injustices by her siblings. I only know her side of the story, about how she was cheated out of art and jewelry that had both financial and sentimental value and had been promised to her by her grandparents. Her parents, siblings, and cousins all knew these items had been earmarked for her. After Caroline's grandfather passed away, her grandmother moved in with Gillian, Caroline's sister, who managed to take possession of all of the heirlooms. Caroline tried to speak up, but Gillian proved to be a formidable opponent, unwilling to negotiate.

No one would stand up for Caroline for fear that Gillian would manipulate their grandmother into cutting them out of the will. Caroline was stuck for years in her anger. It caused her to separate from her entire family. Caroline was so consumed by her sister's unfairness that she even alienated her friends to the point that she rarely socialized. When she came to me, she longed to feel connected, especially during holidays.

In our work together, it has taken years for Caroline to let go of her rage and her obsessive focus on the injustices she perceived. While she could not repair the injustices, over several years she was able to re-channel her energy and resolve most of her anger. Eventually, she felt expansive enough to identify several charitable causes to which she could donate some of her time and financial wealth, and she joined the board of one of these organizations.

On that board, Caroline has met new people and is beginning to build a new social circle. She is taking charge of her life. The key for Caroline was realizing that it was up to her, no one else, to make a life for herself. She couldn't change the past, and after a while she couldn't even find anyone willing to listen to her argue her case. It took her a long time, but she gradually realized the only way out for her was to engage in the present.

Siblings usually have a range of virtues, traits, natural and acquired skills, and deficiencies. Some siblings are polar opposites; others are alike. Either scenario may cause siblings to compete with or resent each other. What's more, when it comes to sibling rivalry, there are few clear winners. You know you can't change the past, and it is unlikely that anyone will help you try to right the wrongs of the past. What you can do is focus on your dreams, let go of the blame, and move forward.

Moving Toward the Bright Side

I recommend staying in touch with family members if at all possible. Even if the communication is merely careful, polite, and cool, it is still healthier to be in touch than to be estranged. The rare situations in which I support cutting off relationships include serious abuse or addiction that could be dangerous to you.

To make staying in touch easier, do your best to ease some of the resentment between you and your siblings by understanding the situation better. Often sibling rivalry comes from the perception that your parents gave more gifts, money, or attention to your sibling(s) than they gave to you. This may or may not be true. Perhaps your sibling(s) have a different perspective than you do. They might think you received more than they did. Even if there were inequalities, it's important to realize that this was your parents' doing, not your siblings' fault. There may be ways you can make an effort to right any lingering inequalities or at least relieve the sting of the pain.

In the business family at the beginning of the chapter, some of the sibling relationships were destroyed irreparably. However, Kathy missed her family. Happily, after all of the accusations and fighting, she was able to establish a positive relationship with Nick, her oldest brother. They grew to treasure their special connection and the sense of family they kept alive with each other.

Exercise 5.3 will help you gain perspective on what you and your siblings might be feeling.

---

e

5.3 EXERCISE 5.3

Sibling Perspectives

1. Do you perceive that your parents gave more gifts, money, or attention to your sibling(s) than they gave to you? If so, what specifically?

___

___

___

2. Do you think your sibling(s) have the same perspective, or might they think you actually received more than they did? Again, include specifics.

___

___

___

3. If there were inequalities, can you view this as your parents' doing, not your siblings' fault? If not, how do you see it?

4. Can you think of ways you can make an effort in the present to right any lingering inequalities?

After you write down your answers to Exercise 5.3, consider asking your siblings to do the same and compare your responses. You may be surprised at how much their perspectives differ from yours. The point is not to force each other to see things in any particular way but to realize that you may not be the only one who feels the other received more.

It's important to realize that even if there were inequities, it is likely that you both received what you needed and, in many cases, gifts beyond what you needed. Sometimes simply talking about lingering resentments can go a long way toward resolving them. Real motivation, you'll find, is key to reaching an amicable resolution for all. And listening—*really* listening—to your sibling(s) may even give you empathy and compassion for their experience. Are you willing to shift your perspective, even a little? If so, talk it over. It's the only way to get through your resentment. "Don't carry a grudge," as comedian Buddy Hackett advised. "While you're carrying the grudge, the other guy's out dancing."

e 2.4

Exercise 5.4:

Gratitude

What are five elements of your relationship with a sibling for which you feel grateful?

5.5 Exercise 5.5

Action Plan

Now write an action plan for beginning to improve your relationship with this or another sibling.

Today's date ______________________

The goal I set for my relationship with one of my siblings is:

____

____

____

____

In order to accomplish this goal, I will perform the following activities:

____

____

____

____

Support people who might assist me include:

____

____

____

____

I realize I may sabotage my plan by:

____

____

____

____

So I will avoid this by:

____

____

____

____

I will complete this goal by ________________________ (date)

(Recommendation: three to six months)

Sometimes the most workable solution to old hurts and the best step toward strong family emotional health is to stretch and be kind, even if you don't feel like it. Console yourself with this certainty: the next generation will benefit from you taking the high road in family relationships.

Embracing, Nurturing
The Extended Family

If the family were a boat, it would be a canoe that makes no progress unless everyone paddles.
—Letty Cottin Pogrebin

Like all the best families, we have our share of eccentricities, of impetuous and wayward youngsters and of family disagreements.
—Queen Elizabeth II

In family life, love is the oil that eases friction, the cement that binds closer together, and the music that brings harmony.
—Eva Burrows

| Relationship elements: | **Values** | **Trust** | **Communication** |

Because the extended family is, well, extended, some of its members may not seem able to impact our daily lives significantly enough to merit an entire chapter dealing with their influence on us. The truth, however, is that the influence that grandparents, cousins, in-laws, steps, and other relations exert on us is pervasive, meaningful, and highly important. The elements most common in these relationships are values, trust, and communication. In extended families, it is challenging and enriching to keep these elements healthy and strong. The effort to do this itself can strengthen you.

Bringing Extended Families Together

Over the years, Colin, who was thirty-five when I met him, found that he was emerging among his extended family members as the only one with the motivation to complete an education beyond high school, the only one willing to develop his business sense, and now the only one willing and able to lead the company. The family business was a highly successful food products company run by a family in which most of the members of his generation dabbled in work or just liked to play—they definitely did not pursue careers.

When Colin's grandfather, whom the family called Papa, first started to accumulate wealth in the 1950s, he set up a trust to benefit each branch of his family. Papa died in the year 2000 and, with Colin's agreement, named Colin as trustee. Before long, Colin had too much on his shoulders; most family members were overspending their income, and deep rifts had grown between branches of the family.

In a nutshell, communication and trust were problems. Significantly, however, the extended family still shared a lot of values. Therein lay their hope.

I started working with this family right after Colin realized that the extended family could not continue together for much longer unless some changes were made. The overspending alone threatened to bankrupt the family within a decade. It was easy to see that the extended family had already lost much of their strength and needed to regain it. We decided to schedule family retreats to work on rebuilding that trust.

During the first retreat, I was amazed to see the shared values at work. We created teams of family members, pairing relatives who normally didn't interact with each other to do exercises. The sharing of values brought out tentative results that would slowly emerge over the course of the retreat. In short, we practiced communication skills that built trust.

Now, several family retreats later, the family owes a debt of gratitude to this young man who brought them together again. The family is pulling together—pursuing education, monitoring spending, and taking part in the business—to sustain the success of the company and the strength of the family. Harmony among the extended family is substantial and noticeable to all.

Common Obstacles to Family Closeness

Families experience various kinds of impediments to closeness with extended family members. Let's explore some common obstacles. We'll discuss possible solutions to these challenges later in the chapter.

Jealousy or Resentment

When your parents resent your grandparents' efforts to connect with you or your efforts to connect with them, sometimes this is caused by jealousy. Some parents feel their parents disapprove of the way they raised you and your siblings. This could be because they think your parents lavished too many material gifts and too little time on you.

Even some innocuous little traditions can cause your parents to feel undercut. For instance, Jim Grubman, head of FamilyWealth Consulting, points out:

The grandpa who slips his grandchild twenty dollars while whispering, "Don't tell your daddy, it's our secret," may cherish the shared moment. But what messages are being delivered with the cash? Children watch their families closely. Is there tension between parents and grandparents around money, roping the child into the conflict? Or are the money messages presented in a united fashion, reinforcing their truth?[1]

Manipulation

Some grandparents, aunts, or uncles put young family members in the middle of problems they have with the parents or parents' siblings. It is difficult to extricate yourself from this position, but it can easily become a negative position for you. The first step is to establish clear and consistent boundaries. In childhood, this requires more strength than most children have, but as an adult, it is important and more reasonable to establish such boundaries. It's one thing to listen to what one person has to say about another; this can be empathetic. It is another thing to indulge in gossip.

There can be a fine line between empathy and gossip. One safeguard against gossip is to only make comments about someone that you would also say directly to them. Beyond this, it is better to ask that conversations and discussions focus only on those who are present. If you do engage in talking about others behind their back, you will likely be tempted to respond or take sides, voluntarily entering dangerous territory. Being a good listener can help people feel understood, process their perspectives, and vent their feelings. However, it is important to resist the temptation to intercede except on clear-cut, established issues, like something that is against the law. Otherwise it is a no-win situation for everyone. Also, there are risks to giving your own opinion. You can be blamed for siding one way or the other. It is better to simply be a good listener and confidence keeper.

Sometimes family members will threaten to withhold financial help or access to family privileges such as vacation homes, yachts, or private jets if you do not agree to certain conditions. For instance, they may insist that your children attend a particular private school even if you don't feel it is the best place for your children. It can be difficult to withstand such pressure.

Grieving

When any family member dies, all of the relationship dynamics in the family shift—some actually change a lot. This is a basic quality of family systems. If family members can grieve the loss of this relative, they will handle their own shifting dynamics better. Many times though, for various reasons, grieving is postponed. This can lead to family and business dysfunction.

On the other hand, when the grieving process is respected, honored, and allowed to progress, the family can engage in intentional and positive changes. If you have any doubt about where you are in the process, there are many resources (other family members, books, clergy, and therapists) that can help you move through your own grieving process with strength.

Distance

In today's generations, families are spread out geographically around the country and even, in some cases, the globe. It's easy, with our busy lives and demands from all fronts, to let time slip by without making contact with extended family members. This can lead to deteriorated relationships, depriving everyone of the richness that can be enjoyed in a strong family. One family member can make a difference by initiating family trips, retreats, or meetings.

Differences in Wealth

When the wealth of different branches of the family varies widely or changes over time, cousins or other family members you were close with in your younger years may drift away. If your family is much wealthier, your cousins may perceive themselves as different—or you may. You might all find that you have less in common with each other. It takes a lot of work for families whose finances have become disparate to remain connected as family members.

Getting branches of the family together can create problems. You may hesitate to engage in the modest travel that is now their norm, or they may not be able to afford fancy restaurants or vacations. Maybe only parts of the family, those who perceive themselves as having more in common with each other, will keep in touch. An effective solution to these dilemmas is to establish a family gathering fund that can be used confidentially by those who need it.

Taking Sides

You can be perceived as being disloyal just for liking someone whom a sibling or your parents don't like. Sometimes parents set up this recipe for disloyalty without even realizing the far-reaching effect of the behavior they model. To be a positive force in the family, be careful about taking sides. It is helpful to cultivate the attitude that you probably can't see the whole picture. It is likely that there are relevant facts and dynamics that you don't have access to. This can help you remember to just be there for your family members without taking sides.

Judgments

When family members who were close drift apart, one or both people may make assumptions about how their relationship got off track. When such assumptions go unchecked and fester, they can turn into resentment. If you care about such relationships, it is worthwhile to submit your assumptions to a reality test. In many cases, people cut off relationships due to a heartbreaking or embarrassing problem in their nuclear family. It could be a divorce or a child who has gotten into trouble with drugs or alcohol. It could be anything, and most importantly, it could have *nothing* to do with you. They may feel they will be judged, so they just withdraw. One of the many advantages of family reunions is that they provide opportunities to rebuild bridges and heal troubled relationships.

Gretchen had been very close to her cousin Keith when they were growing up, but they had become distant over the past few years and she didn't know why. She finally caught him at a good moment during a family gathering, and he told her that honestly, his distance had to do with his daughter, who had gotten pregnant out of wedlock and had kept the baby. No one had ever crossed this line in this extended family before. Keith was still feeling embarrassed and disappointed about it. He was also happy he was talking to Gretchen, relieved she had broken the ice. Gretchen was able to admit to Keith some of her own family's embarrassing mistakes and assure him that she wasn't judging him harshly. She made it clear that she felt she was in no position to throw stones. Their relationship warmed up almost to the point of the closeness that Gretchen remembered from years ago, and Keith was clearly relieved to let down his guard.

Intergenerational Issues

While most of the challenges discussed in this chapter can happen in any relationship, some are more likely to appear across generation gaps. Let's focus specifically on the kinds of issues that tend to present themselves in relationships with grandparents.

Criticism

Criticism can be founded on any point in the spectrum of parenting. You may find that your parents—your children's grandparents—feel you are depriving your children if you don't send them to private schools or fancy summer camps, or lavish them with designer clothes and the latest high-tech gizmos. They may feel that you should use your family's wealth to lavish the children with every material advantage. Others may feel that regardless of the wealth, it's better for children not to receive so many things.

If you feel criticized for spoiling your children, remember that your parents may have grown up in very different circumstances than you have. In many wealthy families, the wealth only goes back one or two generations. You may have been raised in much more affluent circumstances than your parents were. It may be difficult to convince a grandparent who lived through WWII that you are not giving your children too much.

Spoiling

Parents sometimes worry that grandparents are spoiling the children. You may feel helpless to stop the gush of gifts that arrive at birthdays and certain holidays. Many of us have heard the stories of grandparents arriving for a celebration with so many gifts, they can't even carry them all into the house.

This dismays conscientious parents who feel such gifts undermine their attempts to battle the constant barrage of consumerism. The gift giving can actually ruin a celebration when children become overstimulated, crying instead of smiling. Parents often look forward to celebrations as one of their chances to take the lead in parenting and do a good, responsible job, so this kind of behavior by grandparents can be frustrating.

A further complication, as in all parenting, is when both parents do not agree about what constitutes appropriate gift giving. This will cause division within the family and add to the stress of the occasion.

Holidays

In your family of origin, your maternal and paternal grandparents may both insist that you and your parents, siblings and cousins, aunts and uncles spend holidays with them. Often, the family with wealth wins because they're the ones with lovely, big accommodations and—let's face it—sometimes motivated inheritors who want to appease them. They also may get to set everything up the way they want it. It's frustrating for the grandparents who don't have the wealth.

When you marry, your spouse's grandparents, if they are all alive, are part of the package. You may now have to choose between four, not just two, sets of grandparents when deciding where to spend holidays.

Non-Blood Relatives

When non-blood relatives join the family, either as in-laws or step-relatives, it can create emotional and logistical issues surrounding relationships, power, inheritance, and trust. Consider the following challenges.

Trust

One reason some families, especially wealthy ones, keep in-laws on the outside is fear of divorces, splitting up the family fortune, or spreading private, sometimes potentially damaging, knowledge about family members. These kinds of issues have actualized in some families, legitimizing people's reservations in accepting those who are married in.

Do you want to be welcoming and proceed as if people will stay a part of your clan? Or do you feel inclined to protect yourself and your family by reserving the inner circle in case there's a divorce? Finding the right balance can take several years. It's important not to be naïve about the complications that can exist either way.

In-laws' involvement will expose them to family secrets, as innocuous as great-grandma's eggnog recipe or as potentially damaging as serious skeletons in the closet or sensitive business information. If you graft people in and then they divorce or leave, they could talk or write about these secrets, and suddenly you've lost some of your integrity of the knowledge in the family.

Consider, for example, Mary Buffett, who disclosed closely held stock-selection techniques of her ex-father-in-law, Warren Buffett, in her bestselling book, *Buffettology: The Previously Unexplained Techniques That Have Made Warren Buffett the World's Most Famous Investor*. At Christmas, Warren Buffett would give gifts of stock to family members and tell them why he chose those stocks. The shares would inevitably go up in value. Mary's book describing everything she could about Warren's approach to buying stocks could be perceived as a huge betrayal and has undoubtedly caused wealthy families to hesitate in being open with their children's spouses about certain financial issues.

The list of potential risks is huge. The Family Office Exchange's article "The Multiple Dimensions of Risk" lists dozens of risks that wealthy families face, under twenty-six categories! Problems with in-laws appears as only one on that long list of risks. Yes, if you let them in, they will learn about how your family and business operate, your values, and even some family secrets and skeletons. If they turn on you, they have all that personal knowledge of you.

There are also risks associated with not including in-laws—keeping them at bay can backfire. If they feel excluded, they can become resentful enough to divulge anything negative they may subsequently learn about the family. Keep in mind that no matter how hard a family works to keep secrets from in-laws, they will inevitably learn some. Another risk of not including in-laws is that the family and the family business will miss out on any skills the in-laws could share if given the chance.

Rituals and Traditions with In-Laws

Incorporating in-laws into your family can be tricky, especially when there are religious, ethnic, or economic differences between your family and the new spouse's family resulting in different holiday traditions and family rituals. It can be hard to accommodate and honor everyone. This doesn't have to be a showstopper, but be prepared if you encounter these problems. New family members may have a hard time finding a comfortable balance if their family tends to be very tight-knit while the spouse's family is more aloof (or vice versa), or one tends to be lively and loud, the other more reserved.

One family may be eager to welcome new spouses, and many newlyweds may appreciate that, yet at the same time new spouses often also want plenty of alone time, especially during their first year of marriage. It's important that everyone be sensitive, communicate openly, and be flexible.

Some of the challenges include how to welcome new in-laws, how to weigh the relative benefits and potential problems that being inclusive with in-laws can bring, and how to merge family rituals and traditions.

Every family has its own rituals, especially for holidays. It will likely make the new family members feel more welcome, comfortable, and willing to spend some holidays away from their families of origin if they can introduce one or two of their favorite traditions at your family gatherings and celebrations. One client was delighted that her new family was enthusiastic about her family's Christmas breakfast tradition of having each person read a Bible verse that describes something about their year. Another family enjoyed incorporating their new in-law's practice of opening one gift on Christmas Eve and saving the rest for Christmas Day.

Caro Rock, publisher of *Family Business Magazine*, wrote about the many challenges she would face as her two sons and a niece were about to marry. She reflected on how, as her family is expanding so quickly, she will integrate the new spouses into her family. "How do we let go of our young men and allow them to establish family traditions of their own?" she asks.[2] Rock highlights the fact that she and her husband, married for thirty-five years, have never fought over shared time between their families. Rock explains, "This was due in part to my wise mother who, just prior to our wedding, suggested we select one holiday that was special to each family and stick to it."

Holiday division can become complicated in families with several children and spouses. During one of my recent workshops, a participant expressed her concerns: "We have three sons in their thirties, and they are all married, to three extremely different women. They all came from different backgrounds than our sons. How do you acclimate a daughter-in-law, or someone else who comes into the family, who has not been brought up with the same traditions, values, religion, financial background—really, everything?" I answered that the main step you can make is to be kind and inclusive. These people will say things and do things that are difficult for you. Situations will come up that you don't understand. Just continue to be kind and inclusive. Ask your new daughter-in-law to lead your family in one of her holiday traditions.

Another participant suggested hosting a gathering to relate family stories, to help in-laws understand some of the values that come from your family. She also recommended finding a way to incorporate the stories from their families, perhaps by doing interviews of the in-laws, or a skit or game based on their tradition—again, including them in the process and continuing the conversation.

Wealth Division among Stepfamilies

The dynamics of stepfamilies are almost always complex. It's easy to blame a stepmother or stepfather for the breakup of your family of origin and to resent a new stepparent and stepsiblings for invading your home turf, stealing attention from you, and pilfering financial resources from you. Steps bring different values and rules into your home.

If you are a remarried parent, consider how these problems impact your children. Following the breakup of your family, imposing new family members on your children seems like a lot to put them through. Many remarried parents hope they'll recreate the Brady Bunch experience: yours, mine, and ours. But most of the time, it doesn't work that way.

Ideally, the responsible thing to do if you divorce is not to remarry until the kids are eighteen and out of your home. Your children benefit when you keep your focus strongly on parenting until they reach age eighteen. Remember, children don't have options—they have to stay with their parent. When you bring in a person they don't get along with very well, that is unkind. Of course, there are exceptions. You could have a situation where everyone gets along famously and the remarriage adds stability instead of detracting from it. But mostly what happens is they don't get along well.

Add wealth into the mix, and strife, fights, and dislike will probably increase. All of the dynamics get amplified because the stakes are higher. The steps may be viewed as gold diggers who threaten your current lifestyle and your children's future inheritance. On a deeper, emotional level, your children are likely to experience significant confusion about a number of issues:

- Separation and division: These people are supposed to be family, and yet the children may feel the house is divided, which can hijack your sense of family.

- Defining the relationship: Everyone has to have some kind of relationship with other people who are around. Some steps don't even speak to each other, so the relationships become disrespectful and unhealthy.

- Dealing with gold diggers: To most people in our society, it is attractive to marry someone with a lot of money. Sometimes these people just hope to accomplish stability as opposed to love and a sense of family.

Issues with stepfamilies do not end when the children turn eighteen. One client and his new wife each had grown children, none of whom liked this new marriage. The children of the wealthy man worried the second marriage would diminish their inheritance—and it probably will if the marriage survives, as he planned to give a small inheritance to each of his new wife's children. The wife's children, who didn't come from money, were worried about their stepfather taking over all the holiday celebrations and vacation planning, forcing them to lose their family traditions. They felt they would be subjected to whatever he wanted during holidays and vacations, as he was footing the bill.

When we all met together, I suggested that no one expect them to become one big, happy family. They didn't have to love each other as brothers and sisters, but they did need to find some way of getting along. I solicited their input as we brainstormed ideas about how to make holidays work for everyone. The key to beginning this is that everyone needs to feel they have a voice and be willing to speak up.

In another similar situation, each new spouse had three grown children from a previous marriage. The parents had a dream of combining into a happy family together, but they were realistic enough to know that if their kids didn't share that dream, it would not happen. In fact, the children even refused to meet initially. But because the parents hadn't yet transferred any wealth to the children, they knew they had leverage to get their young family members' cooperation for a day. The parents wanted to take everyone on a cruise, but realizing the bad feelings their children harbored, they decided a one-day retreat first could help the cruise vacation go more smoothly.

They wanted me to help them convince the stepsiblings to get along. Many, many issues came to the surface. The husband's children didn't like the fact that one of the wife's daughters had a lot of debt and was drawing on their father's assets as he helped her. The husband wanted to treat everyone fairly and bestow gifts in any way that seemed equal. This was difficult because all six of the adult offspring differed from each other so much. The whole family worked hard in preparation for our day together, completing assessments and private interviews with me. Then at the retreat, they all worked hard again.

Differences were evident, but so was the effort they all made. The parents have stayed in touch with me, and indeed their dream of a cruise became a reality. Everyone was well behaved, and although it was clear that the stepfamily would not become a natural family, it was also evident that they could be polite and give some life to their parents' dream.

Family Business

Managing a family business is especially tricky with extended and non-blood family members. Many married-in people have areas of expertise that might be beneficial to the family and its business. In some cases, in-laws are asked to serve on the board of the family business or participate in the family council or family foundation because they have certain skills. In others, the family is leery of inviting in-laws into the business.

The family of one client I work with, John, has a policy not to include in-laws in the family business. However, John's wife, Elizabeth, is very smart in business, so the family has wanted to bring her in. This has been touchy because she's more skilled than many of the blood family members. They have very quietly given her some strategic roles where they could use her expertise. She has cooperated with this, but she finds she's had to downplay her insight and intelligence because some family members are suspicious and resentful of her "outsider" status. At the same time, many recognize her contribution. Elizabeth is able to manage it well, but it is tricky.

Her involvement has made John's family reconsider its policy of not including anyone but blood relatives. It is a big family with a large family business that has many divisions, a charitable foundation, and several boards. There could be room for those who are married in, but this isn't yet an established policy in this family.

The decision about whether or not to include spouses in the family business is usually a process, and each good experience with a spouse builds it. Some families find this more acceptable now than in the past, as they've had positive experiences with some in-laws like Elizabeth and hope to continue bringing in fresh resources and creating better family cohesiveness.

Finding appropriate ways to reward in-laws who work in the business, serve on a board, or contribute their time or expertise to the family or the business is another concern and may be difficult, especially if blood family members receive shares of stock in a closely held family business in return for their efforts. There are alternate ways to reward in-laws who become involved with the family business. They can be paid money instead of stock, or they can receive stock and be required to sell their shares back to the family in the event of a divorce.

In-laws may feel left out and hurt during family business events that only include blood relatives. Often, the organizers arrange for some superficial activity for the spouses, such as a tour of the resort property, while a family business meeting goes on. It can feel insulting to these spouses to do these activities while they're being excluded from the family. One family worked hard to come up with activities that were more substantial. In a family where all family members enjoy wine, for instance, they offered the spouses wine tastings, which were a big success.

When there is a multigeneration family business involved, many issues can arise, among them:

- Some family members may have privileges that others don't. Certain branches of the family may be favored with employment in the company, while others may not have that opportunity.
- Working with family members forces everyone in the family, whether or not they like each other, to interact and get along with each other.
- Disgruntled family members may want to say, "Give me my money and I'll leave." But cash to buy them out may be tied up in the business and simply not available.

Take a look back at Colin's family, whom you met at the beginning of this chapter. Colin's grandfather, Papa, was so loved and so appreciated that a collective look at his values during our first retreat served as a uniting force early in our work. Virtually every family member saw many of their own values in his, and they realized that it was going to take effort to rebuild family closeness. Everyone agreed that Papa would have wanted this. It was clear that the family business would benefit as well. With Colin's inspiration and with added professional guidance, enough family members realized the value and benefits of improving relationships with each other, and in time everyone was reaping benefits from their work as a family.

Gaining Perspective: The Wisdom of the Old

Many people, fortunately, maintain fond memories of their grandparents as warm, kind, loving people who showered them with gifts and attention. In turn, as adults, most of us reciprocate by attempting to maintain a similarly warm and active relationship with our grandparents, and when the time comes, with grandchildren. Thus, we continue a cycle of multigenerational gifts.

First, we return the favor of love and attention our predecessors gave their grandparents by enriching our own grandparents' lives during a period when many elderly people feel increasingly lonely, less connected, neglected, and alienated. Second, we enrich our children's lives by keeping the bonds of our extended family strong and modeling for them the loving, caring roles we hope they in turn will assume with their own extended families. By doing so, in that we all learn by example, we immeasurably enrich our lives and those of our children. Beyond this personal enrichment, by keeping in touch with our grandparents, we also reap the many other rewards they offer, such as unconditional love, nonjudgmental affection, and sage wisdom.

At times, I know, it may be difficult for the young to accept the insights of the old, but trusting the wisdom our elders offer can prove to be enormously valuable. Let me tell you another story, told to me by my friend and colleague, Jay Hughes:

> Once there was a kingdom in a faraway land. The king was very young, and as you will soon see, stupid. Inexperienced as the king was, he felt threatened by his older subjects, so he sent out a decree that all of his young subjects must banish their parents and grandparents. With great sadness, they complied and forced their older generations to leave the land.
>
> But there was one boy who adored his father and simply couldn't do it. He asked his father if he would please stay and live in their basement secretly. His father agreed to this and stayed hidden from view.
>
> Soon there was a famine, and the crops all withered and died. Within weeks, the people had nothing to eat. The boy told his father about the famine and how everyone was getting anxious. His father told him to go outside and plow up the road. His son questioned him about how this might possibly help. The father said that there had been many famines over the years, and all the elders knew that when the farmers bring their wagons to market full of grain, some of it spills out onto the road. It is pushed down into the dirt and lies there dormant over the years. He told his son that if he would just plow the road up, when it rained, the seeds would sprout and there would be the beginnings of crops again.
>
> So the young man plowed up the road, the rain came, and the crops sprouted. When the king heard about this, he had the son bring his father to him. He told him he was sorry and that he had misjudged the value of his older subjects. He promised never again to restrict the wisdom of the elders.

What we can learn from this story is that in our own families, it is important to honor our elders, seek their wisdom, and always be respectful.

Likewise, all the members of our extended family have the potential to add value to our lives. When we have conflicts with them, it's important to work them out as well as we can. There is no magic wand to fix such conflicts, but you can sometimes improve the situation over time. You can kick off your effort by cheerfully and politely setting up a lunch or a walk in the park with all three generations. If anyone resists, ask if they would be willing to come along *for you*.

The point is not to bring up sensitive issues but simply to avoid cutoff relationships. Talk about the problem candidly only when you have an opening to do so. Getting together even once a year in a group around a table is better than letting the family drift apart. By the way, a round table is always preferable to a rectangular table for a family discussion or meeting.

Understanding Perspectives

Whatever the difficulties between your grandparents and you or other family members, it will help to understand and appreciate each other's perspectives. You can begin to open yourself to their feelings and points of view by using the Multigenerational Role-Playing exercise in Exercise 6.1.

6.1 EXERCISE 6.1

Multigenerational Role Playing

You can do this exercise in person at a formal family meeting or by yourself on paper.

If you are doing this at a family meeting: Divide participants into groups of three, and in each group assign one person to be a child, one person to be a parent, and one to be a grandparent. (Whom they choose to be is their choice—any child, parent, or grandparent in your family—it is up to them.) In each group, have one person address *one* of the following questions from the perspective of the assigned role:

- What does wealth represent to you?
- What has been your greatest joy?
- What is the greatest strength in our family as you look back through the generations?

Talk about this question for a couple minutes. Then rotate roles and discuss the same question from a new point of view. Now rotate once more, addressing the same question from the third point of view.

What observations can you make about your group's answers? After you discuss this within your small group, check with the whole family to see what members have learned. If you wish, you may then cycle back around to the second question and then the third.

This exercise causes everyone to consider the different perspectives of age, which underscores the reality of varying perspectives.

If you are doing this yourself: On a sheet of paper (or in a computer document), write out the first question. Then write a paragraph answering this question from your own perspective. Write another paragraph from the point of view you imagine a parent would answer, and another paragraph from a grandparent's point of view. Repeat this for each question.

Here's another exercise, in Exercise 6.2, that can help promote better understanding and stronger bonds between generations. It consists of eight questions for young family members to ask an elder. Interview an older family member whom you respect or admire—preferably in person.

---

e 2.4

Exercise 6.2:

Questionnaire for Elders: Creating Pathways

Using the questions below, interview a favorite older family member, someone whom you respect and admire. A phone interview is fine if it is more convenient than an in-person interview. If in person, you may wish to record your discussion to share with younger family members in years to come.

1. What is our family's greatest strength? As you look back through the generations, what strengths do you see?
2. Who in the family has shown you the value of generosity? How?
3. What do you have that's special from your mother (tangible or intangible)?
4. What do you have that's special from your father (tangible or intangible)?
5. From whom in the family did you learn kindness? How?
6. Were you brought up in a spiritual environment? What effect has this had on your life?

continued on next page

7. What has been your greatest joy?
8. Who in the family have you had the most fun with? Please give an example.
9. When have you felt your greatest sense of purpose? How did that happen?
10. What is the legacy you are creating? For what will you be remembered?

Moving Toward the Bright Side

Knowing extended family members gives depth and history to your sense of family. There is no substitute for knowing where you come from, the values, the challenges, the losses and triumphs of your family members. There will always be the good and the bad, people you like and others you don't like. It is important to know all of them. It is natural to distance yourself from those whose behaviors are a poor fit with your values, but gather the strength to maintain some contact. Distant and polite contact is fine, but unless there is true danger, keep some communication open. It is important to model the value of family for your children and to give them opportunities to know their relatives.

Colin, brave soul that he is, really stuck his neck out and took a chance when he asked the family to address the importance of and possibility of improving relationships. And this is what it takes: one leader in the family who has a vision of how the family can be great again and then going to the trouble of finding a way to facilitate this.

An Ethical Question

Some inheritors, of course, have an unhealthy relationship with family members who are in charge of inheritance decisions. Young family members may feel a complex mix of emotions: disliking their grandparents yet also knowing that acting on their genuine feelings could compromise their inheritance. This can lead to them maintaining a closer relationship than they want and subsequently feeling guilty about their motivations.

Sam spent years literally waiting for his wealthy father to die. He did not like anything about his father, who had divorced Sam's mother when Sam was young, leaving them without much money for many years. Sam, who was forty-two when I met him, had created his own business success, though it is modest compared to his father's success. Clearly, Sam's success has been fueled by bitterness at times. He struggled with a resentful, vindictive attitude that had created many challenges for him. Just before Sam contacted me, his father had remarried, and the new wife had made it clear that she didn't like Sam. When Sam started thinking about how much his attitude toward his father had cost him, he realized he needed to make some changes so he could manage his life well.

Our work was to breathe new and positive life into his business attitudes so his work could become a positive area for him and he could achieve independence from his father and the would-be inheritance. Another part of our work was for Sam also to build a healthier perspective regarding his relationship with his father.

Accepting money from people you don't like (while they are alive or after they die) raises some important ethical questions. Should you take money from people you dislike or disrespect? Even if your negative feelings for your grandparents stem from a personality clash, you can still find ways to treat them respectfully, show appreciation, and be nice to them.

We cannot control our thoughts or feelings, but we can certainly control our behavior. It is better to maintain a polite, though perhaps distant, relationship with family members whom you dislike or with whom you do not get along than it is to cut off the relationship. If you can find a way to behave in peaceful ways, this will reduce stress for you and for those around you.

However, if your relatives have committed sexual, physical, or emotional abuse, you may feel you deserve the money all the more as compensation for having been abused. Or you may feel their money is tainted and you don't want anything to do with it. I've had clients who walked away from their family fortune (it's rare, but it happens). Sometimes the only way to maintain your emotional health and integrity is to remove yourself from the toxic people and their money.

Most people do make some kind of peace with their inheritance even if they don't like their family members. One of my clients has a high-maintenance relationship with her grandfather. Granted, he is the wealth holder, but her relationship with him is difficult and she has a strong, sincere sense of duty. Although she does not love him, she takes care of the relationship out of a sense of obligation. She feels it's the right thing to do because he is elderly and can't take care of himself.

In most cases, we can behave in a loving manner regardless of how we feel. This does not necessarily prevent us from being true to ourselves as long as we pick our battles wisely. For instance, if a controlling grandparent insists you attend a particular college (or that you send your child there), it may be okay with you. You may not care that much as long as the college has a strong program in whatever you or your child wants to study.

The key in all of these challenging relationships is to be true to yourself. You don't have to agree with people or be a hypocrite to be kind. If you can find the resources within to be kind and even compassionate toward people whom you may not see eye to eye with, then your strength plays a hand in defining who you are. This strength is a gift to your whole family as you create pathways for others who need an example to follow.

Communicate

As we've discussed before, communication is a basic building block for healthy relationships. And yet, communicating well is not widely practiced. Communicating well requires work, constant vigilance, and the willingness to admit mistakes. We can develop communication skills, and as we work to improve these skills, the overall quality of our communication—and our relationships—builds. It is well worth the effort.

Our efforts are usually noticeable—even the fact that we care and are willing to learn counts and can make an impression on people around us. This is especially a bonus in families. Your efforts can have a ripple effect, and the value can extend farther than you realize.

Assertive communication is especially helpful as families work through disagreements. The Assertiveness Guide in Exercise 6.3 is a tool that I have found to be very helpful when planning to discuss behaviors that upset you. It puts the issue on the table so you and the other person can discuss it, and, handled well, it effectively avoids passivity and aggression, steering you straight toward resolution.

An important guideline is that it is only appropriate to be assertive about behaviors that can conceivably change, not about anything people cannot change. For instance, you can ask your sister to stop interrupting you, but you cannot ask her to lower her high-pitched voice by an octave.

The primary goal of this exercise is to have your concern heard; actual change is only a secondary goal. There are two crucial rules to make this tool work effectively.

1. Write one *concise* sentence per step, five in all. Avoid unnecessary clauses! If you keep it lean and focused, you have an excellent chance of being heard. Follow the instructions carefully.

2. Wait to deliver your statement until you have calmed down somewhat. This may mean waiting a day, a week, or a month. Sometimes, though, waiting may make you feel even angrier, so this is a judgment call. Do something that relaxes you before you deliver your assertiveness statement. Try meditating, working out, or enjoying a massage—whatever works for you.

Follow this guide exactly and it will work like magic!

e
6.3

EXERCISE 6.3:

Assertiveness Guide[3]

1. Describe the behavior that you want the other person to change.
   a. Be specific.
   b. Avoid absolutes like always and never.

2. Give the other person a positive reinforcement that is true and related to the behavior you have in mind.

3. Describe how you feel when the person does the behavior you have described.

4. Describe (don't ask for) the change in behavior you want the other person to make.
   a. Make sure your nonverbal messages (eye contact, facial expression, tone of voice) are consistent with your verbal message).

continued on next page

5. Make a summary statement that shows your confidence that the problem can be resolved.

____

____

____

6. Optional and only to be used at a later date (if at all): If the person says no (which is a fundamental right), describe what you believe will happen if the behavior change is not made.
    a. This should be a natural consequence of the behavior, not a punishment.
    b. It should be believable, not far-fetched.

____

____

____

____

Example: Alex, you often interrupt me when we're talking. I love being with you, and talking with you often helps me express my thoughts well. But when you interrupt me, I feel anxious that I will lose my train of thought, and I feel discouraged. I would like for you to wait until I come to a natural stop at the end of a sentence before you respond. In all the time we've known each other, we've worked out many challenges and become closer, so I'm confident we can work this out too. (Optional later comment: If you continue interrupting me, I will get so discouraged trying to interact with you that I won't want to talk with you anymore.)

Please note, there is one concise sentence per step. This Assertiveness Guide is a tried-and-true formula. Do not change the steps in any way. Of the five steps, two are positive reinforcements about the person with whom you are speaking. This keeps him engaged. Even if he starts to feel angry, your presentation of points can go well, and the positive reinforcements can calm his anger when he thinks back on the conversation later.

Let's say a relationship has changed because of competing financial circumstances. This could be with an extended family member or with anyone in your world. Your only chance of taking care of the relationship and fixing whatever bothers you is for you to talk it through with each other. If you're afraid to do that by yourself, perhaps another friend can help you rehearse what to say. Or you can work out your reluctance with a therapist. Do whatever you have to do to gather your courage and take care of your relationship.

It's important to put whatever is bothering you on the table—only then can you talk candidly about it to reach a resolution. Start by letting the person know that you want to talk. You can ask, "Do you have a few minutes?" You are asking your relative to open the door. This is a vital first step.

If you prefer, you can initiate these kinds of conversations on the telephone. This has the advantage of allowing you to read your five statements without the other person knowing you are reading, so you can deliver your message exactly the way you have written it. Or you can memorize your statement to be delivered in person. This is more difficult but also more effective if you can do it. It is important to deliver your statement *exactly* the way you have written it. Many people, in their fear, try to soften their statement by adding phrases, even sentences. Bad idea. If you add words to a well-developed assertiveness statement, you will only create diversions and confusion, decreasing effectiveness.

It is easier to begin your practice of assertiveness statements by working with a relationship that is not central in your life, perhaps an acquaintance or someone whom you see only rarely. If the clerk at the dry cleaner comments about your weight after you've gained a few pounds, you can prepare your assertiveness statement before you go back next time. If a neighbor does something that annoys you, practice an assertiveness statement on her before you do it with primary people in your life or in situations that feel very charged. This will help you practice saying what you need to say with a calm demeanor.

The more confident you are, the more comfortable you will be in delivering your assertiveness statements. You can even get some mileage out of pretending to be confident. Some inheritors are timid about speaking up and feel inclined to hide. It's as if they hardly know what they have a right to say or who they have a right to be in the world. It takes confidence to come out and be who you are. The practice of assertiveness statements not only helps repair relationships, it also helps you be confident in who you are.

Once in a while, a curious and significant outcome occurs when people focus on developing an assertiveness statement. Just as they're ready to deliver it, they observe that the behavior has taken care of itself—there's no need to initiate a focused, intentional statement and say what they had prepared!

While the assertiveness statement can be used for virtually any relationship and conflict, remember there are specific conflicts that are common in situations with extended family members. We'll look at some solutions for those, and you can always use the assertiveness statement—as well as other tools for communicating effectively—in any of these situations.

Holidays

Help your extended family bond by spending holidays with them. This can create challenges of its own, especially when figuring the logistics of which family members to visit for which holidays and ensuring that no family member is left alone for a holiday.

Exercise 6.4 can help you and your spouse identify existing family patterns and preferences around holiday celebrations when you were children. Which holiday gatherings, with which grandparents, created the best holiday memories when you were a child, and which did you dislike?

6.4 EXERCISE 6.4:

Which Home for the Holidays?

Compare your answers to the following questions with your spouse's answers.

When you were a child:

With which set of grandparents did you tend to spend most holidays? What did you like about it?

Me ______________________________

____

My Spouse ______________________________

____

Did this preference lead to arguments between your parents? How were the arguments resolved?

Me ______________________________

____

My Spouse ______________________________

____

Were the grandparents with whom you usually spent holidays wealthier than your other grandparents?

Me ____

____

My Spouse ____

____

With which set of grandparents did you prefer to spend time, and why?

What did you dislike about holidays with other grandparents, if you had them?

Me ____

____

My Spouse ____

____

As an adult:

Which grandparents (or parents) are pressuring you the most to spend holidays with them?

Me ____

____

My Spouse ____

____

If you are receiving pressure from the relatives with whom you do not prefer to spend holidays, how can you and your spouse communicate that without creating irreparably hurt feelings?

Me ____

____

My Spouse ____

____

However heated the holiday division issue may feel for you, it doesn't have to detonate World War III. Avoid going down this road in your own family by taking the following steps:

1. Be aware and honest about these dynamics and how they play out.
2. Be assertive about what you want.
3. Be willing to work out holiday schedules that honor all sets of parents and grandparents.

One client invited her husband's family to a holiday event because his parents and siblings were fun and easy to be with, while her own family was very difficult. By being inclusive, she not only caused her husband's family to feel acknowledged, but she also managed to dilute the tension from her family. This approach—and many other compromises—can be applied to all kinds of gatherings, such as children's birthday parties, graduations, weddings, and others.

Bonding

Bonding across generations can be a challenge when family members have different values, particularly if grandparents want to spend a lot of money on their grandchildren but the parents don't want their children to be spoiled. For that reason, I recommend grandparents focus on bonding with younger generations through nonmaterial means.

Figure 6.5 presents some purposeful and delightful alternatives to material gifts that grandparents can introduce to bond with their grandchildren. If you are a parent, you can encourage your parents to consider these options.

6.5 FIGURE 6.5:

Nonmaterial Bonding with Younger Generations

1. **Education, education, education.** Fund classes or lessons in academics, arts, sciences, and business for your grandchildren. Be involved in each precious grandchild's journey. Support and encourage achievement. As the proverb says: Give a child a fish and he will eat for a day. Teach a child to fish and he will eat for a lifetime.

2. **Investment experience.** Fund your grandchildren's age-appropriate steps in business and investing. Perhaps organize an investment club with all the grandchildren.

3. **Give the gift of time.** Wealth can create availability of time. Choose a regular day every month to spend one-on-one time with each grandchild. Let this child lead and make suggestions about what you do together. Provide a small budget, which will cover a meal and perhaps admission to something of the child's choosing.

4. **Travel.** Take grandchildren to destinations around the world that correlate with places or events the children are studying in school. This helps them gain insight into people living in very different circumstances and also remember their history lessons. And take grandchildren on fun trips too. Unless their parents are homeschooling them, schedule this kind of traveling over school vacations. It is important to build the work ethic that school is to be respected as if it were the child's job.

5. **Philanthropy.** Research, evaluate, and fund philanthropic causes together with your grandchildren. There are many creative opportunities for this, and they can be empowering for all. You also may want to create a family foundation and involve the grandchildren in age-appropriate ways, researching grant applications and recipients, investing the foundation's funds, and tracking the results.

During one of my workshops, a participant told me I made him think twice about taking his kids and their spouses and all their grandkids to Hawaii every year for two weeks. Were he and his wife spoiling their children and grandchildren? I responded that the answer lies in how they do it. If the focus of these trips is on family closeness and strengthening relationships, that is constructive. If the focus is on money and spending, then it's not.

Another grandmother described how she and her husband took their grandchildren, ages ten and seven, to a weekend camp just for grandparents and grandchildren—no parents allowed. The four of them stayed in a lodge all together in a small room with one bunk bed and two single beds. There is enough space for only one person to be out of bed at a time in this room! They eat in the dining hall together, swim together, go boating together, and even do the zip line together. Every hour there are different camping activities. Sometimes one grandparent takes one of the grandchildren to one activity, such as photography, while the other pair does a baking activity.

If you really want to have relationships with your relatives, it is important to make one-on-one or small-group time too. Consider traveling or vacationing together, where you are away from the rest of the family, building special relationships.

Welcome New Members

In wealthy families I work with, I have seen many positive benefits when non-blood relatives are specifically welcomed into the inner family. I believe this is rare but affirming and powerful when families choose to be so inclusive.

While planning family events, one of my clients delegates some responsibilities (such as planning a scavenger hunt, providing entertainment by showcasing a unique talent like music or art, or being completely in charge of a particular meal) to new family members to give them a chance to shine. Figure 6.6 offers some New In-Law Welcome Wagon Ideas.

6.6 FIGURE 6.6

New In-Law Welcome Wagon Ideas

1. **Sharing family history.** Create a family history book or audio or video recording that includes interviews with family members from all generations. Present it to new spouses of relatives. It may focus on the history of the family business that created the fortune, the family itself, the genesis of certain family traditions, customs and rituals, or characteristics of the family. What are some family protocols about gatherings, holiday celebrations, vacations, and education that the family considers to be valuable? Is this a family that only likes very expensive, excellent wines? One that plays and enjoys a certain kind of music? Or one that values handwritten thank-you notes? People will pick up some of these details without such a description, but the information will definitely help.

2. **In-law out-to-lunch day.** Arrange a group of long-time in-laws to take the new spouse out to lunch to give him/her some insights about the family (being careful not to gossip!). This also provides a time and place for the new family member's questions.

3. **Care package.** A welcome wagon care package can include anything to help orient the new family member. Maybe there are favorite treats of each established family member. One aunt might provide her favorite scented candle, a sister-in-law could give box of chocolates, a nephew might put in a book of crossword puzzles if he loves doing them, and the father-in-law may include a small camera to say, "I love photos."

If you want to initiate any of these efforts, you may meet with resistance from other relatives at first. Not everyone understands the need to be inclusive. Some families are very reluctant to change anything. But be gently persistent. This kind of inclusiveness can go a long way toward creating cohesion and goodwill.

Exercise 6.7: 6.7

Gratitude

What are five qualities of your relationship with an extended family member for which you are grateful?

____

____

____

____

Exercise 6.8: 6.8

Action Plan

Now set an action plan for improving your relationships with your extended family. Begin with one important relationship you are confident you can improve.

Today's date ______________

The goal I set for my relationship with one member of my extended family is:

____

____

____

In order to accomplish this goal, I will perform the following activities:

____

____

____

Support people who might assist me include:

____

____

____

continued on next page

I realize I may sabotage my plan by:

____

____

____

So I will avoid this by:

____

____

____

I will complete this goal by ______________________ (date)

(Recommendation: three to six months)

When we begin to build constructive, healthy patterns of behavior in our family relationships, we can then begin to knock down the destructive patterns these relationships had sustained before. An added benefit is that, in doing so, we often pave the way to making similar strides with our friendships and spouse. The next few chapters will help you along that path.

Rich Friends, Poor Friends
The Challenges of Unequal Wealth

Whoever says friendship is easy has obviously never had a true friend.
—Bronwyn Polson

Friends and good manners will carry you where money won't go.
—Margaret Walker

Life is partly what we make it, and partly what it is made by the friends we choose.
—Tennessee Williams

| Relationship elements: | **Trust** | **Competence** | **Giving** |

"Lots of people want to ride with you in the limo," Oprah Winfrey once observed, "but what you want is someone who'll take the bus with you when the limo breaks down." There's no doubt about it—good friends are the ones who'll take the bus with you when your limo is in the shop. It's a quick way, I'd say, of discovering which of your friends are worthwhile and which are just along for the ride. Most wealthy people will never lack for friends, but *true* friends are another thing altogether.

"Hold a true friend with both your hands," urges a Nigerian proverb, for a true friend is rare indeed. Some people never develop such a true friendship. If we are too busy being safe in our friendships, we miss the chance to develop depth.

Some wealthy people choose to be friends exclusively with others who share their financial status. Though secure and comfortable, this circumscribed, insular world deprives many wealthy individuals of life's rich tapestry of potential experiences. If this in fact has happened to you, you may find yourself in a kind of trap, like the golden handcuffs that bind someone to a job that pays well but is emotionally or spiritually unrewarding—or downright boring.

A similar scenario happens when we bind ourselves to a group of people whose common denominator is financial wealth. Many country clubs are a good example of this.

Clarifying Values and Identity

Susan treasured her tight group of six girlfriends. Now in their fifties, these women had been best friends ever since they all had families of toddlers. They had found each other in the early days of parenting and had been fortunate to ride out the parenting roller coaster with their friendships intact.

Along the way, they had weathered many challenges—in their marriages, their health, their children, virtually every facet of life. Susan had always been quiet about her inherited wealth, on the advice of her mother, who had told her that if she ever let that cat out of the bag, all her relationships would change—not likely for the better. Susan's friends were all solidly middle class, and while all were in good shape financially, there wasn't much extra money.

About a year before I met Susan, her mother died. One of Susan's friends, Carolyn, had insisted that she travel to Chicago with Susan to be by her side throughout the days immediately following her mother's death and during the memorial service. Susan was a little nervous because she knew her parents' lifestyle would be revealed on this trip, but she loved the idea of Carolyn being with her. Once they were in Chicago, Carolyn made a few remarks along the lines of "Wow, I didn't realize . . ." but they didn't sound negative in any way.

However, in the months following the trip, Susan began to notice occasional comments by her other friends, implying they all knew she had wealthy parents. Comments like, "Well, for our next trip, we could go to your house in the Cayman Islands." Or "Susan could probably figure out how to get a jet here—I don't think transportation has to be a problem," and "When push comes to shove, Susan probably has connections that could help you out with that bank." Though Susan laughed these comments off along with everyone else, she began to feel uncomfortable. Specifically, she felt different and separate from the group, which came with a sense of loss.

This is what Susan's mother had warned her about. All her friends had begun to make assumptions about what it meant that Susan apparently had wealthy parents. They all saw wealth through their own filter, of course, and it meant different things to each of them, but Susan's sense of separation had set in.

Susan and I worked to clarify her own values and identity. She worked hard to maintain a sense of her worth, even though she felt like she was standing on shifting sand. In the end, she was able to talk with each of her friends, reconnect, and assure them that her parents' wealth and her own inheritance had been relegated to the background of her life, she was the same person they had always known, and she still treasured her relationships with each of them the same as ever.

Differences in Personal Wealth

There's something else about friends and wealth that you're [illegible] money often isolates people. One of the biggest challenges in fr[illegible] ferences in personal wealth, often because of the assumptions othe[illegible]

Right or wrong, people in our society ascribe moral value to fina[illegible] bad—and then attach meaning beyond that. In Susan's case, her friend[illegible] from vacation homes to private transportation to influence at banks to [illegible] [S]usan had said nothing about any of this to them. Sadly, however, when people s[illegible] [t]o see options that the wealthy have access to that they don't have themselves, resentment and separation often result. This painful reality can cause wealthy friends to socialize more with each other, sometimes exclusively. One benefit of this is not having to deal with the complications that the differences can create.

When you surround yourself only with wealthy friends who are otherwise unfulfilling, face it: you live in a materially safe world but one that is severely limited in terms of emotional support and challenge, intellectual support and stimulation, and diversity.

The Traps of Your Trappings

In Figure 7.1 I've identified nine common traps that can damage or even derail friends with unequal wealth. The key to escaping these traps is to discover the values you have in common. If your shared values are strong enough, your friendship will be able to grow. You will be able to plow through each of these traps. Which ones have you experienced with your friends? Have you found effective and comfortable ways to handle these situations as they arise?

---

f 7.1

Figure 7.1:

Wealth Traps in Friendships

Trap 1: Making Decisions about Activities Together: Where to go, what to do?

Trap 2: Taking Responsibility for Paying: Who pays?

Trap 3: Discernment: How can I tell if a friend likes me for me or for my money?

Trap 4: Staying Centered: How can I get beyond feeling self-conscious about my wealth?

Trap 5: Confidence: How can I handle friends who seem jealous of my wealth?

continued on next page

…sy Friends: How do I respond when friends seem too interested in my wealth?

…p 7: Trust: How can I balance feeling distrustful or too trusting?

Trap 8: Knowing My Strengths and Limitations: How do I handle situations when people assume my wealth prevents me from understanding the real world?

Trap 9: Loaning Money: Is it ever okay to lend money to a friend?

In this chapter I describe these traps that can arise between friends when wealth is involved. I also offer trap-specific solutions to help you navigate friendships to more trusting, rewarding, and meaningful relationships. More exercises to help strengthen your friendships follow later in the chapter.

Trap 1: Making Decisions about Activities Together: Where to go, what to do?

If you enjoy frequenting fancy restaurants, popular clubs, or exclusive spas, friends with more modest financial means are bound to feel uncomfortable joining you for nights out. Traveling together can be challenging if one friend wants to rough it by going camping, while the other prefers traveling first class all the way.

Solutions

Exercise flexibility and creativity when a friend can't afford to go out in expensive style. If your friend has a modest budget for entertainment spending, viewing a beautiful public garden, visiting a museum, or sipping tea at an outdoor café makes more sense than taking in a Broadway show or drinking the best champagne. Are you willing to take the subway instead of a cab, or book coach-class seats instead of first class? You may be rewarded as new and different experiences open up in your circle of friendships. Your world may actually become much broader and more varied.

If you typically travel with a driver and prefer to stay at four- or five-star resorts, experience taking trains or buses instead and staying at home-shares in foreign countries. This could give you opportunities to interact openly with local people and learn more about the culture of the places you travel.

Let the less-affluent friend choose where you go together. This way, together you can select venues that fit both your budgets.

Trap 2: Taking Responsibility for Paying: Who pays?

You may be willing to foot the bill all the time, but your friend may feel uneasy with that. Even if your friend is comfortable with it, if you pay all the time, a tricky power imbalance will likely manifest in the friendship. Some people assume that wealthy people have no problem paying for everything. This may be so; nevertheless, you may grow to resent a friend who assumes that because you have more money, you should always pick up the check.

Money is power to many people in our culture. Knowing how to level the playing field can give you your best shot at a give-and-take friendship.

Solutions

Look for ways to balance the power. As mentioned above, give friends with less money a bigger say in what you do when you go out together. You don't need to mention that money is the reason, but invite the other person to choose the restaurant. When the bill comes, approach it as a shared expense.

Be direct with companions who assume you will pay. This doesn't have to be a heated discussion. You can explain that you like them too much to allow money to create an unhealthy balance of power in your friendship, so it makes sense to plan evenings out that both of you can afford. You can say you don't mind allowing your friends to choose evenings out that fit their budget. With your being given the lion's share of power, it can be a challenging and humbling exercise to conscientiously concede much of the decision-making power to your friend. Use the Assertiveness Guide from chapter six to help you with the discussion. For example (notice there is one concise sentence for each step of the instructions):

> Often when we go out to dinner together, you ignore the check when it comes. I love going to restaurants with you, and I always have a great time. But when the bill comes and I feel you withdraw your attention, I feel taken advantage of and angry. I would like you to take the lead in choosing restaurants when we go out so they fit your budget and we can share the bill. We have worked out other differences together before, and I'm confident we can resolve this problem too. (Optional later comment: If you continue to ignore the check at dinner, I'm going to get tired of feeling used and I won't want to go out to dinner with you anymore.)

Trap 3: Discernment: How can I tell if a friend likes me for me or for my money?

Sometimes in friendships this nasty question rears its ugly head. Many wealthy people are inclined to develop relationships outside of their financial world. Naturally, this can be broadening and fulfilling. At the same time, financial differences can create awkward doubts. Fortunately, as in any developing friendship, there are solutions.

Solutions

Pay close attention to every little thing. Does your friend pick up the check at the restaurant half the time? Does she offer to drive or to chip in for gas half the time? Does he more or less reciprocate with gifts? If the answers are no, these little clues can be red flags that your friend is not treating you as an equal. It is a matter of being observant. Without your wealth, you would still need to be discerning and diligent in relationships, and it is the only way you can really observe if people have the potential to be real friends. There is no substitute for your investment of time and attention.

Expose yourself to situations where wealth is not an issue. I began taking classes in improvisational theater several years ago. I thought it would be good for my presentations. After a while, I realized no one who seems wealthy had shown up for the class. On the other hand, it's possible that financial wealth just doesn't show in improv because nothing could matter less in this context. It's also possible that the authenticity required in improv is frightening to people who have not developed their identities well. For those who have, the challenge of focusing completely on the present and having to rely entirely on one's own wits is empowering.

I've found that the people I like in improv, I really like. My feelings, I've discovered, are based on who they are in the present. How much money they have or don't have is completely irrelevant.

Go slowly when discussing the subject of wealth to see if the friendship is one you really want to develop. Does your new friend want to associate with you so she can massage all of her assumptions about the benefits of wealth and its perks? It can be very difficult to sort this out. Time will tell. Slow and steady will get you the information you need.

If you've given the friendship time and feel you are ready to begin bringing a friend more deeply into your private financial life, you can start by extending a question from the Intergenerational Questionnaire from chapter two for you to discuss together. Three good starting questions are (use only one question per conversation):

1. Was money discussed openly in your family when you were a child?

20. Were you encouraged to give time, talent, or treasure to make the world a better place? If yes, how were you encouraged?
23. Was the message you received about rich people positive or negative? What was the message?

These questions will help you get to know each other better and build greater trust and openness. You may have been taught to keep your family wealth absolutely quiet. But what would happen if at some point someone with whom you have been becoming close learns about your wealth somewhere else? Depending upon the friend and the degree of friendship, some friends might take offense. Others might not care.

Realize that many wealth-related problems are created in the mind of the wealthy person. Part of the challenge is to sort out which scenario your life fits with. Just pay close attention. If significant problems arise with your non-wealthy friends and you are paying attention, you will know it.

Trap 4: Staying Centered: How can I get beyond feeling self-conscious about my wealth?

You may feel uncomfortable inviting people over when you know your house is much bigger and clearly more expensive than your friends' houses. Or you may worry they will feel self-conscious having you over to their house if they live in much humbler circumstances. Either way, sometimes this does separate friends from different backgrounds.

Julia had a pretty house in the woods. As a graphic designer, she didn't make a fortune, but she had a respectable salary. She bought the house with inherited funds from a trust. She had carefully avoided having any of her friends over, until one day when her friends wanted to go hiking close to her house. While her home wasn't lavish, it was much nicer than any of her friends' homes.

Sure enough, when Julia's friends arrived at her home, they made some comments. She felt uncomfortable and later came to me for help. When I met Julia, she was in her twenties and near the beginning of her journey as a wealthy inheritor. To help her prepare for another encounter like this one, we role-played the interaction and came up with some responses that she could deliver while maintaining her strength and center. The solution she found most useful follows.

Solutions

Tell the truth, but be discreet about when, where, and how much information you give out. Julia did not want to lie, but she also did not want her wealth to complicate her friendships. She decided to say, "My grandmother died and left some money to me, so I bought this house." It was an understatement, but it was true.

Assign credit to investment. Say, "I'm very fortunate to have some investments that have done well." Most trust funds are invested, so again this is true.

Whatever you say needs to be based on truth so that you can maintain your integrity and move forward in a healthy way in your relationships. One effective strategy is to practice how you will respond if and when a difficult subject arises. Do this ahead of time to find ways to be honest without revealing more than you are ready to show.

Trap 5: Confidence: How can I handle friends who seem jealous of my wealth?

True friendships won't exhibit competitiveness and jealousy. Or if there is a glimmer, true friends will work out the negative feelings soon after they appear.

Jealousy is a form of anger. It is a destructive, negative emotion, and most of us feel uncomfortable when we are the target of jealousy. This can be confusing and can cause us to doubt our self-worth. If jealousy enters a friendship, it needs to be dealt with and resolved or it will compromise the relationship.

Most people are looking for give-and-take in their friendships—for all parties to bring some human, intellectual, and social capital to the relationship. Focus on this as you approach solutions to the problem.

Solutions

Test that your assumptions about the friend's jealousy are accurate. How do these friends talk to you about other people? They will talk about you the way they talk about others. If they are jealous of other people, that's a red flag; they are likely to feel jealous of you as well.

Use the Assertiveness Guide from chapter six to bring up the problem with your friends one at a time. If you love sharing parts of your life with these people but they tend to feel jealous, before you drift away, bring it up. Here is an example of an assertive statement addressing the problem of jealousy:

> Often when we go shopping together, you make negative comments about money when I buy something. I really enjoy your company in so many ways. But when we're shopping and you make these comments about money, I feel self-conscious and pushed away. I'd like you to stop making negative comments about money

when we are out shopping. We have worked out many other issues between us, and I'm sure we can work this out as well. (Optional later comment: If you continue to make these comments, I won't like shopping with you and won't want to go.)

Find or create areas where there is a neutral playing field such as education, sports, recreation, or hobbies you both enjoy. If you have kids who are the same age, this can work well too. Finding common ground can help deflect jealousy. With friends who seem to resent you buying things they can't afford, you could do your best to avoid charged situations, such as shopping together, that fuel the negative emotions.

Watch out for overreacting. I know a man who perceives others' jealousy everywhere around him. His anxiety about what negative thoughts others may be directing at him often causes him to retreat from the world. He endures periods of avoiding virtually everyone while he worries about this. Do your best not to let your worry imprison you like this.

Trap 6: Nosy Friends: How do I respond when friends seem nosy about my wealth?

It may seem perfectly obvious to you that the following questions are inappropriate and violate basic interpersonal boundaries. And yet, you may have encountered people—even friends—who ask you questions such as:

- How much money do you have?
- Who is your family?
- What do your parents do?
- How much did that cost?
- Will you give me a tour of your house?

Some situations can blossom into a series of nosy questions, like when an acquaintance asks, "So how much did this house cost anyway?" Once in a while, people add the quaint phrase, "if you don't mind me asking." Or the question could be, "What is that (fill in the blank) worth?" about any personal item. Sometimes they assume, "Since you don't have to work . . ."

When sheltered teens go off to college, they are often unprepared for questions their new friends ask. Roommates may begin to wonder about wealth when they overhear phone conversations with family members. My colleague Leah K. Hemeyer, MA, LPC, developed a list of tricky questions that may cause unprepared wealthy freshmen to feel confused or defensive:

- How do you pay for school? You have loans, right?
- Where do you get all your spending money?
- How do you afford to fly home?
- Can I borrow some money? Or can you buy the snacks tonight?
- What's a family meeting?
- What are you doing for Thanksgiving, winter break, summer, etc.?

Hemeyer also suggests that new college students think about what comes to them in the mail while at college. Find a safe and private place to keep financial statements, letters, and documents. There are small, unobtrusive safes made for the college student lifestyle. It's also a good idea to think about what to keep in your dorm room. Your furnishings, clothes, jewelry, and photos in frames (at exclusive resorts, for instance) reveal a lot about your family's financial background. If you decorate your dorm room with significantly more expensive trappings than your roommates or friends have, some will notice, question, and comment. The wisest approach is to simply be discreet.

Solutions

Accept that people will be nosy. It is prudent to be prepared for these intrusive questions because they will come. It's okay to change the subject or to give an evasive answer, but it is disrespectful to yourself and others to lie, so don't do it. And it's fine to answer, "That is something I prefer not to discuss." Remember, the queries of these nosy inquirers have more to do with their perspective—their filter on the world—than with anything about you. Don't try to change them; you can't.

Consider the motive. It's usually hard to know what people's motivation might be when they ask such questions. Do the people asking for a tour of your house just enjoy your taste, or do they want to size up how much money you have? To some degree, we invite people over because we want to share part of ourselves with them. But if they cross over a line, it can become a negative experience. Among wealthy people, inheritors are often resented the most because sometimes outsiders feel you didn't earn the luxuries in your life. In response, you may feel defensive. If you earned the money, you are likely to feel less defensive, perhaps only annoyed at the pushiness or nosiness of others. In either case, consider the motive and remember that people are perceiving your wealth through their own filters.

Know your own concerns. My experience, which some inheritors share, is that I feel differently about the money I earn than the money I have inherited. I prefer acknowledgment for having built a business and earning an income over recognition for inheriting.

Most families I work with have significant privacy concerns and would rather not discuss any of their wealth with friends, and certainly not with acquaintances. It's understandable to feel protective of your privacy. The outside world can be invasive, rude, and dangerous, which can cause some inheritors to feel isolated or different when they very much want to be regarded as normal and valued independently of their wealth.

Be realistic. Inheritors often assume other people won't find out about their wealth, especially when they've moved to another city for college or work and if they have a different last name than the well-known family. Understand and accept that people will find out. Determined acquaintances using internet resources can find out who wealthy people are.

You may feel betrayed when you discover that people have been researching you and your family's fortune. After all, you may have thought you were building friendships based on shared experiences, common interests, and matching values. You would rightly question their motives. When you have not offered this kind of personal information, you are not ready to have the information in the relationship yet. It's as if these friends are making an end run around you, rushing you to allow them into your private world.

The bottom line is to respect your intuition. Con artists are a reality, and many are good at pretending to be someone they're not. Distinguishing between a con artist and a genuinely curious yet harmless friend can be challenging.

Trap 7: Trust: How can I balance feeling distrustful with being too trustful?

People with money are often targets for people with bad intentions, so it shouldn't be a surprise that feeling overly distrustful or too trustful is sometimes a hazard of being an inheritor. It only takes one or two bad experiences for someone to become discouraged about others. Trust but verify. Healthy skepticism is a wise approach, and it can be a difficult balance to strike. Too much skepticism can sacrifice close relationships. If you become too skeptical, you will likely be difficult to get along with; your manner can be withdrawn and defensive when you always assume that others' motives are malevolent. It is impossible to establish healthy relationships with this outlook.

Distrust and suspicion are tricky, but a little of each is healthy. Finding the correct amount can be challenging. It is possible, however, to prevent suspicion from swelling into full-blown paranoia.

Solutions

Accept that money is a big source of energy in our society and that many people will take yours if you let them. Almost everyone is a target. Wealthy people are just larger, more attractive targets. In some instances, you can take legal steps to prevent people from cheating you or to minimize the damage if they do. This is one of the main reasons for the creation of trusts.

Don't lend or borrow money from friends or colleagues. There are a very few exceptions to this rule, but the less your relationships are tied to financial dealings, the less opportunity others will have to take advantage of you and the less opportunity you will have to worry.

Educate yourself and be alert and careful about potential dangers. With this approach, you will be open to one of life's greatest rewards: warm, trusting relationships.

Seek professional counseling if you are beginning to feel suspicious of formerly trusted friends and advisors. You don't have to live in a small, suspicious world.

Take baby steps when you are building relationships. Nurture the relationships in which you experience the most evidence of goodwill. Exercise 7.2 will help you do this.

---

e 7.2

Exercise 7.2:

How Much Personal Information Should I Reveal?

1. How long have I known this person? ____ years
2. Is he/she in my inner circle of my two or three best friends? ____ yes ____ no
3. On a scale of 1 to 10 (**1**: *not at all*; **10**: *absolutely*), how much do I trust him/her?

   1 2 3 4 5 6 7 8 9 10

4. What values do we have in common?

____

____

____

5. What priorities do we have in common?

____

____

____

6. How will I benefit from beginning to tell my friend about my financial situation and experiences?

____

____

____

7. How will my friend benefit from hearing about my financial situation and experiences?

____

____

____

8. Can this subject wait? Yes ____ No ____

Why or why not?

____

____

____

9. How do we handle power struggles in our relationship?

____

____

____

10. What do I hope sharing this information will accomplish?

____

____

____

continued on next page

11. What do I risk by not sharing myself?

____

____

____

12. To what extent am I attempting to meet my own needs?

____

____

____

____

13. Is this the right time?

____

____

____

14. How can I say this most concisely?

____

____

____

15. How can I put the focus back on my friend?

____

____

____

If you have known this friend for at least a year, and if your answers to the exercise were positive, you might consider beginning to give your friend specifics beyond "I come from a wealthy family." Still, reveal your precious and private information in baby steps. Observe how each step goes. If you don't like how a step goes, stop.

Trap 8: Knowing My Strengths and Limitations: How do I handle it when people assume my wealth prevents me from understanding the real world?

There are actually two problems here:

1. **Assumptions by other people.** People make assumptions about others all the time. Most of these people are only able to view you through their own lenses and filters. This doesn't have to be your problem.
2. **Self-doubt.** How do you know if you really do understand the real world? How does anyone? Most of us develop confidence that we understand the world we live in, but we may not feel as self-assured when we are outside our normal realm. A savvy politician may feel inept at an arts event. A wealthy person who doesn't work may feel awkward among a group of professionals. Be realistic, take charge of your life, and build your confidence by understanding the world in which you live. This is the world you can master.

Solutions

Find your center. Many people worry about what other people think. They know they shouldn't, but they do. When you find yourself worrying about what other people think about you, you've lost your center. It will help to reflect on who you really are, your values, and how you prefer to interact with people. This will help you center yourself again. There are many ways to regain your center: meditating, talking with a friend, meeting with a therapist, or reading this book or others about spirituality, wealth, or happiness. You might find a helpful book on the resources page of my website, www.thayerwillis.com/books.

Start thinking and talking about your values. Are you handling money in ways that reflect your values? To live intentionally, we need to know our values, set our priorities in accordance with them, and then choose our actions based on our priorities. If you're not basing your actions on your values, you are not only reinforcing the impression that you don't live in the real world, but you are also sentencing yourself to feeling out of sync with yourself. You may want to revisit the list of your top ten values in chapter three.

If you're interested in understanding a broader world, expose yourself to other situations and people: people from other cultures, professions, and interests. The only way to have confidence that you know the real world to some extent is to put yourself in the real world. The more you step outside the bubble of comfort in which you live, the more you can understand different kinds of people, places, and topics.

Volunteer at a community organization to expose yourself to people outside your usual circle.

Take a class in something new. You will develop new competencies and also meet different kinds of people.

Travel with the masses. Let go of first class for a few trips to learn how to maneuver on your own and to experience different slices of life.

It is likely that you will feel challenged at first when you put yourself in new situations. Be prepared to encounter some people who make negative assumptions about you. You may not change anyone's mind, but you will survive the experience—and in the process, you will become more confident.

One inheritor in her late twenties, Ashley, found a volunteer program where she could teach underprivileged children. Unfortunately, the principal of the school figured out she was wealthy and resented her. He gave her a difficult time, refusing to let her implement some of her good ideas and taking credit for many of her successes there. This was a painful but valuable experience about the real world. Ashley learned this is what some people are like. But she made some interesting new friends and learned many lessons that helped her feel more competent and confident about her abilities. Even though it was a tough situation, she survived in a challenging work environment.

Once you develop competence, confidence will follow. As you build your positive outlook, gradually you will realize that being the target of pushy questions, jealousy, curiosity, and assumptions doesn't rattle you anymore. You will see these potential annoyances as other people's problems, not yours.

You may even find that you can be compassionate. Taking on this active role and attitude can empower you. If you focus on staying strong and true to who you really are, you will minimize the impact of others' assumptions about you. And you will have the priceless benefit of enjoying a confident, purposeful, and meaningful life.

Trap 9: Loaning Money: Is it ever okay to lend money to a friend?

If you're at Starbucks with a friend who says she's short for her drink by fifty cents and will pay you back the next morning, it's not necessarily a problem (unless it happens repeatedly). However, I usually counsel people to stay away from giving friends bigger loans because this can be so tricky to manage well without damaging relationships. I am a much bigger fan of gifts. The quality of a gift is clean compared to a loan. That said, there are occasionally circumstances that support a loan. Just be very careful and know that loaning money is a high-risk activity in a relationship with just about anyone.

Solution

Carefully evaluate the situation and what your investment in it might look like. The decision tree in Figure 7.3 will help you consider several factors involved in personal loans that will clarify whether or not it is wise to lend your friend money.

7.3

Figure 7.3:

Decision Tree for Loaning Money to a Friend

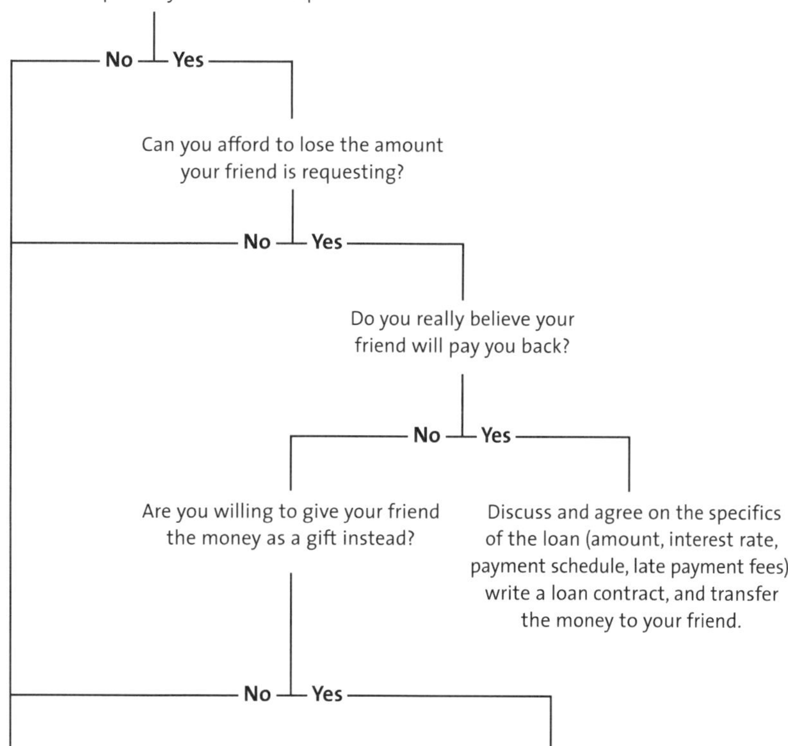

Say no. You may wish to add one of the following:

1. *I value our friendship, and I am not available for a loan.*
2. *I feel uncomfortable loaning money right now.*
3. *I am not available to loan money. Is there some other way I could help you?*

Find out from a financial advisor or attorney if there will be gift tax consequences so that you see the whole financial picture. At this point, you might consider making the money an outright gift. Or write a contract with the condition that if the loan is not repaid by a certain date, it becomes a gift.

Just go straight to making it a gift. Insist, and your friend's response will reveal something to you about his attitude toward you. Maybe it will never happen again, or maybe he'll be back for more next week. Either way, you learn about him.

What Makes a Good Friendship?

We see stories of celebrities surrounded by an entourage of "friends" who hang out together. If you look more closely, you will realize that most of these celebrities are surrounded by sycophants, no one who will give them honesty. Think Elvis, Michael Jackson, or Lindsay Lohan.

When it comes to friends, more is not necessarily better. This is not an area of life where it is wise to accumulate more and more. All we need is two or three close, trusted friends. As I often remind my children, we become like our friends—so choose them carefully. Common values are of great importance. And you will find that different friends have varying roles in your life. You may find you really like working out with friend A, enjoy traveling with friend B, and prefer attending cultural or charitable events with friend C. Friend A may be the easiest of the three for you to confide in, but you may not want to invite her to most social events because she may be rough around the edges.

Amy's and Kate's husbands are business partners, and Amy thinks of Kate as one of the funniest people she knows. Amy enjoys going out for meals and movies with Kate but seriously dislikes shopping with her. The two are both wealthy, but unlike Kate, Amy doesn't shop at designer stores and isn't willing to leave every store with thousands of dollars of merchandise.

Once, after enjoying a nice lunch together in town, Kate asked Amy to shop with her at a favorite store. Amy looked at a few price tags and was quietly taken aback when she saw a belt priced at $1,300—all the prices were at least four or five times higher than what she would be willing to pay. Amy lost interest and sat on a sofa reading a magazine while Kate worked quietly with a very refined sales associate. After a couple hours, Kate's purchase came with a five-figure bill. Not only was Amy a bit stunned by Kate's taste, thinking it a waste of money, she'd been bored while her friend tried on dresses she would never consider herself.

"I can go out to dinner with her and have a great time," Amy told me. "There are certain things I really enjoy about Kate. She's funny and pleasant to be around, but there are some big gaps in our values. I don't see her as one of my best friends. It's more a friendship of convenience, since our husbands work so closely together."

To navigate through situations like this, it may be helpful to identify the strengths and weaknesses of each of your friendships. Where's the balance? What are the demands and rewards of each friendship? Exercise 7.4 will help you create a snapshot of your life with each of your friends.

---

e
7.4

Exercise 7.4:

Interpersonal Needs / Satisfactions Assessment[1]

First, write down the names of your three or four main friends—the people you hang out with the most or with whom you feel closest. Next, fill in each friendship's demands and rewards.

Step 1: My Social Circle

My Main Friendships	Demands	Rewards
1. __________	__________	__________
2. __________	__________	__________
3. __________	__________	__________
4. __________	__________	__________

Next, follow the prompts in Step 2 on the following page to fill in the name of the friend who fills each role related to your social needs and to answer the related questions.

continued on next page

Step 2: My Social Needs

My Social Needs	To whom do I look?	How successfully (as percentage)?	What role does my wealth play in this relationship?	How could I improve this?	Who else might fill this need?
Listening	______	______	______	______	______
	______	______	______	______	______
	______	______	______	______	______
Emotional Support	______	______	______	______	______
	______	______	______	______	______
	______	______	______	______	______
Emotional Challenge	______	______	______	______	______
	______	______	______	______	______
	______	______	______	______	______
Intellectual Support	______	______	______	______	______
	______	______	______	______	______
	______	______	______	______	______
Intellectual Stimulation	______	______	______	______	______
	______	______	______	______	______
	______	______	______	______	______
Play	______	______	______	______	______
	______	______	______	______	______
	______	______	______	______	______

This chart is a snapshot of your interpersonal needs and satisfactions now. You can use your observations from filling out the chart to make a goal to improve a certain area.

e 7.5

Exercise 7.5:

Values Comparison

Considering the friends you named above, identify three strong values you see in each of them.

Friend 1. ____________________

Friend 2. ____________________

Friend 3. ____________________

Friend 4. ____________________

For each of your friendships, identify values you have in common:

1. ____________________
2. ____________________
3. ____________________
4. ____________________

For each of your friendships, identify conflicting values:

1. ____________________
2. ____________________
3. ____________________
4. ____________________

Write your observations about what values may be influencing your friends' actions in ways that impact the relationship you have with them.

____

____

____

____

Moving Toward the Bright Side

It is important to remember that people's actions and behaviors—and the reasons behind why they do them—are their own. You can take charge of your own life regardless of the actions of others. If you are clear on your own values and have developed confidence, you'll be less likely to feel shaken when you're faced with a wealth trap affecting your friendships. You will know what you need and want to do. You'll be able to respond more effectively, usually diffusing the situation early on.

7.6 Exercise 7.6:

Centering Yourself

Look over your Values Exercise from chapter three. Return to step two of the exercise. If you didn't prioritize your top ten values when you did this exercise originally, do so now. Give some consideration to your top three values and how they fit with each of your friends listed in the Values Comparison exercise here. Record your observations below.

___

___

___

Susan, the inheritor from the beginning of the chapter whose friend Carolyn outed her as wealthy, found that with effort she was able to manage her relationships with all of her friends, some better than others. She understood that Carolyn didn't mean to do harm to her but was just unable to keep such big news to herself. Of course Susan would have liked to maintain total control over revealing her family's wealth, but this is not how the scenario played out. What is significant is that Susan's friendships—and her motivation to take care of these friendships—were strong enough that she was able to make her new situation work.

Exercise 7.7: 7.7

Gratitude

What are five elements of your relationship with a friend for which you are grateful?

Exercise 7.8: 7.8

Action Plan

Now set an action plan for improving your relationships with friends. As before, begin with improving one relationship in a specific and measurable way. Part of the goal is simply to accomplish this, so make your action plan doable.

Today's date ______________________

The goal I set for my relationship with my friend is:

In order to accomplish this goal, I will perform the following activities:

Support people who might assist me include:

continued on next page

I realize I may sabotage my plan by:

____

____

____

So I will avoid this by:

____

____

____

I will complete this goal by ______________________ (date)

(Recommendation: three to six months)

Whatever your age or stage of life, and wherever you live, it's wonderful to have trustworthy, loyal, and supportive friends to accompany you. People with whom you share values and background experiences can be friends of ease and provide supportive challenge. While friendships with people from different cultural, religious, and financial backgrounds may prove to be more difficult than relationships with people similar to us, they can still prove extremely rewarding as you open yourself up to diverse and enriching experiences, an expansive world of growth and adventure. Remember, it's important to devote plenty of time, effort, and consideration to those few close friends who make your journey through life deeply worthwhile.

The Eternal Triangle
Man, Woman, Wealth

It is a truth universally acknowledged, that a single man in possession of a good fortune, must be in want of a wife.
—JANE AUSTEN

Love doesn't make the world go 'round; love is what makes the ride worthwhile.
— SHANNON ALDER

*To be fully seen by somebody, then, and be loved anyhow—
this is a human offering that can border on miraculous.*
—ELIZABETH GILBERT

| RELATIONSHIP ELEMENTS: | **Values** | **Trust** | **Respect** |

"THE FIRST TIME YOU MARRY FOR LOVE," said Jacqueline Kennedy Onassis, "the second time for money, and the third for companionship."

"Marrying for love may be a bit risky," comments humorist Josh Billings, "but it is so honest that God can't help but smile on it."

Like God, most of us smile on marrying for love, for we harbor in our hopelessly romantic hearts the belief that love conquers all—despite formidable odds and in the face of insurmountable opposition.

Predictably, it was Onassis's advice on marrying for money that garnered the most opposition. As did a question posted on the internet that asked bluntly, "Would you marry for money? A really rich man/woman asks you to marry them. You don't find them all that attractive, but they're not that bad either. You get on with them OK, but they don't float your boat. They say if you marry them, you'll never want for anything ever again. Would you?"

Among fifty-three posted replies—most of them advising against it—were these two eye-catching comments:

No! Marriage is hard enough with someone you love. If you marry for money, you will earn every penny of it. You will miss out on what marriage is supposed to be about, best friends, emotional support, growing and maturing together. That's what it's supposed to be about.

Money can come and go—marrying a man who does or doesn't have money is no guarantee. People have burned through big loads of cash to find themselves hopelessly in debt and others have persisted despite low paying work to advance financially. Marrying someone who is hard working and responsible with money should outrank their financial status, whether rich or poor.

"*Never* marry for money," similarly cautions a Scottish proverb. "Ye'll borrow it cheaper."

One of the most challenging romances occurs between suitors with significantly less or significantly more wealth than the other. In this chapter you will find tools to help you approach romance with a level head while keeping your heart open. It's up to no one but you. You can have a successful romance if you want it enough to work for it.

Don't Marry for Money

Gary got married reluctantly. It was his girlfriend's idea to get married after dating for three years, and Gary didn't feel he could object any longer. After all, he did like Debbie. He didn't feel like he couldn't live without her, but he thought maybe this was as good as it gets. Maybe this was good enough. The marriage only lasted two years before Gary was so miserable he left.

The fortune he had inherited from his grandfather didn't console him much. Gary had never worked, and he dreaded when people asked, "So what do you do?" in any kind of social setting. It had never occurred to him to work because, well, he had so much money and there wasn't any work he really wanted to do.

The divorce was not without its cost. Debbie hadn't wanted to sign a prenuptial agreement, and she had always been so nice. Gary didn't think it mattered in their case. However, in the end, she hired an aggressive attorney and managed to extract a big settlement out of him. Humiliating. Then every time Gary started dating anyone, he was haunted by insecurity and doubt. He was beginning to fear he would always be alone.

His self-confidence was terribly fragile. He was intelligent and had been managing his money well, but he felt he had completely failed in love. When Gary and I met, he was dating Sasha, but he was reserved with her, constantly asking the emotionally crippling question: Does she love me for me, or is she just after my money? He wanted to know how to find the answer.

It can be a tough question, and it's complicated by the fact that financial wealth is an inextricable part of the package of who you are. Gary wrestled with this reality. I worked with him to help him accept the reality of who he was and then tackle the task of finding the answer to his question. He was willing to take the time to pay close attention to Sasha and her priorities, and he was willing to walk into situations with her where her values would show. Some of these situations were stressful, ones Gary might have avoided in the past, but now he was on a mission to find out Sasha's true nature, so he took the opportunities when they arose.

To Sasha's credit, her behavior was consistent, and her values did show under pressure. They were essentially the same values Gary had been seeing in her. When I last saw them, they were engaged to be married, and Gary was emotionally stronger and more relaxed. The success of his relationship with Sasha was entirely worth the effort he had devoted to it.

Hard Enough by Itself

Romantic love without the complications of wealth is challenging enough for most of us to navigate well. And when we are young adults, we care passionately about making a success of our passion. So we have all the typical challenges of our peers and—just to make it a bit more dicey—if financial inheritance graces our lives, we have another potent complication. In addition to the usual efforts to connect well with a romantic interest, we must also contend with our inheritance, which tips scales and redefines power.

As with friendship, one of the biggest challenges in romance occurs when a wealthy person dates someone with a significantly different amount of wealth. I once dated a man who had children from a previous marriage. I wasn't sure if our relationship was headed toward marriage, but I liked him and his kids. One day we were going out to a party where we all needed to be dressed up. I didn't realize he had taken his kids out and bought them new clothes for the occasion. When they arrived at my house, his twelve-year-old son came in first while my boyfriend and his daughter looked at something outside.

When this young man walked in, I said, "Oh, you look so nice!"

He replied, "My dad got us these clothes, since now that we're going to be rich, we'll need to dress up more."

Hmmm. I didn't like that comment at all, especially because there had already been a couple similar comments. We went our separate ways shortly afterward. The problem wasn't that we came from different economic backgrounds, but wealth amplified our different worldviews.

Crossing Class Lines

Many of the same traps occur in romance as in friendships, which I listed in chapter seven. If you are experiencing any of these traps with a significant other, remember to center yourself in your identified values and to model your actions on them.

8.1 FIGURE 8.1:

Wealth Traps in Romantic Relationships

Trap 1: Making Decisions about Activities Together: Where to go, what to do?

Trap 2: Taking Responsibility for Paying: Who pays?

Trap 3: Discernment: How can I tell if a date likes me for me or for my money?

Trap 4: Staying Centered: How can I get beyond feeling self-conscious about my wealth?

Trap 5: Confidence: How can I handle boyfriends/girlfriends who seem jealous of my wealth?

Trap 6: Nosy Companions: How should I respond when a boyfriend/girlfriend seems too interested in my wealth?

Trap 7: Trust: How can I balance feeling distrustful or too trusting?

Trap 8: Knowing My Strengths and Limitations: How do I handle it when people assume my wealth prevents me from understanding the real world?

Trap 9: Loaning Money: Is it ever okay to lend money to a boyfriend/girlfriend?

Even if your perception is that you have married up or down, coming from different social classes does not doom a relationship. Class is essentially a background experience that can be shared to foster closeness. At best, an inequality in backgrounds can create balance in a healthy relationship. You may gain stability from a less wealthy romantic partner who is not so inclined (and financially able) to bolt when the going gets tough. At the same time, your partner may gain a broader outlook on life from you, as you may have traveled and studied widely.

It's important to use your experiential differences and family cultures to provide the relationship with unique combined strengths as support for one another, whenever possible.

Of course this can be challenging to develop, but ask for help if you need to. It is well worth the effort. Your differences can enable you to offer encouragement and perspective to each other when you find yourselves up against a roadblock. This only works, though, when you have a relationship founded on shared core values rather than on wealth and assumptions.

The relationship between marital success and social station is a sensitive topic, particularly among parents. It may be politically incorrect for parents to be upset about seeing their children marry across class—or religious or ethnic—lines, but the reality is that many wealthy parents strongly object to their children "marrying down." Some fear incompatibility of values, even though in America most values do not differ purely based on class.

Years ago, education and the appearance of wealth were indicators of class, but no longer. Anyone can receive an education, and financial markers such as large homes and expensive cars are now broadly available because of lax lending practices. Values and class are not as identifiable in these outward manifestations anymore. In short, traditional parental concerns based on fear of outsiders, in many cases, require much more effort and depth to assess.

I once helped a client, Kelly, who was very much in love with a firefighter, but her parents disapproved of the relationship. Kelly never wavered in wanting to marry her man. I helped the two of them explore and understand potential difficulties. The biggest challenge lay in finding a proper perspective on Kelly's wealth. After some hard work and success in this, she and her firefighter married and thrived. Both stretched and adjusted, but what marriage doesn't call for flexibility?

I have seen it time and time again. If both partners cultivate focus and commitment and if they have values in common, then social status becomes secondary or irrelevant. Make no mistake: maintaining a successful marriage with differences in wealth requires work and commitment, as do all marriages. So if you have a respectful, kind, loving relationship with your intended, ignore the skeptics, even if they happen to be your parents. Make sure you pay close attention to the first half of that sentence! If you want this marriage, you can have it.

The Delicate Stages of Romantic Relationships

Most romantic relationships build through the following stages. It is my advice to follow these stages as closely in order as you can. They build on one another well, and the time spent in each stage will give you valuable preparation for the next.

You will recognize experiences you have had in relationships as you read through the stages. When you do recall such an experience, take time to consider how that relationship progressed through these stages. Would you do anything differently if you had the chance to do it over again? See what you can learn from your past experiences here.

First Blush

When you first become infatuated with someone, wealth may not seem like an issue at all. In some cases, neither of you may have much sense of the other's financial status. However, one or both of you may have an inkling or make assumptions, consciously or unconsciously, about each other's individual or family wealth.

Values Exploration

It is wise to explore your own and each other's values very early on in the relationship, as values in common play an essential role in the eventual success or failure of a relationship. And there are many types of values to explore. Certainly, the foundational values we considered in chapter three play a large role, and romantic relationships come with their own set of values as well. Marriage and sex can have varying definitions and priorities in people's lives. Other relationship-specific values to consider are argument resolution, gender roles, expectations for work, plans to have children and how to raise them, prenuptial agreements, finance sharing, philanthropy, and the types of friends both partners have.

The sooner you explore these big-picture values, the more likely you are to find priorities in common and to realize where you and your significant other do not align. If you don't agree on something right now, it may not mean the relationship cannot work, but you'll know what areas you may need to discuss at length and compromise on later. At this stage, you're just observing. But it's important not to pretend that conflicting values are unimportant.

Building Friendship

Many successful romantic relationships begin as friendships, sometimes friendships that last for years. However, it doesn't always work that way, and if two people feel the heat of a physical attraction and emotional connection, friendship is often a distant idea.

But while you cannot force a relationship to remain at the friendship level, it is possible—and healthy—to nurture the friendship part of a relationship from the very beginning. To do this, you need to identify the friendship aspects of your connection that feel most powerful. Think: How do I like this person as a friend in addition to a romantic partner?

While lovers tend to put their best foot forward, especially in the early part of a relationship—dressing up, keeping up their guard, hiding weaknesses and shortcomings—friends generally feel more spontaneous, revealing who they really are. What would it be like to just be yourself? What if you didn't have to buy a new outfit for a new man? What if you didn't feel you had to take a new woman to the fanciest restaurant to impress her and instead just met at a park for a walk followed by a visit to an ice cream parlor or café? What if you admitted outright you didn't get a joke, or revealed you were afraid of taking buses, or shared that you were once fired from a job?

You might both find that it's refreshing and relaxing to let your guard down a bit. It might help you bond in your ability to be more real with each other. And it is likely to strengthen an underlying friendship beneath a budding romance.

Figure 8.2 describes differences between how friends and romantic partners tend to approach relationship aspects. In which areas could you relate to a romantic partner better if you considered how you would approach the relationship as a friendship?

8.2

Figure 8.2:

Friends or Romantic Partners?

Traits	Friends	Romantic Partners
Trust/Acceptance	Conditional (you may have one or two very special, old friendships that are unconditional, but this is rare)	Conditional at first, becoming less so with time
Sharing Shortcomings	Generally willing to reveal	May try to hide shortcomings, at least in early stages
Arguments	More open, less to argue about	More often, followed by making up
Jealousy	About attention	About commitment
Gift-Giving	Not expected	Expected
Secret Sharing	Some, depends on the friend	Certain types of secrets
Expectations	Reciprocal effort	Need to be worked out carefully
Duration	Can continue forever on same level	Either get married or break up

continued on next page

TRAITS	**FRIENDS**	**ROMANTIC PARTNERS**
Transition	Friends can turn into lovers	Lovers cannot (easily) transition back to just friends
Intimacy	Emotional intimacy	Emotional and physical intimacy
Conditions	Nonexclusive; relationship is not necessarily central	Exclusive; relationship is central

Opening up a romance to the elements of friendship will help you develop a strong foundation for your relationship as you move from one stage of the relationship to the next.

Meeting Their Friends

You can tell a lot about people by the company they keep. Does your boyfriend socialize exclusively with people in the same economic stratum, primarily those from wealthy backgrounds? Or are your girlfriend's strongest connections with a mix of people from different backgrounds? If a person is from a modest background, does he surround himself with friends who are wealthy? This would be a red flag, as wealth may seem to be the main attraction.

Notice how your date interacts with friends. Observe if there are comments about money or wealth. Are they negative or positive? Do your date's friends assume wealthy people have obtained their wealth through dishonest or even criminal means? Or do they assume wealthy people are generally smart, hardworking, and good in business? How does your girlfriend react when her friends make negative comments about wealthy people? These observations will add to your knowledge of the person you're dating. After all, most people share similar values with their friends.

Common sense dictates being quiet about anything having to do with financial wealth when you are first getting to know your date and each other's friends. Focus on other things, such as the many areas you may have in common: recreation, books, movies, and so on. Keep your financial wealth out of any discussion. It's in bad taste if your date brings up wealth in front of your friends, especially if it's *your* wealth—it's a violation of boundaries and very likely a show stopper.

Visiting Family

When you meet your significant other's family, you're going to learn some things about the person you're dating. It's always interesting; usually everyone's hoping to find a kindred spirit.

How does your boyfriend relate to his mother and father? How a man treats his mother is usually a clue to how he will treat you. Is your girlfriend competitive with her parents? Is your boyfriend an autonomous adult or reduced to teenage behavior in front of his parents? Don't worry so much about what the family will think about you that you neglect to make observations about them. Trust your instincts about the family.

Be yourself and make a conscious effort to use your best communication skills. The basics of improvisation can help you develop these. In improv, you learn to accept and build on what others say and do. So if your girlfriend's family cracks a joke at your expense, laugh with them instead of running from the room. Step into forward motion with it. The same goes for when your boyfriend meets your family. If your father reveals that you flunked out of kindergarten, do your best to go with the flow. You might say, "Yeah, I never did get the hang of finger painting," or "Thank goodness I finally learned how to take naps and share my crayons."

Another helpful maxim to keep in mind during embarrassing moments is to "function in disaster and finish in style." After all, success is one of the elements of strong relationships, perhaps most important in romantic relationships.

Discussing Commitment

When couples begin to talk about commitment, it's usually precipitated by some other event. Maybe your boyfriend needs to move, maybe your biological clock is ticking, maybe your girlfriend is ready to establish a more settled life—any of which are bound to raise the question: Are we together or not?

You might feel afraid of scaring the other person off, but it's important to bring up the commitment question when you're ready. Gather your courage and say, "I'm feeling ready to talk about moving toward a committed relationship. Are you?" If you wait for the other person to bring it up, you could be waiting for years.

If you haven't done so by now, this is the time to openly discuss values and prenups. There are two excellent books to read at this stage of your relationship: *Prenups for Lovers: A Romantic Guide to Prenuptial Agreements* by Arlene G. Dubin and *The Hard Questions: 100 Essential Questions to Ask Before You Say "I Do"* by Susan Piver. Don't delay these explorations. They are much easier in the early stages of the relationship.

Another topic that needs to be discussed if you decide to enter a committed relationship is how to handle your joint finances. By now you should have a clear idea about your future partner's values and money habits. If you have not already discussed areas that may conflict, now is the time to do so. Every couple's situation is different, and as much as we would like a tried-and-true formula for sorting out the details, there isn't one. Your formula must be developed by the two of you. Talk about every aspect of managing your financial lives. The key to your committed relationship's success is to set a solid precedent of speaking your mind (gently and firmly), maintaining a spirit of compromise, and staying true to your core principles.

The step of saying "I love you" is a significant marker in a romantic relationship. During the commitment stage in the relationship, expressing love is appropriate. However, it is not appropriate much before this point. If your love interest is declaring "I love you" too soon and you feel awkward about it, this can be a red flag.

Engagement

When you get to the point of engagement, it is time for each of you to take the prenup discussion to your respective attorneys. By law, you each need to have your own attorney. At this time, both of you will disclose your current income and assets. This may trigger some emotional reactions, so take this opportunity to talk through whatever surfaces.

Your fiancé may say, "When I realized how much money you have, I began to think, *Why am I working at this job that I don't even like?*" It's important to explore the options. How would you feel if your future husband didn't work? How might your future wife feel down the road if she did not have a reason to get up and get dressed in the morning? Is it important that both partners bring money into the marriage? What are the ramifications for the family if your fiancé stops working? What are some alternatives?

This can be an awkward, messy negotiation, so it may help, again, to find a neutral third party—a pastor, trusted older friend or family member, therapist, or counselor—for you to consult. If you or your fiancé express the desire to quit a job, that third party can help you think through the issues.

Marriage

Once you work through these issues and do your best to create a unified vision of how you will live together, the next step will be planning the wedding and beginning to merge your lives as a married couple. We will discuss the many issues that can arise throughout a marriage in chapter nine.

Getting Physical

The timing to begin a sexual relationship is a very personal decision. It has become casual for many people in our society, and sexual relationships are often pursued quickly. My observation is that this is not wise and may very well lead to difficulties in intimacy when couples enter a committed relationship. Therefore, I believe for spiritual as well as emotional and practical reasons, it's best to wait until after marriage to consummate the relationship.

First, waiting serves the purpose of exploring and enjoying true intimacy with the person you will marry. When you experience intimacy and sexuality earlier with other partners, it is difficult to approach your relationship with the exclusive and special status that can be so valuable in marriage. It can even be elusive to create a precious and unique sense of intimacy with your spouse. As a result of a premature sexual relationship, one of the great joys of marriage will be compromised irreversibly.

You may be tempted to think you can manage this without waiting, but you are likely to regret your choice. You can't rewind for another chance to handle this well. Certainly, you can have closeness with your spouse despite earlier experiences, but if you want the highest level of intimacy, it is important to not dilute your potential by attaching yourself to others along the way.

Second is the matter of safety. There are many dangers associated with being sexual with anyone other than your committed partner. Most children learn about these dangers in school sex education programs. Unfortunately, many people think these dangers could never happen to them, so they learn the risks firsthand. Sexually transmitted diseases are widespread, and the only foolproof protection is abstinence.

Wealth is actually another reason for waiting to have sex. It has been said that wealth is the greatest aphrodisiac of all. This is not true for everyone, but it is for a significant number of people. As I mentioned earlier, it can be very difficult to be sure if your girlfriend loves you for who you are or for your money. By waiting to become intimate with your boyfriend, you'll have a much better sense of him as a person, more confidence in the relationship, and trust that he's not just "loving" you for your money.

I recommend an excellent pamphlet, written by Miriam Grossman, MD, about our sexuality and wise choices. It is available to print on the Clare Booth Luce Policy Institute website at www.cblpi.org/senseandsexuality. Its title is "Sense and Sexuality," and it is well documented, well written, concise, and clear. It is written for young women, though it would be a valuable read for young men as well.

Life is unpredictable in many ways, and it's likely that in real life, you have progressed through these steps in your own order, not mine. This is not necessarily a recipe for disaster. The most important thing is to discuss values, take time to build trust, and strive for success together.

Progressing Through the Stages

It's not always easy to know if—and when—you are ready to take a relationship to a higher stage. With the Stages of Romantic Relationships worksheet in Exercise 8.3, identify where you are at the moment in your current romantic relationship. If you are not currently in a relationship, think about a previous romance and how you progressed from one stage to the next, what the tricky spots were, and what ultimately derailed the relationship at whatever stage it ended. If you are with someone now, consider what you would look for to take this romance to the next stage.

For instance, if you are just starting out at first blush, what could you do to initiate a discussion about values with your girlfriend? If you are not comfortable meeting your boyfriend's buddies or family—or he has resisted meeting yours—Exercise 8.3 can help you think (and talk with your boyfriend) about what might change that. You may not be able to fill out the entire worksheet below. You may not be that far into a relationship. Just answer the questions for the stages you have experienced.

2.1 Exercise 8.3:

The Stages of Romantic Relationships worksheet

How would you move from one stage to the next?

What do you look for in your partner?

First Blush

Values Exploration

Building Friendship

Meeting Friends

Visiting Family

Discussing Commitment

Engagement

Marriage

Getting Physical

Most dating relationships do not follow any formula to the letter. Just use the points here to inform you about the quality and progress of your relationship. Above all, use your intuition to guide you. If you are forcing the process, an underlying issue is likely at play and you may need a major discussion with your partner. Don't sweep anything under the rug! It is important for you to be as conscious and honest as possible as you develop your relationship into one of the most fulfilling experiences of your life.

Dysfunctional and Dangerous Relationships

It is critical for us all to understand what makes a relationship healthy and mature and what constitutes an unhealthy relationship. There are two kinds of unhealthy relationships: infatuation and addiction. The first involves attraction based on one specific reason, such as physical appearance or wealth. Addiction relates to believing you should love someone even though you don't, and it results in the bad habit of continuing to be with someone you know is not good for you. Mature love, on the other hand, is a healthy approach to building a relationship founded on values, respect, and communication. Figure 8.4 outlines the signs of three types of relationships.

It is probably not possible to transition from an addictive relationship to mature love, but a relationship can evolve from infatuation to mature love if you stay with it.

8.4 FIGURE 8.4:

Infatuation, Addictive Relationships, and Mature Love[1]

Infatuation	Addictive Relationship	Mature Love
Usually occurs at the beginning of a relationship	A feeling of not being able to live without the partner	Develops gradually through learning about each other
Physical and sexual attraction is central	Insecurity, distrust, lack of confidence, feeling threatened	Sexual attraction is present, but warm affection/friendship is central
Characterized by urgency, intensity, sexual desire, and anxiety	Low self-esteem; looking to partner for validation and affirmation of self-worth	Characterized by calm, peacefulness, empathy, support, trust, confidence, and tolerance of each other; no feelings of being threatened
Driven by the excitement of being involved with a person whose character is not fully known	Fewer happy times together; more time spent on apologies, fear, guilt, and unkept promises	Driven by deep attachment; based on extensive knowledge of both positive and negative qualities in the other person; mature acceptance of imperfections
Involves nagging doubts and unanswered questions; the partner remains unexamined so as not to spoil the dream	Needing the other in order to feel complete	Partners want to be together but are not obsessed with the relationship

Infatuation	Addictive Relationship	Mature Love
Is based on fantasy	Feeling worse about oneself as the relationship progresses	Is based on reality
Is consuming, often exhausting	Loss of self-control	Is energizing in a healthy way
Entails discomfort with individual differences	Making fewer decisions or plans; waiting for the partner to tell what to do	Partners have high self-esteem; each has a sense of self-worth with or without the partner and feels complete even without the relationship
Relationship not enduring because it lacks a firm foundation	Discomfort with individual differences	Individuality is accepted
	Tearing down or criticizing the other	Each brings out the best in the other; relationship is nurturing
	Feeling as though one is "killing time" until with partner again	Partners are patient, feel no need to rush the events of the relationship; there is a sense of security and no fear of losing the partner
	Rushing things, like sex or marriage, so as not to lose the partner	Each encourages the other's growth
	Breaking promises to oneself or others because of the relationship	Is enduring and sustaining because it is based on a strong foundation of friendship
	Being threatened by the other partner's growth	
	Constant jealousy and insecurity	
	Using drugs or alcohol as coping mechanisms	
	Friends or family report that the person is "different" from the way she used to be	

It is essential that you are also able to recognize the red flags of various levels of abuse. Figure 8.5 lists the signs of verbal and emotional violence, sexual abuse, and physical abuse. People in such relationships tend to find creative ways to deny these signs, to make excuses for a boyfriend or girlfriend who displays these behaviors, or they believe the other person will change. Still another possibility is that they blame themselves. For instance, victims in abusive relationships might cling to the belief that "if only I could change, my boyfriend might stop the abuse." Often, such relationships have to hit rock bottom—with the abuse descending to increasingly dangerous levels—before the abused partner will leave. An abused person would greatly benefit from the help of professional counseling.

8.5 FIGURE 8.5:

Relationship Red Flags[2]

Verbal and Emotional Violence

- Name calling—even in "fun"/teasing
- Intimidating looks
- Use of cell phones or smartphones to monitor you
- Making you wait by the phone
- Using *bitch* and other such words as an endearment/loving reference
- Monopolizing your time
- Isolating you from family and friends
- Making you feel insecure or inadequate
- Blaming
- Saying *I love you* too soon
- Manipulation through guilt tactics—leading to you rescuing the partner
- Making threats
- Interrogating
- Humiliating you in public
- Breaking treasured items
- Expecting you to pay for things
- Borrowing money and not repaying
- Making you feel guilty about money
- Telling others about your family or money

Sexual Abuse

- Date rape
- Statutory rape (Each state has its own age-of-consent laws. Generally, if the girl is under fourteen and the boy is twenty-one or older or there is a ten-year difference between the boy and girl with one person being under the age of eighteen, having sex is considered statutory rape.)

- Unwanted touching
- Unwanted kissing
- Any forced/coerced sexual contact

Physical Abuse

- Hitting, beating, shoving, pushing, punching
- Restraining
- Roughhousing/play wrestling
- Any forced physical contact

Sometimes friends and family don't speak up about their concerns for you for various reasons. They may not want to believe the abuse they suspect is happening, they may be afraid of causing more trouble for you, or they may just feel awkward and not know what to say. This is an important area where you can take charge of your life and be realistic about the dangers. You have the right to be treated respectfully, and if this is not happening, take charge and get help.

Moving Toward the Bright Side

Once you are confident that you are in a healthy, positive relationship, it is up to you and your boyfriend or girlfriend to allow and encourage the relationship to mature. The rewards can be great. It is entirely possible to steward your financial assets well while becoming closer to the man or woman whom you will marry.

Fortunately, Gary was able to work through his challenges in his relationship with Sasha. His confidence had been shaken by his experience with his first wife, Debbie, and he was afraid to trust again. Many people can identify with this, and to Gary's credit, he was able to gather the courage to allow his relationship with Sasha to grow and flourish, knowing that he just had to live with the risk that it might go well or badly. He was fortunate that their dating did go well, they grew to love and trust each other, and his financial wealth was not a negative or complicating factor in their relationship.

Use the exercises here to help you foster your own healthy, nurturing relationship.

8.6 Exercise 8.6:

Exploring Marriage Values

Turn back to the Values Clarification exercise (3.1) in chapter three. Using a single color highlighter, mark all the words from the original list that resonate with you. Then do the same with the list of marriage-specific values below. Which do you feel you must have in your marriage?

Love
Shared activities
Alone time
Sex
Arguing style in sync
Gender roles in sync
Work
Kids
Prenups
Friends
Raising kids
Intellectual stimulation
Emotional openness
Agreement about in-laws

How does your list this time compare with your personal list of top ten values from chapter three? What observations can you make about your marriage values?

8.6 Exercise 8.7:

Visualizing What You Want

Get into a comfortable position with your body fully supported by the chair, sofa, or floor. Take two or three deep breaths and allow yourself to focus on the marriage values you just identified and clarified. It is fine to use the papers you have marked to inform your vision. Imagine what a relationship based on your values would look like. Take some time to imagine the details of the relationship as it shows support of each of your values.

Exercise 8.8: **8.8**

Gratitude

What are five elements of your romantic relationship for which you are grateful?

Exercise 8.9: **8.9**

Action Plan

Now set an action plan for one thing you can do to improve your romantic relationship or to be available for the kind of romantic relationship you would like.

Today's date ____________________

The goal I set for my romantic relationship is:

In order to accomplish this goal, I will perform the following activities:

Support people who might assist me include:

continued on next page

I realize I may sabotage my plan by:

____

____

____

So I will avoid this by:

____

____

____

I will complete this goal by ____________________ (date)

(Recommendation: three to six months)

My father rarely gave advice. However, when I was in my mid-twenties, he did offer this stern admonition: "Don't let some boy take all your money." I couldn't understand why he would say this to me. However, I had arrived in young adulthood with more engine than rudder and with the street smarts of a doorknob. I had been well protected by my parents and had learned very little of the ways of the world.

It may seem paranoid to fear that everyone is trying to take your money. And yet, in reality, some people are. I was oblivious to this. My father, with years of experience, understood that some people will say and do anything to separate the wealthy from their money—which is not to say that everyone wants to do this. That is the key: to determine who is trustworthy and who is not. If every human interaction instills fear that someone is trying to take advantage of you, you have crossed the line into paranoia.

With romantic partners especially, there are concerns that a wealthy person will ignore at great peril. I hope this chapter has helped build your awareness of them, given you guidance, and supplied you with tools for identifying positive traits in the people you date. It is important for you to consciously and intentionally bring your own strengths to your relationships and navigate your way through the many challenges wealth will present.

Most of all, it is important to remember that if you truly want it, you can establish a healthy and happy relationship with a person who will walk beside you and bring your dream of marriage to life.

I'm sure you will. I wish you Godspeed.

After the Honeymoon
The Challenges of Marriage

A successful marriage requires falling in love many times, always with the same person.
—Mignon McLaughlin

Love is blind, marriage is the eye-opener.
—Unknown

Marriages and corporate mergers in America have at least one thing in common—more than 50 percent end up on the rocks.
—Rick Maurer

| Relationship Elements: | **Communication** | **Values** | **Competence** |

Self-help author Jack Kornfeld's book about marriage has a catchy title that humorously sums up the rocky road we're going to cover in this chapter: *After the Ecstasy, the Laundry*.

So what can you look forward to when the honeymoon ends? Some of us, long-embarked on the tempest-tossed seas of matrimony, know full well. Others have yet to find out. Whichever group you belong to—no matter how well you and your spouse have prepared for marriage—it's inevitable that you will encounter many challenges, small and large.

Even when you think you've both painstakingly anticipated and come to agreement about the issues, untried circumstances, life stages, and potential problems facing you—and how to handle them—more will come that neither of you has anticipated.

What's more, some of these challenges will be severe enough to test the very foundation of your marriage. Or one or both of you may find that in the harsh light of reality, you feel quite differently about the marriage, more than you dreamed you would. This may lead one or the other to change their mind about lifestyle choices or values on which you thought you were securely aligned.

In this chapter we'll explore many such unexpected challenges you may face, whether you are about to marry, have just married, or have been together for dozens of years.

Marriage—and life—presents a constant flow of new milestones, transitions, and challenges that you'll be called upon to navigate together. Any of the challenges in this chapter could escalate into a danger zone. Without careful, loving, and honest discourse—sometimes with help from an impartial third party—such issues can create serious problems in your marriage

Choices, Always Choices

Carissa and Pascal fell in love in India, where they both happened to be working. Carissa was a researcher from Australia, and Pascal was an apparel company executive from Italy. Just after they married they moved to Italy, because Pascal had completed his work in India and Carissa's work was fairly portable. Significantly, Pascal's family of origin was in Italy too, and so began the journey to know each other's cultures.

At first it was a grand adventure, and everyone was on their best behavior. Then, after a while, the personal work began. Carissa's grandfather had been a tremendously successful entrepreneur, and as a result Carissa had a significant inheritance. She and Pascal hadn't talked about it much when they were dating, and they didn't really want to talk about it now that they were married, but this kind of information is rarely successfully hidden. Carissa worried that discussions about her inheritance might burst the bubble of happiness she and Pascal had found.

However, Pascal's brothers, sisters, and cousins all had ideas about what they could do with even a small part of such a fortune. Carissa and Pascal began to receive requests for money for education, cars, even houses. This forced the couple not only to talk about Carissa's wealth but also to make decisions about it. They often disagreed, and it was after one of these heated discussions that they reached out to me. Because of their different backgrounds and personalities, each viewed Carissa's wealth differently. They were both generous—at least they shared this value. Pascal was inclined to help his family members with loans, and Carissa preferred any money going to others to be gifts. Problems arose when they discussed amounts and purposes of the funds.

What had begun as a loving, caring, passionate new marriage became very strained. Hard feelings had already manifested. When we started our work, all the main areas of life as a couple—family, work, sex, and even where to live—had been impacted. So we began with fundamental couples work: identifying and clarifying values, writing personal mission statements, writing a family mission statement, encouraging openness about personal finances, and building financial literacy in areas that were underdeveloped. We even did some "work" on how to revive play in their lives again.

Slowly, surely their relationship improved. Carissa and Pascal took many practical steps individually, together, and also collectively with the relatives. Practicing new, chosen behaviors is highly effective for reducing stress. For instance, one of their assignments was to practice having a date night once a week. It sounds like it would be easy, but when a couple has gotten off track, it can feel awkward to have fun together again. Though Carissa and Pascal's marriage could have reached the breaking point, and almost did many times, it is now stronger than ever after they've faced these challenges together. And whether we like it or not, we all face similar challenges when we marry.

Conflicting Values

When you and your spouse join your financial forces, money takes on a whole new level of meaning. There is something about stepping into this commitment that intensifies everything and brings issues to the surface that you were not able to see before.

Money is the cause of many divorces no matter what each spouse's financial background is. But often when couples think money is the problem, the root of the issue is actually what money represents. To one spouse wealth may represent freedom, and to the other it may mean security. As you can imagine, freedom and security can quickly become opposing priorities.

I often remember one of the first couples I worked with. They were having trouble agreeing on their vacation (among many other issues). From the husband's point of view of freedom, a distant, expensive vacation destination sounded like fun. But from the wife's point of view of security, a camping trip within driving distance sounded like fun. This couple had major work to do to reconcile their different priorities, and they reluctantly agreed to alternate years for each kind of vacation.

Carissa and Pascal were able to trace their differing perspectives on gifts for Pascal's family members to their opposing values. They had grown up in different countries, socioeconomic groups, and of course families. It was helpful to reconnect with their individual and shared values. Then they could take most of the emotion out of the decision-making process. They used the clarified information about their values to guide them in choosing how to handle all relationships with extended family members and their requests for financial assistance.

Financial Values

Even if you and your spouse come from seemingly compatible financial backgrounds, you may find that you come from very different money cultures. You may have been brought up with different ideas about risk, as fluctuating financial cycles can impact each spouse's family wealth differently.

During a national financial crisis, if your family's wealth was heavily invested in real estate, properties may have suffered significant losses. You may now be very cautious about spending, saving, and investing. If, on the other hand, your spouse's family had relied on cash, certain bonds, and market agnostic investments at that time, it may have emerged from the Great Recession with a portfolio fairly intact. As a result, your spouse may have a more expansive attitude about spending more, saving less, or investing in certain securities.

Other financial issues will arise when a death, divorce, marriage, or illness occurs in the family of origin, influencing how, when, and how much you or your spouse will eventually inherit. You may each have made assumptions about inheritance that turn out to be wrong. How you handle the new reality can challenge your relationship.

One effective approach is to communicate about and prepare for inheritance expectations early. Until the inheritance funds have been transferred to you, your wisest position is usually to assume there may be none or that your inheritance will be modest. Handling an inheritance that is bigger than you expected is often more manageable than handling one that is smaller.

There are some other problems regarding financial values. Some people like to cut corners on their taxes and do anything (legal) they can to keep money from the government. This may be a cultural belief in one spouse's family. Another family might feel fortunate that they make a good income and thus are able to pay taxes and will not hide anything or take shortcuts. This can create a marital clash when the married couple approaches their own tax planning.

Some families use credit and debt in their personal lives. Other families value the absence of personal debt. Imagine if you're married to someone at the other end of the spectrum. It's important to understand each other's backgrounds and how that impacts you today. It's ideal to find a compromise, such as using debt only for assets that build intrinsic value, not for depreciating assets, or only for taking on debt in the business.

Pascal came from a modest background and thrived on budgeting. Living within his budget represented security for him. Carissa had never lived on a budget, and it was not appealing to her. They were drastically divided on this issue when they first set up their household together, but both recognized they had to compromise. Pascal became more flexible about budgeting, and Carissa agreed to budget large categories for Pascal's sake.

Cultural and Family Values

Spouses who come from different cultures may stumble upon differences in their perceptions of the world, their expectations, and what they're used to. Everyone who marries has this challenge, but where there's wealth, differences are often amplified. In one all-American family who treasured burgers, football, and patriotism, the youngest son married a Persian woman. To heighten the stakes, this happened during the Gulf War. The husband's family had a hard time relating to the new bride—not only did she eat different food and abhor sports, some family members actually considered her an enemy of American culture. It took some time and a lot of patience, but eventually both sides of the family found ways to approach each other with curiosity and to learn. They found that many of their stereotypes weren't true and that they had much more in common than they expected.

Beyond ethnic differences, there are additional areas where both partners are likely to bring differing perspectives. And the differences can be telling. What about manners? Manners still do make a difference. Perhaps the difference is more subtle than it was years ago, but manners are a marker by which we often assess how comfortable we are with others. How someone holds her silverware and eats is often a clue to her background. Manners indicate that you have been taught the rules and know how to follow them. All classes have their own rules. In the upper class, the rules are well defined, unless you care to be labeled eccentric or an outsider.

Religious Values

Religious values are often very sensitive. In my experience, the approach that I have seen work best is marrying a spouse who shares the same or very close religious values as you. When two parents have different faiths, I usually observe that the children either have no religious foundation because the parents ignore the spiritual quality of life or the children are exposed to all aspects of both parents' religions so the children can choose. This typically results in confusion and rarely brings any kind of deep spiritual practice for the kids. It is difficult to make a marriage work without a common faith center, so it is wise to marry someone with similar faith convictions.

Many couples seem to meet the challenges of coming from different cultural or financial backgrounds well. But religious values can be more troublesome, perhaps because spiritual beliefs and practices are less tangible and more internal than ethnic and financial values. A marriage between an Italian wife and a Korean husband may require certain compromises surrounding food, travel, and cultural involvement, but a marriage between two vastly different spiritual commitments raises significant issues concerning extended family, how to raise children, and beliefs about the future of one's soul. Certain areas of compromise might not be easy or even possible.

How You Make Financial Decisions

How you and your spouse make financial decisions doesn't have to be a source of stress. The key is to lay issues out on the table when they come up and to talk about them openly. Doing this as soon as a challenging topic comes up can help both of you avoid developing stubbornness.

Still, talking it out on your own may not be enough to reach a resolution. If you need help, get it. Strong people recognize their need for help and act on it. And remember that many financial decisions, maybe all of them, are manageable if you are both willing to talk them through.

Who Controls the Purse Strings?

How does a couple decide how much—and how—they will spend money, how much they will save, and how much risk to assume in their investments? How much should each spouse be allowed to spend without having to consult the other? And who will take care of bookkeeping? Should such decisions be based on who has the money or who has the skill? When spouses come from different financial backgrounds, the person with less wealth may have more skill because the wealthier person may never have needed to budget. Or it could be the other way around.

A husband might feel he has less power or control in the marriage if he comes from a more modest background than his wife. He might regain some sense of control by keeping the records. On the other hand, if he is not accustomed to keeping records with that many zeroes, he might feel intimidated, elated, or just confused. Some couples take turns with the responsibility of bookkeeping.

More often, the person who is better at bookkeeping takes charge of it. It is certainly useful when one person in the marriage is good at such detailed work and is responsible. I have observed that many successful couples find their financial roles in the marriage naturally and with a little effort. Another option is to hire a bookkeeper to keep the family finances on track. This practice relieves both spouses of the burden and potential power struggles. The responsibility for the couple can be reduced to a short meeting once a month. The bottom line is that both partners need to take part in, and stay informed about, their financial household.

There are other ways besides bookkeeping to intentionally balance the power in the relationship. One way is decision making. It's very easy to fall into the pattern of having the wealthier spouse take charge of all the big decisions. Remember the "golden rule" from *Navigating the Dark Side of Wealth*? He who has the gold makes the rules. No couple develops this golden rule on purpose, but it may evolve anyway when a wealthier husband is used to spending and the less wealthy wife is uncomfortable spending what she considers not to be hers.

One way of coping with this is to intentionally put the person who doesn't have financial wealth in charge of some key decisions. Say you're remodeling the home and you disagree on the colors or style. Let the person who doesn't have the wealth—who's not paying for it—make those key decisions as a way of balancing the power. This can be hard for some couples to do, but try it anyway. It will help provide equilibrium in the relationship.

The opposite pattern may also naturally evolve. If a wealthy woman is used to being taken care of and has never taken financial responsibility, she may not yet have developed her own competence and confidence in this area. She may not pay attention when her husband assumes control or see the warning signs that he may be incompetent or untrustworthy. The couple may end up losing part or all of their wealth.

Because many inheritors develop late emotionally, it's important to initiate the work to take charge of your own financial affairs early in the relationship. Find a way to avoid turning over your power to your spouse but at the same time to consciously balance the power in the relationship. It is prudent to track what is happening to see what works best in your relationship.

These financial behaviors are key concerns in marriage. Responsibly managing finances is essential to a successful marriage. However, if the couple avoids discussing these concerns and making conscious choices, their financial differences can fester into problems, creating resentment, insecurity, mistrust, and an uncontrolled financial reality.

Keeping Accounts in One or Both Names

There is no one right way to merge financial accounts. Many couples have a joint account for shared expenses, which both partners put money into, and also each have separate accounts. Some couples pool everything. A few keep their finances completely separate.

In my experience, it is best to pool a substantial amount of money to use for living expenses and to make all substantial financial decisions together. The right amount needs to be determined by each couple. Sharing your money and making values-based decisions for its use is a dimension of marriage that you will miss if you keep all your finances separate.

However, do what's best for you and your spouse. Talk about all the possibilities and decide together.

The income on assets kept in each spouse's name will be taxed, so take this into consideration too. As long as there are deductions and exclusions allowed by law, it is important to check with your estate planning attorney to make sure your approach is best for your situation.

Helping Extended Family Members

It is wise to anticipate and talk through the possibility that members from one side of the family or the other may want or need financial assistance. As we saw with Carissa and Pascal, sometimes relatives of a person who marries into wealth will expect loans or gifts. It's ideal to think about this before marrying and to decide in what circumstances you'd consider making a loan or gift.

The Decision Tree for Loaning Money to a Friend (see Figure 7.3) can help you work through how to handle such situations as they arise with family members.

Pascal expected Carissa to support his entire family of origin. She had bought his mother a house, paid for his sister's education, and covered medical expenses for other siblings. Relative to her wealth, the amounts were modest, but by just about anybody's standards, Carissa's gifts were generous. She justified her decisions simply by noting that she had so much and her husband's family's financial resources were very limited. However, Pascal's family didn't seem grateful for Carissa's generosity. They quickly took the gifts for granted and didn't hesitate to ask for more.

Ungrateful relatives can negatively affect the marriage. The spouse from the modest background may feel he is in the middle, caught between his family's expectations and his spouse's resentment. The best—if not only—way to resolve this is for each of you to talk about your feelings and experience of what's going on, focusing your priorities. Your ability to communicate is your saving grace in this situation.

Carissa sometimes questions Pascal's family thinking her generosity is just the way it should be, but she realizes it is largely a cultural issue. Pascal is from a country where people take care of extended family members. They have reached a somewhat uneasy peace about it, yet it is a peace they can live with.

Whether or not you think this scenario could manifest in your marriage, you may wish to discuss the following questions with your spouse:

- What do each of your families expect of you? If you don't know, can you go to the elders of the family and ask for advice?

- How will you handle requests for money?
- In terms of giving or lending money to relatives, what are you, as a couple, available for?
- Under what circumstances is the wealthy spouse willing to help a family member of the non-wealthy spouse? Here are some examples:

  Medical—life-threatening

  Medical—non life-threatening (such as orthodontia or plastic surgery)

  Loss of business or job

  Education

  Foreclosure on a house

  Down payment for a new house

  Desire to start a business

  Fix a poorly functioning car

  Purchase a new car

  Vacations

  Special family celebrations (wedding party, baby shower, sweet sixteen)

You and your spouse may find most of these potential scenarios to be black-and-white issues. Oftentimes, though, a gray area is a request to finance a business. After all, many wealthy people invest in businesses. In such a case, it is important to request a business plan and have a financial advisor review it. If you have a family office, perhaps you can consult a specific advisor in the office or designate a committee to help you determine which enterprises to fund and under what conditions.

Some couples limit family financial assistance to medical needs and education because these are the only areas where the giver doesn't incur a gift tax. I've had some clients set up a pot of funds for family help and let family members know that funds are available for things like starting a business or making a down payment on a house. Because there is a finite amount of money in this pot, people need to apply, just as they would for a grant.

Applications formalize the process a bit, which can be helpful in deflecting hurt feelings when someone's request is denied. Furthermore, gifts are generally safer than loans in caring for relationships. If you do decide to loan money, repayments must be very clearly spelled out and understood by everyone. What are the terms if those repayments are not forthcoming? Some couples loan money and set a payment plan with the family member but also agree that if the loan is not repaid within a year, the remaining balance is written off as a gift. After this, that family member is no longer eligible for funds. This method protects the relationship from turning into a collections scenario clouded by resentments. The most important point in any of these scenarios, though, is that the responsibility for defining the terms of the gift or loan lies on the wealthy person and spouse. The other family members cannot be expected to think this through so that relationships are not damaged.

It's also important for marriage partners to agree on both availability and method by which they will provide family financial assistance. Each of your families' values will provide guidance. My father, who grew up in a family of modest means, was the second to youngest of eight siblings. His oldest brother put all three younger brothers through college with the first profits from his business. That's part of our family history. With that precedent in my family, I look for opportunities to help family members who cannot afford college. Family loyalty is a top priority on my husband's side of the family. On his side I see a great tradition of support and allegiance that do not waiver.

Conflicting Lifestyle Choices

All marriages face lifestyle choices. Sometimes there is easy agreement, and these choices are not difficult. Often, however, couples find that they have different preferences and must find a way to come together. Compromise and taking turns can be effective strategies. Both require flexibility, and this itself can be a challenge.

The potential conflicts in lifestyle choices are many, but we'll look at a few of the most common ones. Later, we'll explore tools to help you manage these challenges for a successful marriage.

Mismatches in Ambition

There are many permutations of mismatched ambition. Whatever the financial backgrounds of you and your spouse, you may each have very different levels of ambition. Even if neither of you needs to work for financial reasons, one or both may feel the need to work for emotional and spiritual reasons. Work can help develop a sense of purpose in life, which is an essential element of emotional health.

Ideally, the couple will have discussed their ambitions and goals and agreed on how they can best integrate their individual visions. If couples have not discussed this important topic, they are leaving a lot to chance. And of course, over time, individual ambitions can wax and wane. It is important for couples to revisit the subject and find new equilibrium when necessary.

A clash I have seen several times is one in which one spouse, the inheritor, is working to establish professional credibility, which usually requires more effort for the inheritor than for the average person. So this can be a quest of great motivation and intensity. Meanwhile, the other spouse is focused on living in France (a pursuit I have seen more than once), or in some other way having a cultural experience in which the ambition is experience, not accomplishment. Usually this mismatch harbors a clash. Couples can resolve it in many ways, typically with some kind of compromise. With communication and patience, this can work.

Where to Live

You might want to live near one or the other spouse's family, or you may want to live where you work. Your preference may be based on weather or on urban, suburban, or rural concerns. It is important to talk about all of these values while still dating, but again, people develop and change, so you'll want to revisit the discussion several times as your marriage progresses. Priorities, predilections, and sometimes health may mandate a move to a different part of the country. In many ways, wealth provides options that less affluence would not allow. You may be able to afford more than one home and private transportation between them. A private jet or helicopter can reduce the complications of frequent travel between homes. This makes it easier for you and your spouse to both live where you want, at least some of the time.

Sometimes, having many options can also create problems. It may be too easy for each of you to gravitate to different homes, resulting in spending most of your time apart. Physical distance can lead to emotional distance and strains on the relationship. This is an example of how affluence can create challenges that outsiders or newcomers might not anticipate. Sometimes ease, freedom, and choice, if not monitored carefully, can damage a marriage.

Types of Homes to Buy

Carissa and Pascal enjoyed a wide range of choices about where to live. Carissa's work was truly portable, and even Pascal's location could be negotiated. So their decisions about where to live were based on family more than any other priority. For Carissa and Pascal, the main consideration was what kind of house to buy for themselves: expensive, or more modest to fit better with Pascal's family?

People often want to have a home that reminds them of the home they grew up in. For one spouse, that could be modest, for the other, big and spacious. One person may want a high-profile neighborhood, the other, a quiet and modest street. You may love a new, modern house with minimalist furnishings; your partner may prefer an older, stately house full of beautiful art. Many decorators are skilled at helping couples find creative ways to honor both aesthetic sensibilities. This can actually be a fun problem to work through, but as with all differences between couples, it is essential to talk about it.

Spending

Beyond determining who keeps track of the family's finances, couples must find a workable approach to deciding what they buy. This is not just an issue of how much money the couple spends. The couple also deals with the values behind the choices of what is purchased. Your choices about the kind of cars you drive, the décor of your home, where and how you vacation, the schools you send your children to, your jewelry and clothes—virtually all shopping decisions—reflect your values individually and as a couple.

It's been said that if you want to see people's values (or your own) look at their credit card statement. What they buy, how much it costs, where they shop—this information will unerringly inform you. Take a look at your giving. Do you fund every neighbor's children in their school fundraisers, or is it medical research that tugs at your heart? Does your spouse focus exclusively on his alma mater, or is he loyal to other organizations? Is your giving a significant part of your financial records, or is it underfunded? How about travel? Do you and your spouse agree on how to spend travel money? Or does your travel style depend on who plans the trip? Is there a balance between your approach to spending and your spouse's?

Interests

Couples do not need to have every interest in common, but it is essential to have some activities that you enjoy doing together. Even more important, find some common goals to enjoy working toward as a couple. Whether playing tennis or getting tickets to the Masters, hiking, travel, photography, community service, or entertaining, couples are likely to build stronger bonds when they share overlapping passions. It is useful to take a close look at the specifics of your common interests, projects, and activities.

e 9.1

Exercise 9.1:

Interests, Projects, and Activities in Common with My Spouse

Do together:	**Do alone:**
I like to: ____________	____________
____________	____________
____________	____________
My partner likes to: ____________	____________
____________	____________
____________	____________

Common interests can be an indication of common values. If, looking at what you've written on the chart above, you see gaps, take the initiative to look for activities you can enjoy together, all in the name of taking care of your relationship. Naturally, there will still be areas which each of you enjoy on your own.

Sexual Complications

Sometimes money can complicate what goes on in the bedroom. If things are not going well sexually, once a couple starts to look at what is hindering them, they may discover that one person is feeling disempowered. Stress, anger, and insecurity can also erode people's romantic and sexual feelings. Often, the root cause is resentment, irritability, or frustration about some aspect of your financial situation.

One common scenario is when a man has worked hard at a job, making a salary that he always felt good about, and then marries a woman who has three times the amount of his paycheck pouring into her life every month just because she was born into a certain family. He might lose his perspective and doubt the value of his salary. He may even question whether it is worth working so hard just to make what seems like a drop in the bucket. This can confuse his perception of the identity he's built and cause him to feel inadequate. We all need to feel confident in what we bring to the partnership. That can become short-circuited when something you've established as an asset (such as your income) suddenly seems to lose significance.

Understandably, any aspect of this, from work to sexual feelings, can be difficult for couples to discuss openly. While talking is the healthiest and most direct approach, it's not always possible. In the absence of the willingness to talk about a sexual problem, which may be related to a financial situation, the spouse can do some things to make her partner feel more secure.

This calls for experimenting, as successful strategies vary greatly from couple to couple. You might try empowering your partner in the context of sexuality, which could mean that you initiate intimacy, or it could take shape as the exact opposite: allowing him to take the initiative. If you have the tendency to take the lead in general, you could try stepping aside and deferring to your partner, even if it takes him longer or he leads in ways you wouldn't have chosen. Of course, your lack of initiation might be interpreted as disinterest on your part, which might exacerbate the problem, so you may want to at least tell your partner you feel like experimenting. As in many aspects of life, it is always important to positively reinforce any efforts on your spouse's part.

Parenting Conflicts

Children are bound to cause each parent to grow and change both in expected and unexpected ways. In the early days of the relationship, neither of you may realize how strongly you feel about parenting issues that will come up around school, medical concerns, religion, and spending, just to name a few. Chapter ten details the many challenges wealthy couples encounter while raising children as well as tried-and-true strategies for handling them.

Interference from Couples' Parents

As discussed in the extended family chapter, no matter what family you marry into, the patriarch and matriarch of each spouse's family of origin may begin to exert pressure over you and later over your children. Sometimes this control is in the form of trusts or education funds, which may have incentive features, and sometimes your parents or your spouse's may find other means to transfer wealth to their grandchildren. Some people do not want this to happen, but there are instances when they have no control.

Another common concern, when there is a family business, is the assumption that offspring will pursue careers in the family business. Your parents may expect you or your spouse to work there. Your children could be targeted in the same way. There may be financial consequences or rewards. This is an important area for you and your spouse to explore possibilities, consider consequences, and make well-thought-out decisions.

In the context of your marriage, it is important for you and your spouse to work together to reach a unified stance in your attitudes toward the grandparents who are exerting this pressure. Identify and clarify the influences you want for your children. There may also be some areas where you and your spouse are flexible. The key, as recommended before, is to talk about these concerns early and to reach an agreement with your spouse if at all possible.

Once you've reached an agreement with your spouse, the two of you can respond to the grandparents. It is kind to first express gratitude at the grandparents' intended generosity before expressing your concerns about the unintended effects of their gifts. In the end, we all know that we cannot control other people's actions, so you and your spouse may be faced with a management challenge. Except in the event of actual abuse, it is important to take the high road and maintain contact with all extended family members. Remember, the example you set for your children is their most powerful teacher. You may want to describe your guiding values to your kids to reinforce the example you want them to see.

Philanthropy

There can be many areas in which you and your spouse might disagree about philanthropy: how much, where and when, and whether to give publicly or anonymously, to name a few.

Sometimes one spouse is much more inclined to be philanthropic than the other. One might view such gifts as throwing money out the window; the other might see donating as a financial, ethical, or religious responsibility or joy. Some people want to focus their philanthropy only on religious charities; others feel strongly about donating to causes that have affected their families, such as an awareness campaign for a particular disease or disability.

Even when spouses disagree about philanthropy, seldom do these issues become highly charged because abundance is the bottom line; this does not involve any kind of scarcity. I don't know of anyone who has pursued divorce because of differences in philanthropy. As long as couples are respectful, they can generally work this out more easily than disagreements about parenting or spending. It's often relatively easy to negotiate by honoring both partners' preferences: give to your spouse's causes this year and next year to yours, or decide on an amount and give half to each spouse's causes every year.

As for how much to devote to charitable causes, inheritance consultant John L. Levy suggests that a couple should first choose the level of assets and income they wish to maintain and then decide how much of their remaining wealth—which doesn't seem necessary to meet their current and future needs—to direct toward philanthropy. This way, both partners will be assured that even if they disagree about how much to donate, at least their giving will not erode their current or future lifestyle and estate requirements.

Incompatible Retirement Visions

When to retire is a looming question even for couples who have a strong, loving marriage. Husbands and wives rarely want to retire at the same time. They may also define retirement differently: is it leaving a job or totally changing your lifestyle? It's important to define what retirement means to each partner and to discuss the details of how and when before it's just around the corner.

Dana worked for her family's business for her entire career. She was looking forward to retiring in her mid-fifties so she could finally start a business growing and developing a certain genus of flower. To her, retiring didn't mean traveling or doing nothing. It meant she would have time to do what she really wanted to do.

Dana had discussions about her retirement plans with her family of origin as well as her spouse. Her husband initially was more open to her retirement because he saw her interest in flowers and their biology as it developed. He knew firsthand that she was excited to have the chance to pursue the flower ideas she had. He wanted to see her succeed in her goals. Her family was sorry to lose her hand in the family business, but they eventually came to understand her priorities too. After training a younger family member to take over her responsibilities, she retired with their blessing.

Among my clients, retirement becomes an issue only when a couple disagrees about whether to retire or what kind of retirement lifestyle they want. If one person wants to travel with her husband in retirement, that makes it difficult for her husband to continue working if he loves his job. Usually some kind of compromise is called for. Perhaps the retired spouse can travel with others sometimes or the working spouse can reduce his work commitment to part time. It is important for both spouses to feel heard and respected. Be careful not to fall prey to the golden rule of he (or she) who has the gold makes the rules. Make your decisions together.

Estate Planning

Do you and your spouse agree on how much of your combined assets you want to pass on to your children? Are you on the same page about how and when? Couples who are both inheritors probably have different experiences about what it was like to inherit money. If you are an inheritor and your spouse is not, you may feel your opinions should hold more weight because you've experienced the process. However, remember that you'll both have plenty of opinions about how much to pass on, how to do it, and when to talk to the kids about it.

Once again, the key is to talk through your beliefs and feelings, and work to discover values you share regarding inheritance. There are many resources, from books to websites to advisors, available to help couples consider the many issues that arise with estate planning. Before creating a trust document, I strongly recommend that you as a couple focus on values and base all decisions about trusts, trustees, outright gifts, and timing on your shared values.

Financial wealth is part of your legacy as a couple, however that wealth came to you. When your wealth is second-generation or greater, you may be aware of the dreams of the wealth creators. They may have wanted their wealth to benefit many generations to come, sometimes in very specific ways. This can create pressure to steward well, so consider the values of everyone involved and work with your spouse to make the best decisions.

Serious Differences

Usually when couples come to me, they already know that they either want to work out their challenges or pursue a divorce. In either case, it's important to explore the seeds of their problems. If they want to stay together, they need to understand what issues have hurt their relationship before they can move ahead in a healthier, more productive, and loving way. Even if they feel the marriage is unsalvageable, they—and their children—benefit from talking through the problem areas. They may not be able to resolve these differences, but are more likely to separate in a less toxic way, let go of at least some of their anger, co-parent more productively and happily, and move forward with a better grasp of healthy attitudes and behaviors so they are less likely to make the same mistakes in future relationships.

Facing Marital Challenges with Courage

The following exercise will help you and your spouse understand your marital challenges.

First, make two copies of Figure 9.2. You will need three different colored highlighters. For the sake of describing the exercise, let's choose pink, yellow, and green.

---

e **9.2**

Figure 9.2:

Potential Marital Challenges I

Potential Challenges	Concerns
Conflicting Values	Religious values and commitment Cultural/family values Financial values

continued on next page

How You Make Financial Decisions	Who controls the purse strings How to divide financial responsibility Whether it is a good idea for your spouse to take the lead in joint personal finances When to keep accounts in one name or both names Helping extended family members
Conflicting Lifestyle Choices	Mismatch in ambition Where to live Type of homes to buy Spending habits Interests
Sexual Complications	When wealth emasculates (consciously or unconsciously) a man who marries a woman with greater financial wealth
Parenting Conflicts (discussed in chapter ten on parenting)	How to raise the children Where they will go to school: private vs. public, boarding vs. home Religious upbringing Trusts: when to teach about family wealth, when to offer inheritance Next generation financial literacy
Interference from Couples' Parents	Trust documents Wealth transference to your children Expectations of family business
Philanthropy	How much to give Which causes or organizations to support
Incompatible Retirement Visions	When? Where? How?
Estate Planning	Inheritance amounts and timing Trust provisions
Serious Differences	Before you call your lawyer for irreconcilable differences, agree to seek help from a mental health professional, clergy, family member, or friend to help diffuse the situation.

With a pink highlighter, underline any of the concerns you are facing now with your spouse. With a yellow highlighter, underline those areas that might become a significant concern in the future. With a green highlighter, underline any areas around which you feel confident you and your spouse will remain aligned. Meanwhile, ask your spouse to do the same with the second copy of the list.

If you discover several areas one or both of you highlighted in green, take a few moments to appreciate these areas of strength in your marriage. It will be significant if you don't have any green areas you've both highlighted in common. As you reveal to each other your pink and yellow highlighted areas, remember this foundation of the issues that you agree upon. We'll focus on working through the challenging issues in just a moment.

Moving Toward the Bright Side

Your marriage can be strong and positive if you both want it to be. The best marriage partners acknowledge that they both make an effort to keep their marriage strong. In fact, spouses in marriages that are working well often joke that they both put 150 percent effort into the marriage. It's important that your spouse meets you somewhere in the middle. The effort you each invest in your marriage may be inherently different—while you may be the one who found this book, your spouse may come up with rewards for working through sections—but the point is that you both contribute something.

In this chapter you've had the opportunity to focus on what you like in your marriage and what could be stronger. The exercises are designed for you to at long last work through the challenges and find ways to meet them well. You will gather courage as you go, and you will also foster ease and peace of mind in your relationship. You will find yourself remembering your spouse's qualities that you fell in love with and breathing new life into your intimacy. It's the beginning of a new chapter in your lives together.

---

e 9.3

Exercise 9.3:

Potential Marital Challenges II

Revisit the Potential Marital Challenges chart that you highlighted with your spouse. Make a date for an afternoon or evening to first work with the issues highlighted in pink, using the following questions. You may plan to celebrate with a special dinner out or a nice bottle of wine, but save it as a reward for after you've completed this exercise. Keep a light touch in the conversation if possible, and bring your sense of humor to the task. Compromise and above all be kind.

continued on next page

What, if any, concerns has your spouse highlighted in pink that you did not and vice versa? Focus first on these. One or both of you may feel dismayed, hurt, or angry to learn of problems the other has identified of which you were not aware.

Before you dig in your heels, cry, or scream at each other, go back to the Values Clarification exercise (3.1) in chapter three. This is a great time to review strongly held values you share with your partner. Use your list of shared values as a reference point for working through your different beliefs or feelings about the issues in pink on your list. For each of the issues where you disagree, ask what approach you can take that best honors and reflects your top shared values. You just may find you are able to make progress. Your progress will probably come in the form of a compromise. It is important that any agreement does not violate your values, shared or individual. Keep a running list of any differences you cannot resolve using your shared values (hoping this will be a short list!) to be worked on later.

Next, go through each of the areas of concern that you have both marked, and one by one give them the same shared-values test. See how many you can resolve. Again, add any you cannot easily resolve to your list for later.

Once you have worked through all the issues in pink, move on to yellow.

What, if any, concerns has your spouse highlighted in yellow that you did not and vice versa? Work for a tentative agreement about how you will handle these issues or events as they arise. Together, look for how you can prepare for and even diminish some of the potential liabilities.

Reward yourselves for working through these two sets of issues. Schedule another date in the near future to tackle the tougher topics remaining on your list. At that time, first review the areas where you are aligned, and then go over the areas you have added to your list of agreement. It's always encouraging to remember your successes. Then review your shared values, and see if you can make some headway on the challenging differences. For any issues that remain on this list, you may find it helpful to make an appointment with a trusted objective outsider or therapist.

There may be some points where you need to agree to disagree. Sometimes this is the best you can do. If the issues are pressing and need resolution, for the sake of your marriage, it is essential to find help. If you don't, these issues can tear at the foundation of your marriage.

This exercise will feel like work, because it is. All successful endeavors require work, and marriage is no exception. It is important to maintain a delicate balance between flexibility and not caving in to compromises that violate your values or who you are. Remember, it is a sign of strength to seek help when you need it.

Exercise 9.4: 9.4

Gratitude

What are five elements of your marriage for which you are grateful?

Exercise 9.5: 9.5

Action Plan

Now write an action plan for improving your marriage. For this exercise, make a copy of the Action Plan below, so you and your spouse each have one to fill out on your own.

Today's date ______________________

The goal I set for my marriage is:

In order to accomplish this goal, I will perform the following activities:

Support people who might assist me include:

continued on next page

I realize I may sabotage my plan by:

____

____

____

So I will avoid this by:

____

____

____

I will complete this goal by ______________________ (date)

(Recommendation: three to six months)

When you have both completed your Action Plans, you may decide if you would like to share them with each other. If you decide not to, it is important for each of you to choose a trusted friend to share your plan with. This friend will be one of your support people. The accountability will help you to remember to work on your Action Plan. Periodic check-ins with your support person will help too.

Marriage can be one of the wondrous joys of life. In order to be great, it requires nurturing and care. You and your spouse have it within your power to shape your marriage how you want it to be. If you are out of sync with each other, it is very possible that you can fix this. If your marriage has cooled, you can fix this too. Motivation is a big part of the equation. Don't think your marriage isn't valuable just because you have to work on it. The "work" is rewarding, and you can set up any kinds of incentives you wish.

Raising Happy, Responsible, Fulfilled Children

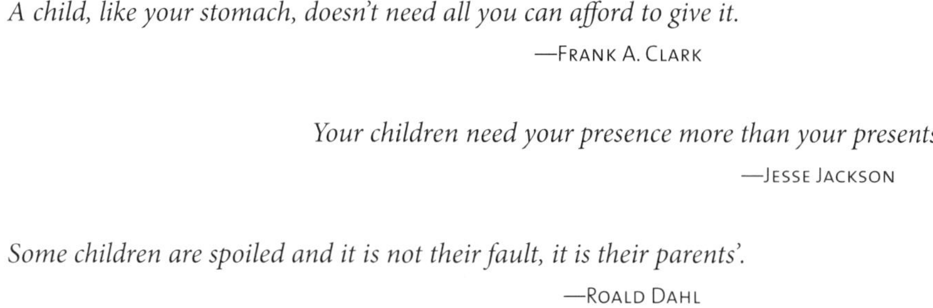

A child, like your stomach, doesn't need all you can afford to give it.
—Frank A. Clark

Your children need your presence more than your presents.
—Jesse Jackson

Some children are spoiled and it is not their fault, it is their parents'.
—Roald Dahl

| Relationship elements: | **Values** | **Communication** | **Trust** |

Good parenting isn't so much about getting children to change as it is about changing yourself. It's about opening your mind and taking a long, hard look at the ingrained habits and beliefs that are keeping you from doing the very best you can to raise happy, productive, responsible, fulfilled, grateful children.

I don't need to tell you that this is no small task. Indeed, it is a monumental one requiring unlimited motivation and unceasing effort on your part. Yet it's a goal of the highest importance that can—that must—be achieved, for your children are the most precious people in your life. And parenting them to the utmost of your ability is your most important task.

The vast majority of parents want the very best for our children, which most of us do our best to acquire by guiding them to become productive, grateful, responsible, and happy as adults.

Meanwhile, it's important to remember that parenting is the only part of the equation of influences that we can control. Many of the influences on our children, such as genetics and some aspects of environment, we cannot control. But there are factors we can control to keep our children from reaching adolescence with unproductive, entitled, irresponsible, spoiled, and incompetent habits. We can open our minds to both the promises and the pitfalls of parenting.

Financial Literacy Can Be Elusive

Henry grew up in a financially wealthy home where his father didn't work. His paternal grandfather and great-grandfather had built the family's fortune in real estate. Henry was a somewhat disoriented young adult because he wanted to work yet had no model for this. He had a terribly difficult time focusing on work at all. When I met him, he lived with an inner conflict of wanting to work yet not being able to sink his teeth into a job, career, or profession.

Over the early years I knew him, Henry essentially dabbled in work while he and his wife had four children. When the children were very young, Henry realized that if he was going to be able to bring up his own children in an environment free of the work-related angst he lived with and with the kind of work ethic he had only dreamed of, he needed to make a drastic change. To his great credit, and with the support of his wife and me, he did two things.

First, he got a job that he liked and made a commitment to stick with it. Second, he hired me to design a financial literacy program for his family, something he had never been taught during his own childhood and that he knew he would struggle to teach his children himself. Finally, tenaciously motivated and possessing the knowledge to make a meaningful change in his children's lives, Henry was able to provide coaching for them in the basics of financial literacy, something he had missed in his youth.

Material Ease versus Productive Good

It is difficult for most wealthy parents to resist the temptation to give their kids a lot of "things." You may want to buy them all the toys you never had—or all the toys you *did* have—when you were growing up and provide them with spending money too. What's wrong with that? The materially easy life can be described as one free of worries, constraints, and hardships. Parents naturally want this for their children. Yet the good life isn't guaranteed by giving them a *materially easy* life with financial gifts. It's all too tempting for them to use money as an avoidance technique and simply forgo adulthood.

Many inheritors lack the impetus to take responsibility for their lives and thus manage to avoid the tough, maturing commitments of life. As a result, they can be much younger developmentally than their non-wealthy peers. Parents unwittingly reinforce the idea that these kids don't need to grow up when they tell their children that they do not need to work. This message implies that their efforts aren't necessary or valuable. Meanwhile, their peers and the media can combine to encourage other pursuits, such as a decadent, fast-track lifestyle filled with parties and shopping. Ironically, the apparent freedom from responsibility and accountability can actually rob a young adult of essential well-being. Their potential is exchanged for a life of carelessness and self-indulgence.

Because financial gifts too often devalue the potential of young inheritors, wealthy parents have the responsibility to help their children understand how to use money in productive, responsible ways. No one has your kids' interests more at heart than you do. Your highest calling as a parent demands active involvement and determination to put your child on the path to true adulthood. This chapter will explore the common hazards parents like you face and will provide you with tools to help your children learn to live well and to represent your family well.

A Tough Fight: Battling Entitlement

Many external factors contribute to children's feelings of entitlement, including the constant barrage of material goods available for consumption, the media that stokes our seemingly bottomless appetite for such goods, and peer pressure—your kids' friends who feed the fad frenzy and their parents who cause you to feel competitive, defensive, or guilty for not giving your kids what they give theirs. These forces that lead us to spoil our children are powerful and hard to resist, particularly when money is no object. I have been dragged along by this tide at times, so I can attest to their powerful allure.

Then there are the internal factors fanning the flames of desire. We indulge our children for reasons that include ignorance, guilt, fear, insecurity, anger, and apathy. We worry that by not giving our children everything their hearts desire, we may be harming them in some way even while we know this isn't true! It seems confusing at times. As parents, we all have our faults, and parenting shines a spotlight on them.

While we struggle to make good decisions as parents, we sometimes look for support from other parents. But ultimately, we need to take responsibility for making those tough decisions. It is up to you, *not* the village, to make those difficult and often unpopular parenting decisions. Or you can give up and give in. It's your choice. There is not a middle ground on your parenting priorities, but you can manage these decisions well as long as you have the common sense, motivation, and courage to resist temptations.

As parents, we may feel an overwhelming desire to give our children the stuff we didn't have. But giving them lots of the material items you longed for is a sure way to snuff out their own developing motivation. Look at how your hard-earned successes have made you the person you are. Do not rob your kids of the challenging opportunities you had and the life lessons you learned from them by giving your children everything they ask for.

Turn back to your top ten values from chapter three's Values Clarification exercise (3.1). Writing them out and posting them somewhere that you will see them often will help you resist spoiling your children by reminding you of the values you wish to impart to your children. For instance, let's say you chose these as your top ten values:

God
Love
Accomplishment
Dependability
Competence
Helping Others
Hard Work
Sense of Purpose
Stability
Discipline

Can you see how providing your children nearly every material thing they want would inhibit their ability to develop such values? How can children who have been given so much develop the discipline to earn life's rewards? How can they feel competent when they have not had to work through their failures or feel a sense of purpose when there's nothing to strive for because they have been given just about everything they want? How can they turn their attention to spirituality or helping others when they are so focused on the next new toy, necklace, or car they know they can have if they just ask?

One attendee at a conference where I presented confided that after a recent liquidity event, he had bought an Italian sports car, a spectacular beach house, and a jet. He had worked hard for these goodies, so he felt he deserved them and had waited for them long enough. But after listening to me, he was thinking about his kids, ages fifteen, thirteen, and ten, and wondering whether all this stuff might actually be bad for them. After my presentation he came up to me to explore this question. I told him he was right to question these luxury influences on his kids. I encouraged him to consider selling them or at least using them quietly with his wife and friends, not with his children. It is a matter of priorities and discipline.

Besides the fact that a sense of entitlement severely limits our spiritual and emotional growth, a supreme irony lies in the limitations that entitlement imposes on us. By regarding only the best of life's magnificent bounty as good enough for us, we deny the cornucopia of truly, deeply enriching experiences. Imagine holding a standard of education that only the

Ivy League schools are good enough for you. Even though the state university offers a degree in psychology, your chosen field, you can't possibly go to such a school because it is simply beneath you. When you don't get into any Ivy League schools, you never go to college—you never explore your passion—because of these self-imposed limitations. Your journey in life would be much smaller because of your choice.

Sadly, the tragedy and waste of our self-deprivation of these deeper gifts is easiest to acknowledge in retrospect. It is why so many inheritors, insulated from making their own decisions, learn too late how much of life's infinite bounty they've squandered through their self-deception. Entitlement is limiting.

The Best Gifts

It is *not* harmless to simply go along with the societal pressure to give our children only the biggest and most expensive gifts. Unless we go against the grain and offer positive experiences in the family, we have little chance of giving joy. It does change the emphasis of giving to think about the gift of your time and presence. Fortunately, some wealthy families are wise enough to know that the smartest gifts are those that build human capital in the family.

If you embrace the idea that happiness does not come from material goods, Figure 10.1 offers some ideas for giving the gift of time. Parents can ensure their children feel loved without lavishing them with expensive toys and material items. The gift of time can be far more valuable. It certainly can counteract the temptation for children to feel entitled to the latest gadget when they see their parents prioritizing time with them over material items.

---

f **10.1**

Figure 10.1

Giving the Gift of Time

- Floor time is a great way, if you have young children, to let them lead. The focus is on experience and just being together. Just get down on the floor together and let the child lead the direction of your play.
- Game night is most effective with less competitive games like Charades, Quelf, Life Stories, Balderdash, or Apples to Apples (the junior versions are best with children).
- Song night might involve singing together, karaoke, or if you and your children play instruments, learning to play a duet or jamming. You can also create playlists to enjoy while driving together.

continued on next page

- A hike or a walk around the block, downtown, or on a nearby trail requires no planning and can be a great time to let your kids talk about what's on their mind. Keep cell phones off!
- A family retreat with extended family members, all expenses paid, can become an annual tradition planned by family volunteers. Be sure to include a fun committee.
- Volunteer together. This will also reinforce the value of giving back to the community for your children.
- Watch a movie as a family and then talk about what you liked and did not like. With kids ages ten and up, some of the first movies to watch and discuss are *The Ultimate Gift*, *Greedy*, *Wall Street*, and *The Pursuit of Happyness*. For older teens you can add documentaries such as *Born Rich* and *The Ascent of Money: The Financial History of the World*. See the resources section for a longer list of feature films and documentaries you may want to watch with your kids. When parents watch these films with kids, the discussion afterward adds great value. Here are some steps you can take to get the most out of the experience:

1. Choose a movie or film to watch with a family member.
2. Ask if he or she is willing to watch it with you. Only proceed if the answer is yes.
3. Watch the movie.
4. Discuss what you watched. Ask open-ended questions like:

   How did [the main character] evolve in the story?

   What revelation did you see a character experience in the movie?

   How did it affect the story?

   What conflict did you see in the movie? How was it resolved?

   What was a major theme in this story?

   What did you learn about your life?

Tip: Ask open-ended questions, not ones that can be answered with a simple yes or no. Also, be grateful for any discussion. If you disagree, you can say so, pointing out that in excellent films, often there can be more than one valid point of view. Be accepting and kind.

Developing Strong Character

Your children's preparation for the financial and psychological realities of inheriting depends to a great extent on their overall character development. Ideally, it includes all of the building blocks that are best for everyone: training in how to build and maintain physical health, including nutrition and fitness; intellectual development and education; development of emotional well-being and coping skills; spiritual foundation and practice.

All of this culminates in a wide range of skills that will help your children as they approach work, relationships, and a meaningful life.

Good character includes fighting the impulse to feel jealous of others who seem to have more. It is human nature, especially for children, to compare themselves to others and to feel deprived when others have things they don't have. When you hear your children express jealousy of a friend, you may want to relate a story that motivational speaker Mark Scharenbroich often tells about when he was in first grade. Mark's teacher had told everyone in his class to bring a box of crayons. His parents had bought him a brand new box with five crayons. He sat next to a girl who reached into her "leather-bound, school-supply Gucci attaché case and pulled out a beautiful box of what looked like five thousand crayons. It had a flip-top and a real sharpener on the back."

The little girl turned to the young Scharenbroich and matter-of-factly announced, "I have six colors of orange." He looked at his box and thought, *I don't even have orange.* The teacher observed this exchange and said to Mark, "Stop counting crayons. Just draw pictures."

Children often compare themselves with others, and sometimes these comparisons make them feel like they have less or are not as good as others. It can be about clothes, looks, toys, or athletic abilities. It is important to help them focus on what they are doing with the talents they have and resist the temptation to measure themselves against others.

Discouraging Bad Behavior

Not long after my husband and I gave our then fifteen-year-old daughter a puppy, we happened to be standing at the bottom of the stairs when she came down wearing sunglasses, having clearly chosen the newest and most fashionable outfit she had (the top was even low cut) and with the puppy sticking out of a pink purse.

My husband asked her, "What are you doing?"

"I'm going to Starbucks," she answered.

My husband told her to sit down and then explained, "There are two celebrities we are going to talk about. First, we're going to talk about the woman you know as Elaine on *Seinfeld*—her real name is Julia Louis-Dreyfus. She stands to inherit a tremendous fortune, but you probably don't know that because she is a hardworking actress who has become an immensely successful comedian, has built a career, and has established her own wealth independently of her family. She has made a lot of choices along the way—a lot of good choices.

"On the other hand, there is Paris Hilton, whom you seem to be trying to emulate. She shows up at parties. She made a sex tape, a mindless TV series, and nothing much else that anyone can think of. You have choices, dear."

Our daughter got the point. She went back upstairs, took the puppy out of the purse, and thought of something else to do.

We all have choices. It is easy to see a teenager's battle for identity, but we adults also make identity choices all the time, and sometimes we are tempted to step into the dark side. Whenever we choose to take the high road, we build our character with what I call bright-side attitudes. When we make these choices, we cultivate character in our children because they notice how we live our lives. By setting an example, we give them a good chance of growing up to become a gift to the world.

While parenting when children are young has its inimitable challenges, it is easier to encourage the behaviors we want to see them develop when they are young. All of the same principles can be learned by young adults; the dynamics are simply changed. Influencing adult offspring can be tougher. If your children have reached adulthood without financial values or maturity, the transition to a healthy relationship between parents and children may be difficult. It's still possible, just tougher.

Ten Financial Lessons for Children

Use these ten financial lessons to teach your children financial literacy. Not only will you be teaching them valuable information, but you'll also be building a bond between you and your children. They'll know they can trust you to provide them with positive learning experiences, and you'll know they'll be ready to inherit when the time comes.

These lessons are best imparted in age-appropriate steps. I'll provide general age guidelines, but every child is different. Use your judgment. When I first tried to teach my daughter about investing, she was eight. I was so excited, I didn't even consider that she might be too young for this lesson. Partway through the lesson, I looked over, and there she was, head down. She had fallen asleep! She was completely bored by this, so I learned that, at least for this one child, eight was too young. Later she did become interested in investments, but it's possible to try to start too early. Some children may be ready that young, but ten or twelve is more likely.

Keep in mind, too, that all these lessons are applicable as children grow older. If your children are teenagers but have not yet learned to save or keep a ledger, now's the time to get started. Even if you have adult children, it's never too late to work on building their financial literacy.

1. Save (beginning at age five to seven)

Why should wealthy children have to learn how to save when they (you) can afford to buy so much? Thomas J. Stanley and William D. Danko's book *The Millionaire Next Door* emphasizes that it is important to save money because it is an attitude that will support the behaviors that support effective stewardship. If I allow my children to grow up as spendthrifts, in thirty or forty years, there will be no family fortune. However, if I impart to them the importance of saving and investing, their assets are more likely to grow.

As an exercise in teaching children age ten and up the principal of compounding interest—the eighth wonder of the world—give them this challenge: Offer to give them three hundred dollars today or to give them one penny today, two pennies tomorrow, four pennies the next day, eight pennies the next day, sixteen pennies the next day, and on and on, doubling the amount each day for thirty days. Which would they like to take? Which would you take? You'd be smart to take the pennies because when you compound them for one month, you end up with $1.3 million. The principle of compounding interest is fairly simple for kids to understand. Show them what happens when they start saving a regular amount at age fifteen, and what happens when they start saving that same amount of money at age thirty-five.

2. Keep a Ledger (age six to seven)

Provide your children with an old-fashioned ledger book to record all the money (allowance, earnings, gifts) that comes into and goes out of their life. You'll need to set this up and assist them at first. The process of writing every amount down and seeing how much money is left after taking some out teaches the value of a dollar. This can progress into more sophisticated steps, such as a checking account or even a credit card—which should always be paid in full every month. All these practices will help your children develop good habits and learn to handle a budget well. By this age most children are handling some money coming in, whether from an allowance or just birthday cash. Work with them to designate some of that money for giving, some for saving, and some for spending.

My husband and I started both of our children with ledgers when they were six or seven. It is amazing how quickly kids learn to do this. I thought it would take our kids much longer to understand than it did, but they got right into it, and for a while neither one of them picked up their wallet to go somewhere without making a note in pencil in their ledger. One day when my son was nine, I asked him to bring me his ledger. This is what I saw: allowance +$4, watering plants +$3, offering at church –$3, allowance +$4, watering plants +$10—that must have been a big day, a hot day. He was very meticulous.

In between each entry, we have them enter a balance so it's easy for them to see how much money they have. It does require some parental supervision, and it's important to check it every month or two to make sure that the money they actually have matches the money that's in the ledger. Sometimes the numbers don't match, and at first we just adjust it. They learn. This needs to be guided with kindness and with a trend toward accuracy. There are so many lessons to be taught with the ledger. You see how easily and quickly money can go out of your life, and how long it takes and how hard it is to build up money. This practice teaches accountability and responsibility.

3. Earn Money (age seven to eight)

Working can be a great experience, and sometimes scary stuff can happen. Your nine-year-old daughter might be doing yard work for a neighbor who asks her to do something she doesn't know how to do, and she might feel afraid to tell him lest she lose the job. Or your teenage son's boss might tell him to do something that he doesn't believe in, and he may not know how to handle this. Earning money can come with some very testy situations. Making it through such challenges is one of the key ways young family members will mature.

Most of us look back on our own early jobs and view such experiences as valuable, so I encourage you to require young people in your family to work. They can work for an employer or build a business. Find out if your children would like to develop a business mowing lawns, babysitting, pet sitting, or something else.

As a young adult, I wanted to earn money, but I was very unsure about how to begin. My father discouraged me from finding a job, telling me that I would never have to work. This kept me young on the financial front and also in a lot of other ways. I know my father meant well. He meant for me to have the freedom of youth that he never had. But I was always curious and wanted to see what working was like. Also, I wanted the confirmation that I could produce work that was valuable to an employer. I felt sort of left out of that world.

So in my twenties, I secured contract jobs doing work I knew how to do—training horses and writing. Good experience. I developed a habit of overspending, though. When I was thirty, my father, who was tired of my overspending, set up my financial life so that I had to work with a trust officer on everyday personal finance. It was a life-changing experience, and in order to live within the budget we created, I got a full-time job. Then I really learned some lessons. This time it was great experience. And I have always liked being able to relate well to people who work. I never wanted to be remittance addicted; instead, I wanted to take charge of my financial life.

You can insist that your children earn half of the cost of a big-ticket item they want as a way to begin learning how good it feels to set a goal and achieve it. This is also an opportunity to teach them about banking concepts such as interest and the value of setting money aside to save for a particular purchase.

4. Learn high-road values (age eight to ten)

If you're modeling high-road values, children will begin to learn them from infancy. Age eight to ten is a good time to start having discussions about them, though. There are many opportunities to be creative in using your wealth to teach your values: working hard, offering your children cash rewards for accomplishments you value, and planning achievement-oriented travel and philanthropy.

You may value certain books highly enough to pay your kids to read them. Non-parents are usually horrified by this, and it would be ideal if kids would just sit down and read the books we present to them, but on a practical level, if you want to get the knowledge into their minds, a cash reward, paid *after* reading, *after* discussing salient points with Mom or Dad, can be very effective.

Cash rewards for behaviors you want to encourage is a controversial idea. Here's my take: If you have a healthy, high-functioning family in which everyone knows they are loved no matter what, cash rewards can work well. If you have a dysfunctional family in which love is perceived as conditional, cash rewards will come across as punitive and controlling. Incentive trusts function in the same way.

Travel is a great opportunity to teach your values. Take your children to see places that are different than the world in which they live. You can take them on a church mission or a trip to help natural disaster victims.

Philanthropy is not only an excellent tool for teaching values; it is also a great way to instill financial literacy. For instance, have kids research and build a case supporting a cause in which they believe. The money management of the organization needs to be described as well. Then have them present the case to your family. Only when you are convinced of its merit will you make the gift together. (See more ideas about community service and philanthropy below.)

You can ask elders in your family to relate stories from their lives that demonstrate the way family values have helped them. Some questions could include: Who were your favorite aunts and uncles, and what did you like about them? Who in your family has best exemplified generosity? Audio or video record their stories if you can—the tales they remember about their lives, or that their mother or father told them about their lives, often reflect the values of your family.

My father was a humble man, and I remember well how much he liked to dress for work. He wore a suit to work every day, and he dressed very carefully. I remember him expressing his gratitude for the kind of work he did on more than one occasion. He was very respectful of everyone he worked with: suppliers, customers, his brothers, and everyone who worked for Georgia-Pacific. I knew that a great part of his appreciation was that he had succeeded in escaping the tedious farm labor he had grown up with and securing the kind of job where he could sit at a desk and use his mind. To him, it was a privilege to work in an office.

5. Develop community service (age eight to ten)

There are many ways to cultivate community service in your children's lives. You can raise money for causes that you care about, sign up with your children to work in a soup kitchen, or work together building a house for Habitat for Humanity. There are a lot of environmental concerns that you can work on together. My family lives by a park where the ivy grows up the tree trunks and can eventually choke the trees. When our children were young, we went out as a family to ivy-pulling events organized by the park rangers. We pulled ivy off the trees as a family to save the trees and be part of a community effort.

There is tremendous value in doing community service together as a family. It will help your children gain perspective on what is truly important in life. If you believe that happiness comes from within, and if you recognize that the mainstream in our culture promotes happiness coming from without, the clash is obvious. Helping feels good. We're all part of a larger society, and if we contribute to it, it thrives. If we don't, it might not. It is up to you to take the initiative to help your children develop a healthy perspective.

6. No debt (age ten to twelve)

This is perhaps the most important lesson, and it would be wise to teach it to your children as early as you think they can understand it. Debt can be a big problem in wealthy families, especially if children have not become responsible with how they handle money.

I recommend that wealthy clients carry no credit card debt, no mortgage, and no car payments and base lifestyle choices on what they can afford in the present. I agree with investment manager Jeff Auxier's advice: Never borrow against depreciating assets. Never borrow for consumption. And if you believe you must borrow, only borrow for well-thought-out business purposes or assets that are building intrinsic value. You would be doing your children a huge favor by modeling this behavior and teaching them to do the same. You can explain to them that if you are living on the money that you actually have, then your lifestyle is true and you are living within your means.

Certainly your children won't be buying houses or taking out business loans when they're twelve years old, but they're starting to develop the way they see the world and how it works. As they get a little older, work with them to understand debt even more. One credit card is okay for convenience as long as your children pay it off in full every month. This is not mainstream American thinking—only 35 percent of credit card holders pay off their balances in full every month according to Yahoo Finance.[1] But if you've taught your children about interest and the value of a dollar, they'll quickly catch on to the dangers of debt.

Many of us constantly receive offers to apply for credit cards, to refinance our mortgages, and other ways to take on debt. Sometimes we receive a page of checks with the credit card bill. These are all insidious ways of trying to "help" us—help us go into debt that is, and at ridiculously high interest rates. Point this out to your kids the next time you or they receive a new credit card solicitation. These offers come with a lot of encumbrances, and it's difficult to get off their mailing lists.

To teach what you believe about these solicitations, when your teen gets one of these credit card offers, tell him that the best way to handle unsolicited credit card offers is to shred them. Or better yet, have him find the paper that has his name printed on it, hand him a Sharpie, and have him write in big, bold letters, "No, thanks!" Then fold all the papers that came with the offer, including the envelope they came in, and stuff them all into their postage-paid return envelope, seal it, and put it in the mail box. This gives your teens a graphic example of how you think about the dangers of credit cards.

7. Become a Choosy Consumer (age ten to twelve)

Do *not* model the saying, "When the going gets tough, the tough go shopping." Instead, teach your kids to be smart shoppers. When you go shopping, you can find one of those short-sleeved polo shirts at a large-volume store for twenty dollars. Or you can find the same shirt in the same color, possibly made in the same factory, but with a little emblem on the front, at a high-end store for eighty dollars. If you give teenagers the chance, they often will choose to buy the one with the emblem, and some adults will too. But help kids understand what they are paying for. The point isn't to tell them that they can't buy the one with the emblem but to help them understand that they are paying a premium for the emblem. Ask your teens if they think it's worth the extra cost. Ask them what they could buy with sixty dollars. Help your children appreciate that along with privilege comes responsibility to make wise financial decisions. Exemplify and cultivate a grateful spirit.

In their book *Kids, Wealth, and Consequences*, Jayne Pearl and Richard Morris suggest some conversation starters to help your children learn the financial value of distinguishing between wants and needs:

1. When is it appropriate to spend on luxuries, and when might it be okay, or even better, to choose less expensive items?

2. Do we choose luxury items based on quality or a desire to impress and keep up with our friends?

3. What are some categories of purchases for which we would not mind spending much less, and why?

4. Why should we think about spending less when we can afford more expensive things?[2]

Another thing you can do while you are shopping is to ask your children to take a moment to think about how fortunate your family is to have everything you need and so much of what you want. Many people in the world don't have this.

Give ample consideration to the funds that leave your hands. Teach your children to do this as well. Waste not, want not. Cultivate a grateful spirit. Help your children appreciate that along with privilege comes responsibility to make wise financial decisions.

8. Invest (age ten to twelve)

You can start to teach your children about investing at about age ten, though it may make more sense to wait on investing in public offerings until age sixteen or so. Before a child begins investing in public offerings, provide business experience and reading in investment texts. Invest in your child's business or allow your child to invest in yours. Study your common investment together and share the profit. Then encourage investing in stocks and bonds on a regular basis and use the dollar-cost averaging method.

We started this step when our daughter, Julianne, was ten. My husband and I decided to give her $1,000 to invest in some stocks, which she would choose, so she could watch them grow. We sat down and started looking at companies that sell items kids are interested in—products she would recognize.

Julianne picked out Disney, Toys R Us, and Krispy Kreme. Unfortunately, no sooner had we bought them than they all started down! I thought if we waited a while, they'd come up again, right? But after two years, these three stock prices were not coming up. I called our financial advisor, Jeff Auxier, and he suggested we all come in because by then our son, Clay, had turned ten and we wanted to give him $1,000 to invest too.

When Jeff started talking about the stocks my daughter had purchased, she listened to him for a while and then asked, "Can I invest in my mom's company?" Jeff thought that was a very good idea because it would help her to learn about business as well as investing. My business is straightforward, so we decided she would make her investment, we'd figure out the profit at the end of the year, and she'd get a percentage. In the process, she'd learn about return on investments and other basic business concepts. Then our son said, "Can I invest in my dad's company?"

We thought that was a good idea too. My husband's business is a partnership, completely different than mine, but a good one to study. Clay actually decided to take the diversified approach, investing half of his money in his dad's company and the other half in my company. An unexpected result of this for me was that the heat was on now with two little investors.

This has turned into the education that I was hoping for. You do not have to be a financial wiz to take charge of financially educating your children. But you may want to consult your advisor *before* you get started to avoid getting off on the wrong foot!

There is another kind of investing, which parents can bring up for their children to consider. Ask your children, if you gave them ten cents for every kind word they ever spoke and took away five cents for every unkind word, would they be rich or poor? It's a question that underscores the value of kindness and the existence of rampant unkind behaviors, which seem to be accepted in our society. The fact that unkind behaviors are so prevalent certainly doesn't make them any less harmful. This challenge also imparts the message to stand up for what you know is right.

9. Be authentic (age thirteen and up)

Exemplify your values and be yourself. If you like to wear your Burberry blouse when you serve at the soup kitchen with your family, wear it! Just put it in context for your kids as in, "I really enjoy wearing this top, and I really enjoy serving in the soup kitchen. What's important here is helping others and making sure they have a good experience with us."

Be real. This is a great lesson for teenagers, most of whom are busy trying to figure out who they are. When teens notice you being confident in who you are in the world, especially when your actions fall outside the mainstream, it's a powerful model for these young people. Most teenagers and young adults are not going to throw any praise your way for this, but they will notice.

10. Be a leader (age thirteen to fifteen)

Last but not least, teach your children that very few, if any, of their friends will handle money in the ways this chapter suggests. Leaders are made of people who withstand peer pressure to stay true to their values. When this authenticity shines through, others take notice and often follow their example.

Learning these steps of financial literacy will set your family members apart from their peers. Most other young people will not learn to manage their financial lives in these responsible ways. So it is important to alert your kids to the fact that when their peers are submitting credit card applications for "free money," yours will understand the folly of this course of action. For them, the process of studying and practicing financial literacy and responsibility will minimize temptations and entitlement.

There are excellent books that supplement the examples and lessons you offer as a parent. The first is a fantastic book with (sorry) a horrible title: *The Complete Idiot's Guide to Money for Teens* by Susan Shelly. It is well organized, clear, and comprehensive. *The 7 Habits of Highly Effective Teens* by Sean Covey is another book that tremendously benefits teens. For adults who are already in trouble with their personal finance, I recommend Dave Ramsey's *The Total Money Makeover* and its accompanying workbook.

When you and your family practice these ten financial rules, your children become competent and confident in their financial affairs.

Parenting Adult Offspring

When children are grown, the shift to adult-to-adult interaction within the context of an ongoing parental relationship presents one of the most challenging dilemmas for many families. The presence of wealth adds a layer of intensity and complications. However, the following strategies may help smooth this transition. Ideally, it is great if you can start teaching financial values and skills while your children are young. If you haven't done so, or if your efforts to date have not yielded the results you had hoped to achieve, you can still work with your adult offspring.

Virtually all of the principles I outline in this chapter apply to adult children, especially if you still have leverage—if you have not yet given your adult offspring the financial wealth you intend. But even if you have distributed significant financial wealth to your grown children, if they are not using it wisely, you may be able to exert some influence to encourage them to take charge of their lives in positive ways. Your simple willingness to spend time with them can make a difference. It may mean getting to know each other all over again, this time as adults.

We can all strengthen our families by reviewing and revising our own roles and boundaries, tuning up our communication practices, and working to extend trust and love. We can stretch to take the high road in life's many decisions—sometimes making painful compromises—and learn to focus on ways to love and accept one another regardless of life's circumstances.

Parenting adult offspring is challenging in ways that are unique to the generations living today. Older parents are enjoying longer, healthier lives. Their family presence is expanding as they remain vitally engaged in managing their family's finances, businesses, and philanthropic efforts. Yet they also wrestle with how to parent their adult children and find appropriate ways to provide input and guidance to younger family members. Some parents expect their relationships with adult children to evolve into friendships, while others continue to relate to them as children. The transfer of wealth can all too easily become a tripping point as the parent-child relationship evolves.

Adult children do not have it any easier. They battle with a range of conflicting emotions and thoughts. This may originate from a continuing reliance on parents' financial support, especially as many young adult offspring delay assuming independence from their parents. They frequently are not prepared for a career until they reach their mid-twenties or early thirties.

Additionally, more young adults are returning home after completing college or having lived on their own. Some of them are expected to—or expect to—work in a family enterprise headed by a parent, which can further delay independence and strain relationships. When young adults join the family business, their positions are rarely negotiated in the way other jobs would be, and the option of leaving is often loaded with implications and consequences. One way to minimize young adults' loss of independence in this scenario is to require each young family member to work outside the family business first. It is wise to set up this requirement with the stipulation that the young adults be promoted to a level of responsibility above the level where they started. After this point, they can apply to join the family business. This way, young family members gain independence, gain "real world" work experience, and enhance their skills before joining the family business, thus providing safeguards for all family members and protecting the family business from the business family.

Further complications in the lives of wealthy adults can come from their parents' largesse. I have seen these arise from annual gifts ranging from $13,000 per person per year (the amount that is currently allowed tax-free) up into many more digits, cash or its equivalent to help with the purchase of a home, the opportunity to buy hand-me-down vehicles from parents, exotic family vacations underwritten by the parents, tuition payments, or savings plans for a grandchild's private education. None of these gifts are inappropriate in themselves, but they do affect the relationship dynamic. Adult children may feel overly controlled and resent any perceived intrusiveness; they can also feel embarrassed by their lack of independence, particularly when it comes to finances.

Here are six tips for helping your adult children improve their relationships with others in the context of wealth.

1. Establish healthy communication patterns.

The rules of healthy communication are deceptively simple, beginning with speaking only for yourself, followed by listening to others. Further communications skills that are also vital to building strong family bonds include: avoiding criticizing, belittling, or insulting others; being assertive, not passive or aggressive; remaining in the present and jettisoning past offenses; and showing respect to one another.

2. Teach and learn assertiveness skills.

Assertiveness is the mastery of standing up for yourself and communicating your needs in a manner that minimizes the potential for offending the other person. Simply put, assertiveness is the ability to say yes if the response is yes, and no if the response is no. Assertiveness is a mainstay of healthy communication, and many adults struggle in applying this skill to their relationships with their parents, offspring, and others. True assertiveness is more challenging than many believe. It is a skill that needs practice. The need for it and the difficulty of it are heightened when offspring fear reprisal from their parents, particularly the loss of financial support. The Assertiveness Guide in chapter six is a step-by-step method for developing an effective assertiveness statement.

3. Actively build trust.

Trust is an ongoing process that requires acceptance, dependability, honesty, accountability, and openness. Building trust takes time and attention. There is no shortcut. It is only over time that we have the opportunity to see each other in all kinds of situations, and this range of situations will unveil new behaviors, revealing the maturity levels of everyone involved.

4. Set appropriate roles and boundaries.

When children reach young adulthood, definitions of roles and boundaries need to evolve. Parents are bound to encounter problems if they continue to attempt to set limits on an adult offspring's behavior—unless these actions are directly affecting the parents. Providing choices with associated consequences is also inappropriate in most cases. In healthy adult relationships, the parental role shifts from authority figure to advisor. It is important to note here that if parents didn't take on a parental role while children were young—abdicating their responsibilities to nannies, for instance—acting as an advisor later doesn't work very well. If the parental role does not shift from authority figure to advisor, frustration and rebellion can result. This often leads a child to distance himself from his parents, or conversely, it perpetuates an ongoing parent-child relationship that continues an unhealthy childlike dependency. Set appropriate boundaries and expect everyone to treat each other with respect. An excellent book that offers guidance for learning the rules of relationship both horizontally and vertically is *Hats Off to You: Balancing Roles and Creating Success in Family Business* by Ernest A. Doud Jr. and Lee Hausner.

5. Allow family members to make choices and experience the consequences.
In families in which children have not been required to accept responsibility for their actions while growing up and their lives have been cushioned by their parents' wealth and power, the development of personal responsibility is often delayed. This can lead to poor behavior patterns, including addictive behaviors. As these children become older, parents will find it more and more difficult to help. Allow children to learn that all actions have consequences and to figure out how, knowing this, they want to make choices for their own lives.

6. Separate love and acceptance from competence and responsibility.
In many highly successful families, parents unwittingly communicate that their love and acceptance is tied to their children's performance and achievement. While it is important to raise children with a sense of personal competence and responsibility, family members need to know they are loved and accepted regardless of what they do. This can be a difficult message to deliver consistently. Yet the message of unconditional love is powerful, and it is an essential support to healthy psychological and emotional development.

In addition to helping offspring learn relationship skills and manage relationships well, it is important for parents to decide how inheritance will be handled in the family.

Making Wise Decisions about Inheritance Issues

If you have not written a will or created an estate plan for the next generation, it is your responsibility to do this as soon as possible. First you need to identify your family's unique circumstances, needs, and values.

Take a few moments to consider your own experience as an inheritor, in Exercise 10.2.

10.2 EXERCISE 10.2:

How Did You Learn About Your Family's Wealth?

How and when did you find out about your family's wealth, and what was that like for you?

Do you wish you had learned about the wealth earlier or later?

How might you have been better prepared to handle the information?

What has worked well about the way your parents informed you? What has not worked so well?

What has worked well about the way your parents and/or earlier generations set up your trusts? What has not worked well?

Have you taken charge of your financial life, including a clearly defined role for your trusts, in which you feel financially mature and grateful? Were your benefactors too restrictive or lenient?

Did, or do, you work well with your trustee?

You and your spouse can compare your answers to these questions and discuss how your own experiences are influencing you as you decide how to communicate to your offspring what you want them to know about the family wealth.

Then, it's important to find an estate planning attorney who will take the time to understand your family's circumstances, needs, and values. You may find it helpful to discuss with your spouse the questions in Exercise 10.3, created by wealth consultant John L. Levy, author of *Inherited Wealth*. Then ask the same questions to estate planning attorneys you interview to find out whose answers align best with your own and those of your spouse.

e 10.3

Exercise 10.3:

Estate Planning Questions for Attorneys[3]

1. What are some advantages and disadvantages of parents keeping their children informed about the family wealth? About their likely inheritances?

2. Is it a good idea for parents to involve their children in the process of estate planning beyond keeping them informed factually? How about meeting with them individually or collectively to discuss the whole process? What's likely to happen if parents encourage children to express their own wishes, hopes, concerns, and fears regarding the process and their own inheritances? Is the resulting estate plan likely to be more or less constructive when children participate in the process?

continued on next page

3. If a family meeting is held, in which parents discuss their estate planning with their children, who else should attend? Attorneys? Financial planners? Accountants? An objective facilitator? What about the children's spouses?

4. What are some advantages and disadvantages of incentive trusts, which financially reward heirs for certain behaviors?

5. What are some pros and cons to generation-skipping trusts, in which grandparents bequeath some of their wealth to their grandchildren?

6. In distributing their estate, should parents treat their children equally? Are there situations in which fair doesn't mean equal—perhaps different children receive different amounts or under different circumstances or timing? What kinds of situations? If parents are considering these questions, how should they go about determining the best course of action?

Even when you have your estate plan in place, your work in this area is not finished. It is important to review and update your will and trusts every three to four years. Why? Tax laws change. Your children grow and evolve. They may become more (or less) responsible with money over the years. As they go to college, pursue a career, marry, have children, or divorce, you may be more or less inclined at any specific period of their lives to offer financial help, protect your estate, or possibly protect them from their own irresponsible decisions.

Parents' Top Five Estate Planning Questions

Following are the top five questions I hear from parents who are developing their estate plans. The estate tax laws are complex, and over a period of years, they develop into moving targets. Estate planning attorneys can provide the technical expertise you need to create the plan you want, but you have a lot of work to do before you ever see the attorney. There are five important questions to answer first:

1. Should I treat each child equally?

In most cases it is not entirely possible to treat each child equally. The beach house you leave to one of your offspring may simply not be the direct equivalent of the antique car collection left to another. Treat each of your children fairly but not necessarily equally. Each heir is different and will have different needs and financial abilities. Tailor the various aspects of your estate plan accordingly. In a family meeting with everyone present, explain your decisions.

2. How much should I leave my children?

It's important to determine your priorities early in this process. If your priority is to see your offspring grow up as motivated people who each want to make a life for themselves and to make their mark—however they define that—then it will be important to allow them to develop some hunger for life. No one who has navigated this hunger successfully would trade it for anything.

Many wealthy families, such as the Gates and the Buffetts, have chosen to give most of their fortunes away and leave their children, as Buffett described it, "enough to do anything, but not enough to do nothing."

3. When should I begin transferring wealth to offspring?

Until you have seen how your children handle their financial lives, set up your plan to transfer money to them later rather than earlier. When they are very young, it is wise to set the age of transfer high, as in fifty or fifty-five. Give them some wealth at ages twenty-one and twenty-five or thirty to practice with, a very small percentage of what they will eventually inherit. This becomes part of their financial literacy education. If they do well, investing the money and growing it, perhaps the ages of inheriting larger amounts could be lowered slightly toward forty or forty-five. Be careful that you do not rob them of the motivation and the opportunity to make a life for themselves.

4. How much information is wise to tell children about what they will inherit, and when should we tell them?

It is most effective for children to earn information regarding their inheritance, and it is best acquired in stages. The early tasks for earning family wealth information are: success in keeping a ledger or a personal balance sheet, handling an allowance well, having a summer job, and making good decisions about spending, saving, and giving money away. Once they show their competence in these areas, they have earned the right to be introduced to some aspects of your estate plan. No numbers yet, only the concepts and likely progression.

Have your older teens take a university class in accounting. Accounting is the language of business, and learning it is an important step in their financial literacy. Under most circumstances, do not discuss the actual amounts they will inherit until after they reach age twenty-one, sometimes well after. One effective strategy is to tell them that they will be getting what investment advisor Dirk Junge calls a great starter kit: an excellent education, money to get started in a house, maybe some money to start a business, but they won't be getting so much that they won't need to work.[4] It's important for offspring to go through an era of working to learn how to do a job well for pay.

Consider being open with your adult offspring about what's in the will or possibly including them in your estate planning process. This is not always appropriate, but at the very least tell everyone what you are deciding to do. This communication can prevent misunderstandings and avoid hurt feelings. Be kind.

5. What is the best way to structure trusts?

Trusts can sap beneficiaries' drive and ambition. To avoid this, sometimes wealthy people explore the idea of incentive trusts. But these are very difficult to write well. Whatever outcomes you are trying to avoid by creating conditions for the wealth can have serious unintended consequences later if the conditions come across as punitive. There are many kinds of trusts and other estate planning vehicles. Take your own well-researched information about your priorities to your estate planning attorney for help identifying the best legal tools for you to accomplish your goals.

Don't assume your estate plan will play out as you expect after your death. Offspring change, laws change, and the value of the assets can change. When you review your estate plan every three or four years, make sure you are consistent with your values. Be careful to raise your children in ways that reflect the legacy you intend. As John L. Levy cautions, "Don't bring up your children on steak and then send them out in the world to live on hamburger." If you value philanthropy and intend to leave gifts to causes you now support, share your passion for this with your children and offer to involve them if they wish.

You can make your estate plan an instrument that will enhance and reflect the legacy you intend in addition to the financial wealth you want to pass on to future generations. The final stage in the cycle of life is described in many cultures as a time of divestment, a progressive stripping away to leave the world as we entered it: with nothing. It is arguably more important than the accumulation phase because of the familial element. Deciding how much to leave, what, and when cannot be determined once and for all, never to change. It is a work in progress. As you pass on resources to those who will outlive you, you will experience a continued sense of involvement and connection to that future.

Everyone wants to create a legacy that shows the best of who they are. Your children can be your finest work. What they do with the values and wealth you give them goes on and on in the world.

Moving Toward the Bright Side

It is entirely possible to teach and model good behaviors and habits for your children. The surest way to find the path to these behaviors is to focus on your own top values and to let them guide you. If you value lifelong learning, it is easy to make sure you are always learning in some way. You might be taking a class, researching, writing, or leading a discussion group, to name a few activities which can engage you in learning. Your children, even adult offspring, will notice and be influenced by your lead.

You can offer to develop something together, even with adult offspring. If neither you nor your son is good at tracking personal income and expenses, you can both start a record-keeping program together, written or digital. I prefer the written ledger, since I believe you get more out of the exercise, though if computer records are significantly more appealing to you, then keep your records electronically. Set a time frame, stick to it, and set up a reward at the end. For this example, maybe one year is a good time frame, with smaller rewards along the way.

Philanthropy is another area where a project together with your young or adult offspring can be very effective. The overall lesson is for the parent to stop preaching about financial literacy and get involved. Any teaching you do will be turbocharged and longer lasting if you do it together.

These are the kinds of behaviors that Henry, whom you met at the beginning of this chapter, didn't have the benefit of learning from his parents. But he was astute enough to realize that he didn't want the same experience for his own children. It was hard for him to create a different financial upbringing for his kids, but he did it, and it became an important building block of his legacy to his family.

Exercise 10.4: **e 10.4**

Gratitude

What are five elements of your relationship with one of your children for which you are grateful?

____

____

____

____

10.5 EXERCISE 10.5:

Action Plan

Now set an action plan for improving your relationships with your children. For practicality and to increase your odds of accomplishing your action plan, begin with one goal with one of your children.

Today's date______________________

The goal I set for my relationship with one of my children is:

____

____

____

In order to accomplish this goal, I will perform the following activities

____

____

____

Support people who might assist me include:

____

____

____

I realize I may sabotage my plan by:

____

____

____

So I will avoid this by:

____

____

____

I will complete this goal by ________________________ (date)

(Recommendation: three to six months)

Parenting provides some of the toughest relationship challenges. Certainly there are oases and times of joy along the way, and thankfully many heartbreaks are healed and forgotten. But the fact remains that parenting is very difficult to do well. When children are young, we have the best chance to reach them, yet many healthy parent-child relationships falter when offspring become teens. Conventional wisdom tells us that this is nature's way of preparing families for young adults to leave home and make their own life, but knowing this doesn't lessen the pain of parenting teens or, for that matter, the pain of teens being parented. Take time to remind yourself to let your values guide you. Growing kids need parents to help them navigate the maze of temptations, discouragement, and their own fears. Your support on their journey to adulthood is the most precious gift you can offer. You can provide the circumstances for their identity and the motivation to grow.

Most relationships with adult offspring are still full of possibilities to grow strong and close. Sometimes steps of maturity, forgiveness, and humility are essential on the part of both parents and offspring. The dynamics of relationships with adult children need to evolve, and an adult balance must be found. The underlying principles of strong, positive relationships—identity, values, respect, competence, trust, communication, and generosity all apply. Prioritizing your relationships with your children, no matter their age, is the key to fostering better relationships. If you need help in this process, don't hesitate to ask a professional.

Creating, Enhancing Healthy Professional Relationships

If you think hiring professionals is expensive, try hiring amateurs.

—Unknown

I want to work with the top people, because only they have the courage and the confidence and the risk-seeking profile that you need.

—Attributed to James Joyce

When planning for a year, plant corn. When planning for a decade, plant trees. When planning for life, train and educate people.

—Chinese Proverb

| Relationship elements: | **Communication** | **Competence** |

Many types of professional relationships require us to be competent, confident, and calmly assertive—traits many inheritors lack. So we continue now on our journey mastering the bright side of wealth by identifying some of the challenging situations you may encounter at work with supervisors, coworkers, and employees; at philanthropic organizations with those with whom you interact; and in personal matters with financial advisors, managers, accountants, trustees, and lawyers.

This chapter explores common misunderstandings that develop between wealthy people and the professionals around them and will give you insight into how to handle these situations. We'll look at the conflicting agendas, inaccurate assumptions, and negative emotions that cause and exacerbate these difficulties. I'll also outline methods for interacting with these professionals in healthy ways that will help you build and maintain your sense of confidence, self-sufficiency, and business acumen.

Achieving Financial Competence

When I met Margaret, she had an uneasy relationship with her investment manager, and virtually all her relationships were troubled. Her father had died when she was fifteen, and her mother knew little about financial management of any kind. Her mother believed she herself would be taken care of for life, and that was pretty close to the truth. But she was little help to Margaret.

Margaret's inheritance was in a generous trust, and for the first few years, all her interactions with her trustees were straightforward enough. When Margaret was in school, her spending habits were not that different from other students, but she did enjoy spending money. Her spending began to grow when she finished college, and by age twenty-five, when a third of the trust was distributed to her, she had developed a habit of shopping to ease the stresses of life. She worked part time in the retail fashion industry, but she moved around a lot and usually made minimum wage.

When she received the first third of her trust, she opened an account with an investment manager, one whom she had known through the bank where the trust was located. Just as she received the funds, he left the bank to join a private firm. Margaret liked him, and it was easy for her to imagine working with him, especially since he had known her father too. They had barely started their work together when he noticed that her spending was outpacing the ability of her account to generate income and even outpacing the income the trust, still at the bank, would generate. When he brought this up with her, she admitted that she had a "little problem" with overspending and asked him to tell her when she was spending "too much."

Thus began a relationship in which the investment manager became the authority figure and Margaret the child. This continued for years, including two more trust distributions, the final one when Margaret was thirty-five. When I met her at age thirty-eight, her relationship with her investment manager had grown tense due to her erratically checked spending, his admonitions, and her insecurities. She relied on him to tell her when she was spending too much, but her degree of cooperation varied. She had spent a lot of money over the years and was now worried.

The course of our work began with basic financial literacy. Margaret needed the tools, the language, and the confidence to take charge of her life financially, something she had never done. She was motivated by fear that she could run out of money, and when she told me the numbers, I too could see that this was a real liability. To her credit, Margaret worked hard.

At first it was three steps forward, two steps back, but she had become highly motivated, and this was her biggest asset. She established many new and healthy habits, such as keeping track of all of her income and spending, planning big purchases well ahead of time, and getting a full-time job. Significantly, she developed new coping strategies for her stress management, techniques that did not involve shopping and cost little or no money. Her relationship with her investment manager also evolved. He was skeptical about her ability to change at first, but after a while Margaret's responsible behaviors won him over. He began relating to her as a financial advisor rather than as an authority figure. She has stopped moving and settled down. She speaks highly of her friends and family. Her future looks bright.

Working with Supervisors, Coworkers, and Employees

This can be a delicate balance to establish and maintain, especially when the people you work for, with, and above, know *or think they know* about your financial resources. You will encounter their assumptions and their attitudes. Some people will believe that you just got your job because of who your family is, or that because you don't really have to work, it's okay if they try to take advantage of you, or that you've had it easy, so you can't really be any good at what you do.

Most of the time, it is wise to simply do your job as well as you can and not directly address the assumptions and attitudes of others. You may benefit from the attitude that, as an inheritor, you need to do your job twice as well as others to overcome their assumptions that you rely on your wealth more than your work ethic.

You will encounter conflicts at work, just as everyone else does. Don't think you must simply put up with trouble because of assumptions others may make. Talk with your supervisor or at least with a coworker you trust, and expect yourself and others to make every effort to resolve the problem.

If you need advice or a reality check, you can explain the situation to someone you know outside of your job, someone whom you trust. This might be a friend who is successfully negotiating a job and liking it, or it may be a professional or other neutral third party.

It is helpful to keep your values fresh in your mind; focus on your work; remember that sometimes you will encounter unfairness, just as others do; and make an effort to be respectful and kind. If you have work you really like that helps you follow your dreams, the effort to maintain your focus will be worth it.

Interactions at Philanthropic Organizations

Like work situations, relationships at philanthropic organizations can be difficult due to others' assumptions and attitudes. You may encounter politics in these organizations and have difficulty seeing what their agendas are at times.

Again, it is important that you maintain your focus on your values, why you are volunteering for the organization, and what you want to accomplish. Your hard work will speak for itself. Sometimes it is helpful to volunteer to do tasks that no one else wants to do. In this way you increase your value to the organization. Be true to yourself when it comes to making financial gifts, and know that the organization will likely expect something from you. Give what you are led from within to give, and follow through to see that your gifts are used in the way they agreed to use them. This kind of participation, of both time and money, can be a great source of inspiration and fulfillment if you manage it well.

Choose your volunteer work carefully and hold high standards of performance for yourself. This is an opportunity for you to experience the benefits of working at a purposeful job, even though you won't have to go through a big hiring process and will only have to commit part time. It can be the best of both worlds for you if being paid is not a concern. Volunteers are not usually held to high standards, though, so challenge yourself to surpass these low expectations. If you just show up at board meetings and do little else, you will miss the opportunity that this kind of engagement can be.

Before you begin volunteering, think about what you are available for and what you are not available for in terms of time, tasks, and donations. It is very important for you to stake out this territory before anyone asks you to do anything. I know of a wealthy woman who handles her foundation well, has a great staff, and is clear about her mission. Still, she is often asked to take on a new responsibility or to repeat gifts she has made before. Sometimes she feels as though people *always* want something from her. "I feel cannibalized," she has said. So be clear—to yourself and to the organization—about your passion, what you want to give, and what you want in return. The tough job is to keep the balance.

Beyond working with other professionals in job or volunteer capacities, you will also need to build a team of financial professionals to help you manage your wealth.

Working with Advisors

In order to take responsibility for your wealth, you need to know how to work effectively with your legal, financial, and investment advisors. It is important to remember that these professionals are working for you, and you will handle the relationships best if you take the time and care to manage them well. This means understanding what each professional does for you, showing interest in their expertise, and participating in all these professional relationships with an attitude of cultivation. You will be wise to learn the language of your advisors' expertise and to develop at least a superficial knowledge of their professions. Communication skills are of the utmost importance in these relationships, especially in the context of inquiring about fees, asking about concepts you are not familiar with, and clarifying expectations on a regular basis.

Although Margaret, whom we met earlier in the chapter, didn't approach her relationship with her advisor in this way for many years, she reached a point in her life where she was ready, willing, and able to do the tough work of acquiring financial literacy, which drastically improved her relationship with her advisor. This had many secondary benefits as well: she improved her life with friends and family, she settled down and became less anxious, and she received many compliments and great encouragement from her advisor, friends, and family. She hadn't realized her life could be so much better.

Ted Austin, senior vice president and market leader of US Bank's Private Client Reserve, once shared this observation with me:

> Of all the trust beneficiaries I have worked with, the ones who are the most grounded seem to use their trust and the trust income that it generates almost as if it were an "employee" that works for their company and generates additional income "for the company." They have jobs and responsibilities that have absolutely nothing to do with the trust or the amount of income that comes to them, but they continue to watch the portfolio and stay in tune with the investments as they would an employee whom they had trusted within their company.
>
> The income from the trust is simply additional income and often is plowed back into the trust; or if required, is taken and invested outside of the trust for additional growth. When the trust becomes distributable to them in their mid-thirties, they are the ones that typically make the effort to create their own trusts and think about stewardship of these assets for their children more than they think "the money is finally mine." The folks that I worry about think of the trust conversely as their employer: as a dead-end job that they don't particularly want but cannot get away from.

Hartley Goldstone, Founder of Navigating the Trustscape and author of *Trustworthy—New Angles on Trusts from Beneficiaries and Trustees*, wrote a paper titled, "On Becoming an Excellent Trust Beneficiary," in which he explains that the "hallmarks of the excellent trust beneficiary" can be found in both intellectual capital and human capital:

> The excellent trust beneficiary will address the fact of her trust's existence and its implications for her life at increasing levels of understanding, moving from assimilating fundamental information, to successfully managing relationships, to seeking personal well being and fulfillment. Each level of understanding will present its own tasks for the excellent trust beneficiary to master. As she integrates her learning, the excellent trust beneficiary will reframe her trust from a focal point of her life to a supporting role as financial capital in service of her journey toward excellence.[1]

Once the excellent trust beneficiary begins taking charge of her interactions with her trust and trustees, she will mature in her financial literacy and in her confidence. At first, many inheritors are intimidated by their advisors, some to the point of being afraid even to ask about their fees. Often, inheritors fear they will be offensive by asking questions about the financial realities of the arrangement, or they fear they won't understand the answer. They often lack basic competence and confidence about trusts and other financial and legal instruments that greatly impact their lives.

Another reason some of my clients who are inheritors are reluctant to ask about fees is that they have been trained to be polite and they feel that asking about fees is rude or aggressive. I coach my clients to ask all of their advisors about their fees specifically. After they ask the questions, I ask them what they found out. If they answer, "Well, I don't know. We talked about it, but I don't really remember what was said," then I tell them it's important for them to go back and ask again. And again, if necessary, until they're sure of the answers.

Many courses and books cover basic financial literacy in accessible formats. The Institute for Private Investors offers a one-week course through Wharton business school and Stanford University called Private Wealth Management. It is usually offered once each year at each location. The courses are designed specifically for people who have earned or inherited wealth. Many clients to whom I have recommended it have found it enlightening and empowering. They return feeling more educated, confident, and competent. They have hope for their future in all financial interactions with advisors. The provided glossary of legal and financial vocabulary alone, when diligently studied, helps inheritors learn the language needed for meeting with advisors.

If inheritors don't learn the language of their advisors, when they encounter jargon they don't know, they suddenly feel lost. Typically their eyes glaze over and the meeting becomes boring. Learning the vocabulary and basic concepts of wealth management will—in addition to making these meetings much more interesting—make the meetings more effective. Without financial literacy education during their formative years, the majority of inheritors think being an inheritor is a passive situation and they're just at the mercy of the trustee or the bank. They don't realize they can use their own roles and responsibilities as beneficiaries to take charge of their financial reality.

Furthermore, financial professionals will have more respect for you when they can interact with you more, and you'll be more comfortable doing this when you fully understand your situation. It is important that you and all the professionals you work with are clear about what's in your trust, how it's managed, and exactly what your rights and responsibilities are. In *Family Wealth—Keeping It in the Family*, wealth advisor Jay Hughes points out that in more than three decades of his law practice, very few inheritors have understood—or even tried to read—the terms of the trust of which they are the beneficiary. "Clearly, you can't expect good relations in a complex legal relationship if one party to the relationship hasn't even understood her or his basic rights and responsibilities. Frankly, no beneficiary can honestly know if the trustee is or is not performing correctly without understanding the trust instrument."[2]

A Healthy Trust Perspective for Beneficiaries to Develop

Here are six concrete steps beneficiaries can take to become responsible, high-functioning adults:

1. Read the document that created the trust.

Be sure to understand the roles and responsibilities of the beneficiary, what the terms of the trust are, and what power and authority lies with whom. If you do not completely understand the trust as it is written, make an appointment with an attorney and ask for an explanation. It's best to do this with an attorney other than the one who wrote the trust in order to gain an unbiased perspective. Then, when and if you do speak with the attorney who wrote it, you will have this perspective to add to what she says.

2. Understand your roles and responsibilities and those of the trustees.

These roles and responsibilities are listed in Figure 11.3. Respect these. Jeffrey R. Lauterbach, an independent attorney, advisor, and consultant focusing on human capital and wealth planning, offered this advice for me to pass on:

> The trustee can't change the governance of the trust. The trust isn't magic. It's a business. A respectful relationship between you and the trustee takes effort on both sides. Don't ask your trustee for the fifth time to pay for your daughter's wedding, when you've already been told four times that they can't. Put yourself in their shoes. Realize that part of their compensation is psychological. They typically derive some gratification from being involved with all of that money, but they don't get paid that much. A good working relationship is essential.

Hughes outlines the roles and responsibilities of beneficiaries in *Family Wealth*, which are presented in Figure 11.1.

11.1 Figure 11.1:

Roles and Responsibilities of Beneficiaries[3]

Each beneficiary has an obligation to educate himself or herself about the duties of a beneficiary, as well as the duties of the family trustees. Here are specific responsibilities of beneficiaries:

- To gain a clear comprehension of each trust in which the beneficiary has an interest and a specific understanding of the mission statement for each trust as prepared by the trustees
- To educate himself or herself about all trustee responsibilities
- To understand the trustee's responsibility to maintain the purchasing power of the trust's capital while maintaining a reasonable distribution rate for the income beneficiaries
- To have a general understanding of "modern portfolio theory" and the formation and process of asset allocation
- To recognize and look for proof that each trustee represents all beneficiaries
- To meet with each trustee once each year to discuss his or her personal financial circumstances and personal goals and to advise the trustee of his or her assessment of the trustee's performance of the trustee roles and responsibilities to the trust, to the beneficiary, and to family governance
- To become knowledgeable about the functions and importance of each element of the family's trust governance structure
- To attend the annual family business meeting and to accept responsible roles within the family governance structure based on his or her qualifications for such roles
- To develop a general capacity to understand fiduciary accounting
- To demonstrate a willingness to participate in educational sessions and to become financially literate (through family seminars and family-funded educational programs)
- To know how and in what amount trustees and other professionals are compensated and to obtain a general understanding of the budgets for the trust and investment entities in which the trust will be invested

Beneficiaries should also understand what to expect of their trustees. Hughes's roles and responsibilities of trustees is laid out in Figure 11.2.

f 11.2

Figure 11.2:

Roles and Responsibilities of Trustees[4]

Each trustee has an obligation to educate himself or herself on the duties of a trustee as well as on the duties of the trust beneficiaries. The trustee's specific duties are as follows:

- To be fully aware of the grantor's original purposes in creating the trust and the current purposes of the trust, if these have changed over time
- To guide his or her decisions by these purposes
- To act so that the actual operation of the trust is empowering to the beneficiaries, within the provisions of the trust
- To put mechanisms in place to increase the level of financial awareness of the beneficiaries and to see that such financial education of the beneficiaries is carried out effectively
- To meet at least annually with each beneficiary in order to renew the beneficiary's understanding of the trust, as well as to obtain from each beneficiary full information, financial and otherwise, about his or her personal situation
- To educate himself or herself about all beneficiary responsibilities
- To evaluate and advise each beneficiary on how well he or she is meeting the roles and responsibilities of a beneficiary
- To implement effectively the trust's general policies and procedures as they relate to the following:
    1. The trust's investment goals and acceptable risks
    2. The selection and/or provision of investment advice and management to accomplish such investment goals within the given risks
    3. The trust's tax position and the selection of tax services, and
    4. The trust's legal position and the selection of legal services

3. Compartmentalize your trusts.

Trusts create a safety net that has been placed in your life by someone else. Relegate your trust(s) to the background of your reality. It is important to devote some time and attention to stewardship, but keep the trust in its place. Do not sit in the safety net. Decide what the trusts will be for (e.g., emergencies, philanthropy, education for yourself and future generations), and stick to this decision. Make a life for yourself apart from the trust funds.

4. Make a plan for your life.
Your life plan includes developing competence in an area of interest. Yes, commitment too. "Half the failures of this world in life arise from pulling in one's horse as he is leaping," pointed out Augustus William Hare. Make a plan, set a goal, and leap. People are there to help, people who have the skills and experience to sit down with you and help you develop a plan. You may find another family member, a trusted professional advisor, or a mentor of some kind to be a great resource.

5. Develop financial literacy.
This is an ongoing process, and some of your education will be relevant to your trust(s). You will want to understand the concepts of financial responsibility. These include theories of investing, asset allocation, accounting, trust governance, and fees.

6. Remember, you have just as much right to a fulfilling career and fulfilling relationships as a non-inheritor.
And you have just as much need for them. Don't be deterred by family pressures. Hughes's book *Family Wealth* provides much useful information toward these six goals. The trust as a legal instrument is meant to be a positive concept. The hope is that you as a beneficiary are able to fund the best of what you can be. Yet blessings and curses are two sides of the same coin. The threat is that a trust could derail your development. There is so much more at stake for you as a beneficiary than material well-being. A life well lived is a promise fulfilled.

Once you understand the basics of wealth management and the roles and responsibilities of inheritors and trustees, you will not only be able to work more effectively and efficiently with your trustees and advisors, but you will also be able to intelligently evaluate whether you want to use the same investment, legal, and financial managers you "inherited" from the previous generation. Chances are, you will want to build your own team with at least some advisors of your own choosing.

Hiring New Advisors

Sometimes the advisors you inherit are a good fit, but you may not want to work with all of them. Not only should you feel confident about their competence, but it's wise to also have a good rapport with them. Before you look for new advisors, read some books and develop some questions for interviews. Before you choose attorneys to interview, read *Your Lawyer: An Owner's Manual* by Henry C. Krasnow. And before you look for a new financial advisor, read *The Elements of Investing* by Burton G. Malkiel and Charles D. Ellis. Both of these books will inform and orient you.

Furthermore, you will find your own important questions to ask. Draft the questions you want to use in interviewing a prospective attorney or financial advisor so you will feel a sense of control. This is an important process. Listen carefully, ask questions, take notes, and think about the answers you receive. Look for someone who, under different circumstances, could be a friend, someone you'll look forward to seeing at meetings. Never hire a professional advisor who isn't smarter than you are.

If you and your family decide to work with a consultant, be careful when choosing this person or firm. Take your time to interview and wait until you find someone who has the expertise and skills you want. In addition to the qualities you want for your family, again, the rapport, the style, even the gender are important to consider. Wealth management is cumbersome when interrupted by hiring processes, and in some families you don't get a second chance, so take time up front to find the best fit for your family.

As a result of making a poor consultant choice for my family of origin several years ago, I developed a curiosity about how a successful choice can be made. One of the main steps I took to figuring this out was joining the Family Firm Institute and enrolling in its Certificate in Family Business Advising program. After completing the certificate, I understand much better how our family's process went wrong. There are some basic guidelines for making a good choice, which I was unaware of and thus did not follow. So you may benefit from the knowledge I've gathered, here are the guidelines:

1. Match your family's needs with the consultant's expertise.

First, assess your needs as specifically and thoroughly as possible. Is your family in business together? Is it the family business or the business family that needs help? Has the family business sold, leaving the family members still working together to manage the wealth? What are your concerns? Are your challenges financial, legal, or psychological?

It is highly unlikely that you will find one consultant who can provide expertise in all these areas, though you will find consultants who will tell you they can do exactly this. To have success, it is important to match your family's needs with the consultant's expertise.

Don't rule out working with a team. Some consultants prefer to work in teams, some are willing to call in experts when needed, and some will work with the advisors you already have. Working with a team may cost more, but you will likely have access to more expertise and varying perspectives. Ask for relevant references.

It can be helpful to ask for suggestions from friends, colleagues, and peers when seeking a consultant, but what may be a good fit for one family may not be for yours—again, be sure the consultant you are considering understands the unique needs of your family business or your business family.

2. Check the consultant's references, license, and credentials.

Yes, experience and training do matter, so verify potential advisors' licenses and credentials. Your consultants will need skills for analyzing, teaching, facilitating, and advising. Make sure their expertise is the right resource for your family's challenges. Do not make an exception.

You may want to request proposals from the consultants you feel are most qualified. Make sure you know what the fees are. Do your best to compare the services they offer and the fees charged for those services.

Take the time to check their references and make sure the consultant you hire is the best fit for your family. David Bork, in his book *Family Business, Risky Business*, has a good list of questions to ask references when looking for advisors.

3. Expect your family to maintain interest, energy, and commitment to the work.

Sometimes people attribute too much power to a consultant. Make no mistake about it—the responsibility for initiative, motivation, and success is squarely on the shoulders of the family members. Some people are more motivated than others—that is normal—but it is the family who must do the work. You may wish to build in incentives to help keep up the motivation.

4. Keep firmly in mind that consultants are your *guide*, nothing more, nothing less.

Don't let advisors make decisions for you or try to fix your problems for you. That task lies squarely with you. It's important to learn to fix your own problems, and the best advisors are those who will help you acquire the skills you need to do it on your own.

To that end, you and your family members must be willing to be open and honest with your advisors. Consultants can only be as effective as the information they are provided—if it is incomplete or untrue, they cannot do their jobs, no matter what level of expertise they have.

5. Allow time for the process to work.

Don't expect results too quickly. The families who hire a consultant and are the most satisfied with the work accomplished are the ones whose objective is to move toward their long-term goals. They know better than to focus on achieving a particular outcome in a short time frame. Often, the problems families need advisors' help for have developed over years. Resolving them will take time—especially if interpersonal problems are a necessary focus. Sometimes a family is wise enough to hire a consultant to help them define their goals. Or they recognize the potential for trouble and want guidance in setting up a governance structure to keep family concerns running as smoothly as possible.

Building an Advisory Team

Once you are working well with each of your advisors, it's a great idea to ask them to collaborate. You can bring together your accountant, financial advisor, attorney, banker, and trustees for full team meetings. This is not common practice, but it is cutting-edge and can lead to breakthroughs in how you manage your wealth with professional advice. An advisory team allows for an exchange of expertise that builds the whole stronger than the parts.

As an advisor in the psychology of the family, I collaborate with lawyers and financial professionals because it is the highest service we can give to our clients. And we collaborate because we have confidence that not only is our own expertise valuable and precious, contributing to the benefit of the client, but the expertise of our co-collaborator is also valuable and precious. Most importantly, we know that together we can do more for our client than any of us can do alone. As Lynne Twist articulates in her book, *The Soul of Money*, "existing resources, when brought together in collaboration, create a new source of prosperity."

As professionals, advisors are often accustomed to running our own turf, and for most of us, most of the time our only assistance comes from people we have hired to work for us. When we collaborate, though, we must learn to accept that all advisors have valuable input for the client.

In a notable meeting with a client, Ava, and all her advisors, collaboration was the main objective, and each advisor had been asked to give it the highest priority. The advisors in this meeting were all highly accomplished and respected in our fields. To our immense credit, all of us rose to the challenge, and the meeting met many objectives. In fact, without stating it, we agreed to add a dimension to Ava's work with the advisor team, the "new source of prosperity" Twist referred to.

The prosperity showed in the objectives we met. The single most important accomplishment this attitude of collaboration (with a willing lack of egos) yielded was that Ava clearly emerged as the head of the team. This was evident in that all advisors focused on how we could help each other to help her. It is such a shift in thinking that it requires uncharted effort for most advisors. The key in this instance was that for every one of the advisors, Ava is highly valued, so the motivation to respond to the request from her for this type of meeting was great.

Another important objective accomplished was that new information was communicated. Ava began with an opening statement highlighting top life priorities, which none of these advisors had heard stated so clearly before. With everyone present in this meeting, we each were able to acknowledge her direction and purpose. This acknowledgment became a commonality among us.

We also accomplished the objective of working together. As we explored the risks that Ava is likely to encounter, we brainstormed together. We collaborated during the meeting as we put ourselves in Ava's shoes to develop a comprehensive list of the risks for her. It was an exercise in building on each other's ideas, which is useful to all of us.

Collaboration is a huge buzzword in the field of wealth management. Everyone claims to think it is a brilliant idea with undeniable benefits to the client as well as possible benefits to the advisors. The challenge is that it is very hard to do. What gets in the way is ego, turf, insecurity, absence of trust, fear of conflict, poor communication, lack of commitment, and avoidance of accountability, all on the parts of the advisors. Ego is the biggest one. That same ego that has carried each of us to success in our respective businesses must be set aside for any significant collaboration to take place. This is harder than it seems at first. If we can set aside our egos and simply let our expertise work for the client, we can avoid all these related obstacles.

Collaboration can only be accomplished with humility and an open mind. Whether we are seasoned professionals or rookie advisors, it is humility, an open mind, trust, generosity, and an attitude of service that enable us to work with others for the benefit of the client. We must focus on developing the whole to be stronger than the parts. It is an exciting way for all of us to take the high road. With courage, collaboration can be a welcome friend, not a secret foe.

Guiding your advisors to work as a team requires focus, communication skills, persistence, and patience. The benefits of this effort will become evident over time. First, you and your family benefit from their coordinated efforts. Second, you reduce the risk that their work for you is focused on them and their agenda rather than you and your agenda. Third, your advisors will benefit from the experience of true collaboration.

Moving Toward the Bright Side

For many families, focused work with a consultant clearly provides the ticket to better relationships, fulfilling work, and more meaningful lives. Often there is only a rare window when enough family members are open to outside professional help that a working contract with a consultant can begin. Take time and care at the outset to research and interview candidates, respecting the importance of finding the right consultant for your family. It is the wisest investment you can make in this potentially healing and unifying resource.

Beyond fostering relationships with advisors, inheritors need to nurture their relationships with themselves and clarify their goals. Goldstone recommends that at least once a year, beneficiaries take time to reflect on the big picture. The excellent trust beneficiary will:

> reflect upon what her trust has made possible during the past year. She will identify one or more positive experiences, large or small, and will relive and savor those experiences. What occurred? How did she feel? The more detail the better. She will look ahead to the coming year or years and envision what the trust will make possible. Again, the more detail the better. She will reflect upon how she may positively affect others in the coming year.[5]

He also recommends that beneficiaries prepare well for their annual or quarterly meetings with trustees. This includes drafting an agenda that outlines the beneficiary's goals for the meetings, desired outcomes, and a possible post-meeting action plan. Trustees, says Goldstone, should also review the trust agreement and trust statements, and make a list of any questions that come up while reading those documents.

Next, it's important to review their notes from the previous meeting, including the action plan from that meeting. Consider what has been accomplished, what has not, and why not. If an unrealized goal is still desirable, it can be folded into the new action plan. Last, beneficiaries should list any life changes the trustee should know about, including births, deaths, and marital status changes.

11.3 Exercise 11.3:

Advisory Team Agenda

Date, time, and location of advisor meeting: ______________________________

Team members present: ______________________________

From among the following paperwork: trust document(s), investment policy statement(s), estate plan documents, tax documents—mark any relevant documents for this meeting. Questions or points to address:

____

____

____

____

Goals for this meeting:

____

____

____

____

Desired outcome:

____

____

____

____

Action plan (developed during meeting):

____

____

____

____

Exercise 11.4: **11.4**

Gratitude

What are five elements of one relationship with an advisor for which you are grateful?

Exercise 11.5: **11.5**

Action Plan

Now set an action plan for improving a relationship with an advisor. Remember to make your action plan specific, measurable, and small enough that you are likely to accomplish it.

Today's date ____________________

The goal I set for my relationship with my advisor, ________________________, is:

In order to accomplish this goal, I will perform the following activities:

Support people who might assist me include:

continued on next page

I realize I may sabotage my plan by:

____

____

____

So I will avoid this by:

____

____

____

I will complete this goal by ______________________ (date)

(Recommendation: three to six months)

In relationships with supervisors, coworkers, and employees; with those with whom you interact at philanthropic organizations; and with financial advisors, managers, trustees, and lawyers, many of the same interpersonal skills apply. It is important for you to keep in mind the seven elements of successful relationships: identity, values, respect, competence, trust, communication, and generosity. Realize that everyone you come into contact with will have their own assumptions and attitudes about inherited wealth.

Don't make the mistake of assuming that if you don't tell those with whom you work about your family or its wealth, they will not know. People figure this information out with deft ability. They will know. Just be yourself, do your work well, and the rest will have to take its course. Some things are indeed beyond your control. The biggest favor you can do yourself is to take time to identify work you love so you bring genuine enthusiasm to your responsibilities every day. Stick with it and develop competence.

In your relationships with advisors, find out their expertise, determine what they love about their work, learn their language, be interested in what they are doing for you, and always be respectful. With a strong understanding of yourself, your values, the financial world, and the people around you, you are sure to build strong relationships with other professionals in your life.

Stepping Back, Taking Stock
Putting It All Together

It's not that I'm so smart, it's just that I stay with problems longer.
—Albert Einstein

Lasting change only occurs when we change ourselves.
—Lou Ludwig

The readiness is all.
—Shakespeare

Stephen Sondheim's musical *Sunday in the Park with George* features a delightful song containing these buoyant lyrics that sum up this climactic chapter:

Bit by bit,
Putting it together . . .
Piece by piece—
Only way to make a work of art.
Every moment makes a contribution,
Every little detail plays a part.
Having just the vision's no solution,
Everything depends on execution:
Putting it together—
That's what counts.

Putting it together—that's what counts, indeed. Throughout this book you've read about the many potential pitfalls wealthy people encounter in challenging, improving, enhancing, and solidifying their relationships with family, friends, and professionals. You may have already applied some of these techniques I've presented to improve your vital personal bonds and professional liaisons. If so, and you've succeeded, I commend you heartily and trust you feel encouraged and empowered by these successes, however minor they may seem at first. At the very least, it's likely you've come away with a better understanding of why certain relationships have become troubling to you, even though you may still not be entirely sure just how to fix them. Don't worry—you will. All you need to do is persevere.

Simply getting to know what you have to do, though, isn't the answer. It's a great start, but the hardest part is following through with what needs to be done. First, let's pause, step back, assess what we've learned, and pull everything together.

This chapter will help you assess and assemble what you've learned from previous pages. It will help you plan how you can more consciously—and conscientiously—interact in healthier ways with the people in your life.

How Far You've Come

On our journey this far together, we have explored the seven elements of healthy relationships. To review, they are: identity, values, respect, competence, trust, communication, and generosity. I certainly hope you have seen how they apply in each kind of relationship you have in your life. If any of them is missing, it is very difficult to forge a strong, positive relationship. Doing so even *with* them is difficult. The good news is that healthy relationships are entirely possible. And the work to maintain them is rewarding in itself through the moments of success and joy along the way.

In the introduction to this book I gave you my core principles, which guide me in my work. Because these principles are good reminders about why we do the work to repair and reinforce relationships, I offer them to you once again as you decide how you will improve the relationships in your life.

1. People in families want to get along.
2. People want to be able to forgive.
3. People want to take charge of their lives and have access to the resulting happiness and freedom.
4. People want their children to be happy.
5. We know why we do what we do.

6. Gratitude is a powerful attitude.
7. Wellness is essential.
8. People love meaningful work.
9. Helping others is the greatest source of happiness.
10. A deep commitment to your spiritual practice becomes security in life.
11. Each person has their unique story about everything.
12. People have to want change.

In chapter two, I asked you to take the Wealth Attitude Assessment. Now I'd like you to take this assessment a second time in Exercise 12.1. Ideally, you will have spent precious time doing the exercises in this book, considering alternate points of view on wealth issues, and practicing new attitudes and behaviors. If you have skimmed through this book in two days, your Wealth Attitude Assessment score will not have changed. A changed scored will necessarily be based on reflection as well as new attitudes, behaviors, and experiences.

---

e 12.1

Exercise 12.1:

Wealth Attitude Assessment II

Today's date ____________________

Please rate, on a scale of 1 to 5, how true each belief is to you at this moment.

1: *Never/Disagree* **2:** *Rarely* **3:** *Sometimes* **4:** *Usually* **5:** *Always/Agree*

_____ 1. When I think about my wealth, I feel guilty.

_____ 2. It's hard to have a sense of my own identity because I feel like I'm living in someone else's shadow.

_____ 3. I feel alienated or isolated from the relationships I would like to have.

_____ 4. I have not yet taken charge of my life or my wealth.

continued on next page

_____ 5. The abundance of choices I have in my life feels like *too* many choices.

_____ 6. It would be hard for me to think of something I did this past week in which I really feel a sense of accomplishment.

_____ 7. I am not happy with my spending practices and habits.

_____ 8. I don't enjoy doing many of the things I feel I should do.

_____ 9. I know that just about anyone would say I have plenty of wealth, but I have trouble achieving a healthy perspective on this.

_____ 10. I am never satisfied with the amount of my wealth.

_____ 11. I know that others envy me, but they can't possibly imagine how troubling, exhausting, overwhelming, and frightening my life feels at times.

_____ 12. Charity is a social or moral obligation to me, something I have not figured out how to enjoy.

_____ 13. Without my inherited wealth, I would be scared and would feel I had lost an important part of my identity.

_____ 14. I am afraid to ask for help for fear of embarrassing my family..

_____ 15. I long to have something of value other than my wealth.

_____ 16. I wish I could live a normal life with a normal job and a normal amount of money so I would not have to deal with my wealth.

_____ **Total Score**

A high total score, 45 and above, on this assessment indicates that you need help with your attitudes and behaviors. A medium score, ranging from 29 to 44, indicates that you can use help but you have worked out some of these important concerns. A low score, 28 and below, is the range of healthy wealth attitudes and behaviors.

Notice how your scores have changed from when you first took this assessment and which specific attitudes have shifted. Any progress you have made is worthy of note. You may want to take this assessment again when you do further work on your attitudes and behaviors to track your progress.

Strength in Hard Times

Fostering familial relationships is incredibly important, primarily because family members rely on each other for strength in hard times. When financial times are good, it is easy to say you prioritize human and intellectual capital. But when times are tough, everyone's priorities and communication skills are put to the test. Are family members fighting about money, or are they pulling together, remembering that values are more important than money?

Most wealthy families experience an economic downturn as a damaging force. Though wealthy families possess stronger financial resources than lower-income families, they may lack the emotional competence and depth to weather a crisis well when their financial reality takes a hit. As a result, when portfolios suffer dramatic decreases in value, some affluent families argue over current risk and look for someone to blame for their deflated assets.

In financial hard times, otherwise easygoing, reasonable family members may develop short tempers or depression or both. Depending on the type of assets each family member has and the state of the economy, some people may incur much larger losses than others, which can easily complicate relationships even within normally tranquil families. In such crises, families quickly find out how well they understand each other and their family dynamics. Those who have truly developed core family strengths will reap the benefits of their work, weathering the storm with intact relationships at the very least and increased human, intellectual, and financial capital at the most.

The person to start with is you. As you know, we cannot control the actions or attitudes of people around us. But we can decide to change our own beliefs and behaviors. Focus on the skills you've learned in this book, particularly on your values, forgiveness, and using assertiveness statements. Don't forget to use your observation skills to understand what is troubling your relationships and how you can heal them. When you do, you'll find that many family members and friends begin to shift the way they interact with you.

You know which relationships are most in need of your attention. Consider the relationship that has come to mind most as you have been reading and completing the exercises in this book and start with this one.

Family Meetings

Many wealthy families hold regular family meetings. Most do this annually, some quarterly. Often, these events focus mainly on the business of the family, including wealth management, and the work consists of reviewing the performance of investment managers and advisors as well as resolving any issues or changes concerning trusts. If there is an active family business, that is often the focus of family meetings. Family members spend time evaluating performance and other business concerns, and comparing these to previous quarters or years.

Other families use family meetings for education about investing, basic personal finance for younger family members, communication skills, relationship management, or prenups.

Philanthropy is another popular topic of family meetings. If the family has one or more private foundations or charitable trusts, family members may use this time to review assets and grant requests and to make decisions about which charitable causes and organizations will receive donations.

It's wise to incorporate fun, recreational activities into family meetings. This may sound frivolous, but recreation can be even more important than the business activities because it helps the family develop stronger bonds. These fortified relationships make the tasks of working together on the family's financial, legal, and psychological issues easier and more effective. Fun and recreation also create experiences that family members look forward to, and this engages almost everyone's interest in attending family meetings.

You can use improv to help build your family's communication skills while showing them a new kind of fun. You might have the group tell a story using the *yes, and . . .* method. Everyone is in a circle, and one person starts a story. The next person in the circle says, "Yes, and," then adds another line to the story. The yes portion of this activity teaches participants to accept the situation they find themselves in and to continue building the story. You could also play a game called No S's. Two family members begin the scene. The actors decide on a place, relationship, or activity and then create a scenario about anything in that scenario with only one rule: no one can say any word with an s in it. It's hard! And fun. When you inadvertently say a word with an s in it, you "die." It's even important to die with energy and positivity, like there's nothing you'd rather do—and this is when a new actor steps in. When players get exhausted avoiding s's, a third person offstage can pick another letter to dance around. It's an entertaining way to engage family members of all ages. Once when I played this game, I uttered the forbidden letter in the very first word out of my mouth. Then I found myself faced with the challenge of completely switching my focus and remembering to die exuberantly. It was a lesson in embracing change. Is it hard? Yes. Impossible? No.

If your family meetings focus on just one or two categories, such as business and play time, you may want to discuss with the organizers the possibility of adding new elements, such as education and philanthropy, being careful to add new elements one at a time.

Family meetings that are structured in an informal way can be very effective, but so can those with detailed agendas and trained facilitators. I've found that when there are contentious issues or people who tend to behave badly, the family is wise to engage a facilitator who can keep discussions focused on the agenda, assist family communication, and handle disruptive family members effectively. One of your existing family advisors may be a trained facilitator who could add this helpful dynamic to family meetings.

Whether or not your family decides to use a trained facilitator, meetings can get off track and sometimes develop into arguments. Much of this can be avoided with a code of conduct such as the sample one in Figure 12.2. Develop your family's unique code of conduct as a group effort. At the beginning of the meeting, have everyone offer points for the family code of conduct, and then agree to honor them.

e 12.2

Figure 12.2:

Sample Family Meeting Code of Conduct

We will be respectful to each other.

We will be on time.

We will be present in every sense and will turn off smartphones, cell phones, and any other electronic distractions.

We will practice active listening.

We will not interrupt each other. We will wait to speak until the speaker has completed his or her statement.

We will not use loud voices, screaming, or yelling.

We will not use derogatory body language such as eye rolling.

We will be honest and specific during our family meetings.

We will be as concise as possible.

We will strive to behave assertively, not passively or aggressively.

We will check all assumptions with the person who is speaking.

We will speak directly to any person about whom we have something to say. In other words, we will not talk behind anyone's back.

continued on next page

We will always do our best.

We will limit break time and the number of breaks.

We will speak loudly enough and clearly enough for everyone to be able to hear.

We will focus on problems, issues, and behaviors, not on people.

We will allow humor.

We will speak only for ourselves. No one is allowed to speak for someone else.

We will practice confidentiality. What happens here, stays here.

We will respect each other's personal boundaries.

We will be kind.

Another good meeting opener is to ask a question from the short version of the Intergenerational Questionnaire in Exercise 12.3. This can be a terrific tool for understanding family members better.

e

12.3 EXERCISE 12.3:

Intergenerational Questionnaire: Short Version

What do you have that's special from your father?

What stories did your mother tell you about her childhood (about anything)?

What is your family's greatest strength? What strength can you see through the generations?

Were you encouraged to give time, talent or treasure to make the world a better place?

If yes, how were you encouraged?

From whom in your family did you learn kindness? Give an example.

Who in your family has shown you what a great sense of humor is? Give an example.

Were you taught gratitude by your parents? If so, how?

What has been your greatest joy?

What is the legacy you are creating? For what will you be remembered?

Invite everyone—including advisors, if they are present, and young family members—to share their answers. If most attendees find this a positive experience, consider opening each future family meeting with a different question, followed by sharing and observations about the comments.

Beyond family meetings, these questions work well as openers for holiday gatherings, Sunday dinners, or even informal conversations with your immediate family. These questions and answers take you into the inner world of your family members, where you are communicating about values and true identity. When family members share answers, it is possible to gain insight into how your family came to be the way it is. It is important to let people volunteer information to share and not to pressure them to say more than they want to.

Every family has its own reasons for holding meetings and its preferences for how to do it. One client's family meetings usually had a serious component in the morning and then an afternoon recreation. They played a number of different games, sometimes using a questionnaire with questions like:

- What's the craziest thing you've ever done?
- What was the most unusual place you've ever traveled?
- What are your favorite foods?

Then the meeting coordinators use the questionnaire answers to put together a Jeopardy! game with statements such as:

- This family member has watched a sunrise in the past year.
- Someone who makes apple pie from scratch.

This personal interaction helps members of the growing family learn about each other—and have fun while doing it. Such activities can help extended families of different generations get to know one another while discovering unusual interests they have in common, all the while growing closer.

One Chicago family often had a tough time getting everyone to attend all of their sessions. Some people would go off to play golf while others would gravitate to the bar and miss sessions they deemed unimportant. So they held one of their gatherings on Lake Michigan on a private boat ride with dinner and mingling opportunities. Once they were on the boat, nobody could leave, making for an effective—and enjoyable—opportunity for family members to interact.

More Exercises for Healthy Family Relationships

Following are more exercises you can do to move toward building healthier relationships in your family.

Shareholder Equity

Take stock of your family's shareholder equity by asking these important questions from the Family Shareholder Equity Assessment in chapter two:

1. To what extent have individual family members taken charge of their lives?
2. To what extent are individual family members successfully pursuing happiness?
3. How evident are each family member's strengths?
4. To what degree are human, intellectual, financial, and social capital increasing as a result of each family member?
5. To what extent are family assets stronger than liabilities?[1]

If the answer to any of these questions for any family member is a low percentage, you have work to do! In your family you may be the one to encourage others. These questions suggest standards by which you can measure your family members' progress.

The Seven Habits

Read Stephen Covey's book *The Seven Habits of Highly Effective Families.* Better yet, read or listen to it *together*—it's available in print and audio. If you listen to the audio and if your children are still young enough to be living at home, it can serve as the focal point of a weekly meeting in which you savor this book's pearls of wisdom as a family—one habit at a time. Another place to absorb this author's insights and inspiration is on a car trip together or at a vacation destination. In our family, we listened to the book on Sunday afternoons and discussed each habit as we worked our way through the text.

Brainstorm Together

Gather your family to brainstorm opportunities for strengthening the family. This requires a stretch in perspective, so capitalize on the strength of specific family members to get this effort out of the starting gate.

Family Dinner

Plan a family dinner and ask each person to bring an item that is meaningful to the shared family history and be ready to tell its story.

I sincerely hope this book helps you work through the difficult relationships. Even if you're still feeling stuck, at the very least, you are likely to have developed a lot more clarity about what is working and what is not working in your relationships. And if you decide that you could use the help of a mentor, pastor, therapist, or friend to help you improve relationships, having read this book will give you specifics with which to begin the process.

Where to Go from Here

Because you are the one in your family who is reading this book and you have explored concepts, attitudes, and new behaviors regarding wealth, you are the one in your family to take the lead, right now, to build your family capital.

Here's how to start: Take a moment to think about a difficulty in one family relationship, one you would especially like to improve. What is one thing you've learned in this book that you can apply to make a difference in this relationship? Could you apologize? Forgive? Is there someone you need to call, maybe someone you haven't spoken to in a year . . . or ten years? Would someone welcome a handwritten note? Is there a financial wrong you could right?

Don't allow yourself to think, *Well, you don't know my family; they are impossible.* Or, *I've tried and nothing works.* That is not the point. The point is for you to take the high road and keep extending your caring into your family. As Mike & the Mechanics sing in "The Living Years": "Don't give up, don't give in, and don't wait until it's too late." Remember that you *can* improve relationships, even when you can't see how at the beginning. Stay on the bright side. And gather your courage to do what you know is the right thing to do.

Remember, *you* are the agent of change in your family. Think about it often. You are the one who is learning and growing. *You* are the one who is amazing, and you know it. Think of the ripple effect of what you have learned and continue to implement from this book. *You* are the one who has found the ideas that inspired you to improve your family relationships.

A Heroine's Inspiring Wisdom

Before we reach the end of our journey together, I'd like to share an inspiring client story. Ellen and her husband, both attorneys, made a decision before their children were born to live on the money they earned and not to use Ellen's inheritance for living expenses. They had two boys, two years apart, and for many years, Ellen stayed home to be a mom. Both boys became Eagle Scouts, played football in high school, and went on to do well in Ivy League colleges, not to mention many more informal accomplishments—like standing up for bullied kids.

Over many years, Ellen worked on a letter of life advice to her boys. When we spoke about it, she was not yet sure when she would give it to them, as this depended partly on how they developed into adults and partly on how their education about family wealth took shape. She revised the letter from time to time, adding more of her perspective as she went.

Ellen is bright, articulate, wise, and a master of common sense. With her permission, I share with you her words, although I've changed the names. As you will see, her Christian faith is her guide, and it is through her knowledge of the Bible that she has developed her understanding of her situation. While I believe that most of her words are relevant to all of my readers, I acknowledge that you may need to rephrase it in places to fit your own spiritual practice.

> Dear William and Michael,
>
> By now you should be aware that you have or will inherit what now seems like a great deal of money. This is in many ways a wonderful blessing. However, I must admit that your grandparents and your parents have significant concerns about providing you with such a fortune. You have both shown yourselves to be mature, responsible, and thoughtful young men, so we have no qualms about your character. Instead, we are afraid that by giving you such a large sum of money, we will rob you of some of life's most enjoyable aspects—a sense of accomplishment in your own activities and in overcoming barriers to your own success. We are also concerned that your inheritance will get in the way of your relationships with other people and with God. So please forgive your old mother for giving you some unsolicited advice:
>
> **Always remember that it is God's money. He has only made you a steward.** There is no explanation for why our family was made wealthy while other, equally

hardworking families didn't enjoy such success. Some of the credit is due to the fact that your grandparents and parents made good decisions and worked hard. But lots of people make good decisions and work hard. Truth is, we are blessed beyond any measure and beyond my own understanding. As a result of such blessings, we now have responsibilities and duties that other people don't have. We also have temptations and dangers that other people don't have to endure.

Forget that the money is there. Truth is, inherited wealth ruins more people than it helps. That is because the person inheriting the money no longer feels the need to work and achieve a goal. While they might have otherwise gotten satisfaction from their work, many, if not most, people will readily quit their jobs when they come into money. Even if they don't quit, a lot of people will lose their desire to work, set goals, and accomplish something with their lives; instead, they find their ambition diminished. Other men who inherit wealth become discouraged and take the attitude that they shouldn't even try to succeed because they could never measure up to the ancestor who made the fortune. In either case, those who inherit become lost wanderers. If giving you money results in diminished ambition, your grandparents and your parents will have done you a terrible disservice.

My advice to you and your families is to forget that the money is there. Don't live on it or see it as your principal income. Instead, use these funds to provide enrichment to your families, your church, and your communities. Use the money in ways that are not obvious to friends or family. Do not live at a level that is much higher than your earned income would reasonably provide.

Money can come and go, so don't count on having or keeping an inheritance.

Inherited wealth is not an achievement, but it isn't anything to be ashamed of either. Your father and I are very pleased with the character development that you have each displayed, so I hope that by the time you read this letter, you won't really need to discuss false pride. But as a reminder, I want to point out that neither of you can be proud of the fact that you inherited money and property. That pride belongs to your grandparents who earned the wealth through hard work, sacrifice, and a certain amount of luck. Inherited wealth isn't an accomplishment; it's an accident of birth. However, it isn't something to be ashamed of either. Inherited wealth is simply a fact, like being tall or having blond hair. The goal is to not let the money define you. Instead, be defined by your character and your accomplishments.

Wealth and possessions are actually a burden. Owning stuff just means that you have to keep track of it, maintain it, and insure it. Having money just means that you have to spend time taking care of it: investing, accounting, moving funds, etc. Possessions can get to the point that you feel like they own you instead of the other way around. So before you buy something, think about whether it will become just another burden. (Don't get me wrong; not having money is a big burden too!)

Raise your children as middle class kids. Okay, the truth is your dad and I could have bought you boys any toy or bauble your heart desired. But we wanted you to have the experience of not getting something that you wanted, even from an early age. You needed to know how that felt and to realize that you could be happy not getting what you wanted, whether it was material goods, honors, or even earned achievements (like making the baseball or football team).

If you use your connections to "make things happen" for your children, you will rob them of some of life's greatest rewards. It may also give the children the impression that you don't have faith in them, that you don't believe that they can do it on their own. So, bottom line, raise them as middle class children, demand that they develop the tools needed to succeed, and then let them make it on their own without help from you.

Give anonymously. The Bible makes a very strong case for not letting your good deeds be known. It also makes the case that the ability to give generously is a spiritual gift on par with the gift of prophecy and teaching. You must remember that your donations should always be to the glory of God and not to you. You can't take any particular pride in the fact that you gave money. Instead, you have to thank God for the opportunity and ability to be His tool. This is much harder than it seems.

Don't let anyone know that you have money. There are three main reasons for this. First, you set yourself up to attract the wrong people: "hangers on," high-maintenance women, and unscrupulous solicitors and advisors. Second, when people discover that you have money, even if they are old friends, it usually changes the relationship. All of a sudden, you aren't like them anymore and you begin to feel isolated. Some may even become a little jealous, especially in light of the fact that the wealth is inherited. You may feel a lack of respect from others. Third, there are safety issues to consider. The more people know that you have money, the more physical danger there can be for you and your family. Be very careful about who knows your financial status.

Don't rely on your wealth. Rely on God and Jesus Christ. Do you know why the Bible says, "Blessed are the poor"? It's because the poor have to look to God and rely on God for their every need. When you have to rely on God for your basic needs, you have no choice but to stay close to His side.

However, with money comes the illusion (and it is just an illusion) that you can take care of yourself. As a result, you no longer stay near Christ's side. You tend to look to your bank account for security instead of relying on your Savior. This is very dangerous indeed. Once you begin to think you are self-sufficient outside of God, you tend to become your own "god."

In closing, I should also tell you that wealth can be a great blessing. It does free you from some of the everyday trials that many families endure. It also allows you to be the instrument of God in blessing other people. Since giving generously is a spiritual gift, I recommend that you pray to God for wisdom in the way that you handle financial matters. Both of you have become young men to be admired and respected. You have each grown in your faith and demonstrate a desire to be God's man. No parents could want more of a son. Your father and I believe that you can handle this blessing. We have faith in you and your judgment.

I believe in you, and I love you more than life itself,

Mother

Ellen has a tremendous heart. Fortunately, she is also intelligent and wise. I have no doubt that as her boys grow into men and as she and her husband both mature, she will relax and develop confidence that her boys will indeed flourish. Though her advice may sound negative or harsh to an outsider, her strong and thriving boys are proof positive that the values and priorities she and her husband chose for their family are playing out well.

During our journey through this book, I trust you have gathered inspiration and tools for improving your relationships. Your primary concern may be your children, as Ellen's is, or you may want to reconcile with a sibling. You may be ready to devote a renewed focus to your marriage or grow up in your relationship with an advisor. As I know you understand, there are many, many opportunities for you to enhance your life by improving your relationships. I also know you can do it.

The very fact that you have stuck with this book until the end tells me that you are brave and motivated. And you now have the knowledge, the tools, and the power to change. Your legacy can be to make a difference.

Godspeed on the Bright Side

Our journey together is over, dear reader. I leave you now to continue on your own.
Godspeed on your exploration of the bright side of your wealth.
"Happy trails to you," as Roy Rogers and Dale Evans sang.
Happy trails until we meet again.

Prayer of Saint Francis of Assisi

Lord, make me an instrument of your peace.
Where there is hatred, let me sow love;
where there is injury, pardon;
where there is doubt, faith;
where there is despair, hope;
where there is darkness, light;
and where there is sadness, joy.
O Divine Master, grant that I may not so much seek
to be consoled as to console;
to be understood as to understand;
to be loved as to love.
For it is in giving that we receive;
it is in pardoning that we are pardoned;
and it is in dying that we are born to eternal life. Amen

Guard your heart above all else,
for it determines the course of your life.
—Proverbs 4:23
New Living Translation ©2007

Endnotes

CHAPTER 1

1. Graeme Wood, "Secret Fears of the Super-Rich," *The Atlantic*, April 2011, http://www.theatlantic.com/magazine/archive/2011/04/secret-fears-of-the-super-rich/8419/2/.

CHAPTER 2

1. These specific forms of capital were first identified by family wealth counselor James E. Hughes Jr., owner of Families of Affinity, www.jamesehughes.com.
2. Adapted from James E. Hughes, *Family Wealth—Keeping It in the Family: How Family Members and Their Advisers Preserve Human, Intellectual, and Financial Assets* (New York: John Wiley & Sons), 2004. Used with permission.

CHAPTER 3

1. Erik H. Erikson, Identity: *Youth and Crisis* (New York: W. W. Norton & Company), 1968.
2. Adapted from Hughes, *Family Wealth—Keeping It in the Family*, 2004. Used with permission.

CHAPTER 5

1. Benedict Carey, "Study Says Eldest Children Have Higher I.Q.s," *The New York Times*, June 21, 2007, http://www.nytimes.com/2007/06/21/science/21cnd-sibling.html?pagewanted=all.
2. Del Jones, "First-Born Kids Become CEO Material," *USA Today*, September 3, 2007, http://www.usatoday.com/money/companies/management/2007-09-03-ceo-birth_N.htm.
3. Studio M Publishing, "The Birth Order Bugaboo," September 19, 2011, http://www.lakeprofile.com/2011/09/the-birth-order-bugaboo/.
4. Petter Kristensen and Tor Bjerkedal, "Explaining the Relation Between Birth Order and Intelligence," *Science*, June 22, 2007, http://www.sciencemag.org/content/316/5832/1717.abstract.
5. Marianne Neifert, MD, *Dr. Mom's Parenting Guide: Common-Sense Guidance for the Life of Your Child* (New York: Plume Books), 1996.
6. Adapted from Erik H. Erikson, *Childhood and Society* (New York: W. W. Norton & Co.), 1993.

Chapter 6

1. James Grubman, "Of Treasured Kids and Treasure Hunts," *Pitcairn Family Newsletter*, winter 2011.

2. Caro Rock, "In-Law Integration," *Family Business Magazine*, Autumn 2010, http://www.familybusinessmagazine.com/index.php?/articles/single/in-law_integration/.

3. Adapted, with permission, from *Assertiveness Guide* by Susan Christiance.

Chapter 7

1. Adapted from N. L. Tubesing and D. A. Tubesing (Eds), *Structured Exercises in Wellness Promotion: Vol. 1* (Duluth: Whole Person Press), 1983. Used with permission.

Chapter 8

1. Dr. Jill Murray, *But I Love Him: Protecting Your Teen Daughter from Controlling, Abusive Dating Relationships* (New York: Harper), 2000. Used with permission.

2. Adapted from Murray, *But I Love Him*, 2000. Used with permission.

Chapter 10

1. Meg Handley, "Consumers Still Buried in Credit Card Debt," *US News and World Report*, March 12, 2012, http://finance.yahoo.com/news/consumers-still-buried-credit-card-162849304.html.

2. Adapted from Richard A. Morris and Jayne A. *Pearl, Kids, Wealth, and Consequences: Ensuring a Responsible Financial Future for the Next Generation* (New York: John Wiley & Sons), 2010.

3. Adapted from John L. Levy, *Inherited Wealth: Opportunities and Dilemmas* (Charleston, SC: Booksurge) 2008.

4. Thanks to Dirk Junge for this description.

Chapter 11

1. Hartley Goldstone, "On Becoming an Excellent Trust Beneficiary," *Navigating the Trustscape*, February 22, 2012, http://navigatingthetrustscape.com/index.php/on-becoming-an-excellent-trust-beneficiary.

2. Hughes, *Family Wealth—Keeping It in the Family*, 2004. Used with permission.

3. Hughes, *Family Wealth—Keeping It in the Family*, 2004. Used with permission.

4. Hughes, *Family Wealth—Keeping It in the Family*, 2004. Used with permission.

5. Goldstone, "On Becoming an Excellent Trust Beneficiary."

Chapter 12

1. Adapted from Hughes, *Family Wealth—Keeping It in the Family*, 2004. Used with permission.

Acknowledgments

My desire in writing this book was to make the text as useful and as thoroughly accurate as possible. I want to thank many experts and resources for their generosity. Every one of these outstanding, amazing people helped me with crucial information and insight: Kay Abramowitz, Ted Austin, Jeff Auxier, Charlotte Beyer, Susan Christiance, Shelley Darcy, Kathryn Davison, Bev Dolan, Steve Duin, Hartley Goldstone, Ann Hargrave, Leah Hemeyer, Jay Hughes, Henry Krasnow, Dirk Junge, Kathleen Lansing, Jeffrey Lauterbach, John L. Levy, Daryl Olson, Stuart Patterson, Michelle Rand, Bob Sanders, and Karen Vinton.

Many have helped me bring this book to its current rendition, and I wish to thank each one. These are the accomplished professionals who have helped me structure the book and make it inviting to read: Ali McCart, Lionel Fisher, Martha Gannett, Vinnie Kinsella, Amy Miller, and Jayne Pearl. Thank you.

My biggest gratitude is to my husband, Jon. He is the world's best collaborator and editor. His understanding of the points I write about never ceases to amaze me. He often helps me with reality checks, and when he deems something important, he doesn't back down. The most remarkable aspect of his availability is his willingness to consider anything. My children, Julianne and Clay, almost grown now, provide frequent inspiration as they mature into strong, positive adults. I feel blessed to be in my precious family.

Resources

Recommended Books

Books are tremendous resources. In recommending a book, we can impart valuable knowledge, share our values, or suggest a new way to look at something. Following is a list of many books I have found useful in developing the concepts, principles, and strategies I teach. The list is varied, as they further develop insights included in all the chapters of this book. If you are focused on growing with or providing help to a family member, choose a book and read it together, discussing the salient points of each chapter as you go.

Bradley, Susan. *Sudden Money: Managing a Financial Windfall.* New York: John Wiley & Sons, 2000.
Sudden Money *is the definitive book on how to handle unexpected money. Read this book before you do anything.*

Brooks, Robert and Sam Goldstein. *Raising Resilient Children: Fostering Strength, Hope, and Optimism in Your Child.* Chicago: Contemporary Books, 2001.
Raising Resilient Children *is one of the best parenting books there is, for any family.*

Buffett, Mary. *Buffettology: The Previously Unexplained Techniques that Have Made Warren Buffett the World's Most Famous Investor.* New York: Fireside, 1997.
Any study of Warren Buffet's investing is a valuable read. Mary Buffet's book is the most user-friendly one I have found.

Burrough, Bryan. *The Big Rich: The Rise and Fall of the Greatest Texas Oil Fortunes.* New York: Penguin, 2009.
Burrough's book gives the reader plenty of grist for the mill if you have ever wondered how Texas oil fortunes were created.

Cline, Foster and Jim Fay. *Parenting with Love and Logic: Teaching Children Responsibility.* Colorado Springs: NavPress Publishing, 2006 edition.
This book is full of great parenting advice, and teaching children responsibility is essential to everything else I teach.

Cochell, Perry L. and Rodney C. Zeeb. *Beating the Midas Curse.* West Linn, OR: Heritage Institute Press, 2005.
This book addresses the many pitfalls of traditional estate planning, and in it the authors give great, practical advice on both estate and financial planning.

Collier, Charles W. *Wealth in Families.* Cambridge: Harvard University Press, 2006.
Collier's main focus is on philanthropy, and he wisely addresses the many facets of wealth management, including family relationships and values.

Covey, Sean. *The 7 Habits of Highly Effective Teens.* New York: Fireside, 1998.
Sean Covey, Stephen's son, has written a highly useful book for teens. The habits he describes and teaches are the same as his father's, only with perspective and material especially for teens.

Covey, Stephen. *The 7 Habits of Highly Effective Families.* New York: Golden Books, 1997.
Covey's comprehensive book illuminates and teaches the basic foundation of the family. He does this in a practical step-by-step manner, which is inspiring and easy to work through with all family members.

deWitt, Patrick. *The Sisters Brothers.* New York: Ecco, 2011.
If you have ever wondered about alternative lifestyles and views of wealth, and if you can stomach a fair amount of violence, this is a provocative novel.

Domini, Amy, Dennis Pearne, and Sharon Rich. *The Challenges of Wealth: Mastering Personal and Financial Conflicts.* Burr Ridge, IL: Irwin Professional Publishing, 1988.
Some of the first research and thoughts on the challenges of wealth in our modern era are written in this book. It is interesting as a historical reference point.

Doud, Ernest A., Jr., and Lee Hausner. *Hats Off to You 2: Balancing Roles and Creating Success in Family Business.* N.p., 2004.
In this book you will find the guidance you need for how to balance roles and create success in family business.

Dubin, Arlene. *Prenups for Lovers: A Romantic Guide to Prenuptial Agreements.* New York: Villard, 2001.
This book is a gem for taking what is possibly the most unromantic subject there is, prenups, and presenting it in a positive light. Valuable for anyone contemplating marriage.

Ellis, Charles. *Winning the Loser's Game: Timeless Strategies for Successful Investing.* New York: McGraw Hill, 2002.
Ellis's book is a useful primer on investment basics for those of us who are not experts in financial matters.

Gallo, Eileen and Jon Gallo. *Silver Spoon Kids: How Successful Parents Raise Responsible Children.* New York: McGraw-Hill Professional, 2001.
The emphasis on taking responsibility makes this parenting book useful.

Gersick, Kelin, et al. *Generation to Generation: Life Cycles of the Family Business.* Cambridge: Harvard Business, 1997.
This is the definitive book on family business, including all aspects of generational changes in leadership.

Gill, Michael Gates. *How Starbucks Saved My Life: A Son of Privilege Learns to Live Like Everyone Else.* New York: Gotham, 2007.
Gates tells his own story in this memoir, and his evolution is nothing short of profound. An inspiration.

Godfrey, Jolene and Kit Hinrichs. *Raising Financially Fit Kids.* Berkeley: Ten Speed Press, 2003.
This is an excellent how-to book on raising financially literate kids.

Goleman, Daniel. *Emotional Intelligence: Why It Can Matter More than IQ.* New York: Bantam Dell, 1995.
Goleman's classic is full of insight on the important role our emotions play in our lives. He includes examples to learn from and skills we can develop and apply.

Goldstone, Hartley and Kathy Wiseman. *TrustWorthy: New Angles on Trusts From Beneficiaries and Trustees.* Denver: Trustscape LLC (2012)

In Trustworthy *Hartley Goldstone and Kathy Wiseman have created inspiration and guidance for all who have any involvement in trusts. The reader will come away from their stories with hope and confidence in the power to shift to a better outcome.*

Goleman, Daniel. *Social Intelligence: The New Science of Human Relationships.* New York: Random House, 2006.

Social Intelligence *is focused on our relationships, and in this book, Goleman describes the many scientific aspects of relationships. He coaches the reader on how to use this knowledge and develop skills for relationships.*

Hartley, Bonnie Brown and Gwendolyn Griffith. *Family Wealth Transition Planning: Advising Families with Small Businesses.* New York: Bloomberg Press, 2009.

With a focus on strengthening family businesses, Hartley and Griffith give excellent advice on a tough challenge: transition planning.

Hausner, Lee, PhD. *Children of Paradise: Successful Parenting for Prosperous Families.* New York: Tarcher, 1990.

Children of Paradise *has been immensely helpful to many wealthy family members in understanding the landscape in which they live. This book offers guidance on parenting in this specialized, privileged situation.*

Hausner, Lee and Douglas K. Freeman. *The Legacy Family: The Definitive Guide to Creating a Successful Multigenerational Family.* New York: Palgrave Macmillan, 2009.

As generations multiply, the odds are against families striving to keep their legacies and their relationships intact. Hausner and Freeman's book details the practices that help families succeed in defying the odds.

Hughes, James E., Jr., *Family: The Compact among Generations.* New York: Bloomberg, 2007.

Hughes gives us the benefit of his eloquent gifts in describing the challenges for families to stay together and thrive over generations. He also gives us his observations of strategies that work.

Hughes, James E., Jr. *Family Wealth: Keeping It in the Family.* New York: Bloomberg, 2004.

This is the most substantial book on family wealth that we have. My clients love to read this book and discuss it on their way through. Sometimes we stay on one chapter for many explorations before moving on.

Hughes, James E., Jr., Susan Massenzio and Keith Whitaker. *The Cycle of the Gift: Family Wealth and Wisdom*. Hoboken, New Jersey: Bloomberg Press, 2012.

The Cycle of the Gift *is about giving well. When handled correctly, giving offers the opportunity to know yourself and recipients better. As shown in this book, giving can promote the well-being and growth of all involved.*

Jacobs, Deborah. *Estate Planning Smarts: A Practical, User-Friendly, Action-Oriented Guide*. Houston: DJ Working Unlimited Inc., 2009.

The title says it all. In a field that is sensitive to frequent changes in laws, Jacobs has crafted advice to help the reader take care of all the important facets.

Krasnow, Henry. *Your Lawyer: An Owner's Manual: A Business Owner's Guide to Managing Your Lawyer*. Evanston, IL: Agate B2, 2006.

This is one of my favorite books. Krasnow's sense of humor brings levity to a subject that can be intimidating. Beneath the fun ride of his style, he gives sound advice on practical legal matters.

Levine, Madeline. *The Price of Privilege: How Parental Pressure and Material Advantage Are Creating a Generation of Disconnected and Unhappy Kids*. New York: HarperCollins, 2006.

In a world in which many wealthy parents agonize over "stuff," this book sheds light on how our materialistic society is hurting our kids and what we can do about it.

Levy, John L. *Inherited Wealth: Opportunities and Dilemmas*. North Charleston, SC: BookSurge Publishing, 2008.

Levy is a pioneer in the field of the psychological challenges of wealth. He is an eloquent writer, and his observations in this book are extremely valuable.

Lewis, C. S. *Mere Christianity*. San Francisco: HarperCollins, 2001.

This book is for those who desire to examine Christianity with the hardest questions and with strong intellect. Because spiritual dimension is an asset in relationships, finding your spiritual focus is tremendously valuable.

Malkiel, Burton G. and Charles D. Ellis. *The Elements of Investing*. Hoboken, NJ: John Wiley & Sons, 2010.

I recommend this little book as the best, most user-friendly summary of the basics of investing.

Morris, Richard A. and Jayne A. Pearl. *Kids, Wealth, and Consequences: Ensuring a Responsible Financial Future for the Next Generation*. New York: John Wiley and Sons, 2010.

There is outstanding advice in this book for parents who are seeking guidance on how to impart financial literacy to their kids.

Nicholson, William. *Shadowlands*. New York: Plume, 1991.

This play is the story of growing up and learning to love. It reminds us to treasure each day as a precious gift.

O'Neill, Jessie H. *The Golden Ghetto: The Psychology of Affluence*. Milwaukee, WI: Affluenza Project, 1997.

O'Neill explores the emphasis our society places on material wealth. She encourages us each to acquire a healthy perspective on our own relationship with money and gives us guidance on how to do this.

Pipher, Mary. *Reviving Ophelia: Saving the Selves of Adolescent Girls*. New York: Ballantine Books, 1995.

This is the best book available on parenting girls. Pipher's ability to express her insights is exceptional, and any parent of a girl will benefit by reading this book.

Pipher, Mary. *The Shelter of Each Other: Rebuilding Our Families*. New York: Grosset, 1996.

In this book, Pipher turns her attention to the family and, as in Reviving Ophelia, *she writes with clarity and expertise about how to build strong families.*

Piver, Susan. T*he Hard Questions: 100 Essential Questions to Ask Before You Say "I Do."* New York: Tarcher, 2007.

Piver's book is exactly what the title says it is: the essential workbook for marriage, to be completed before the wedding.

Ruiz, Don Miguel. *The Four Agreements: A Practical Guide to Personal Freedom*. San Rafael, CA: Amber-Allen Publishing, 1997.

This little book packs a powerful message: simple, practical instructions on how to achieve freedom and happiness. An inspiring read for anyone.

Ruiz, Don Miguel. *The Mastery of Love: A Practical Guide to the Art of Relationship*. San Rafael, CA: Amber-Allen Publishing, 1999.

The Mastery of Love *offers practical, simple yet sophisticated advice on how to love others. Ruiz leaves us with hope and excitement to practice the principles he describes.*

Shelley, Susan. *The Complete Idiot's Guide to Money for Teens*. New York: Alpha Books, 2001.

Though I always introduce this book with an apology for its title, I love the book itself. Concepts are laid out in the most logical, practical manner imaginable. Shelley's descriptions are perfect even for mature teens, and her style of writing inspires confidence.

Smedes, Lewis B. *Forgive and Forget: Healing the Hurts We Don't Deserve*. San Francisco: HarperOne, 1996.

As I have said before, forgiveness is the single most powerful tool we have in relationships. Smedes's practical book can fill our wounded hearts with courage and hope.

Stanley, Thomas J. and William D. Danko. *The Millionaire Next Door: The Surprising Secrets of America's Wealthy*. Lanham, MD: Taylor Trade, 1996.

An insightful look into the private realities of the quiet ones among us who are wealthy. This book is a look at the best practices of the financially successful.

Stovall, Jim. *The Ultimate Gift*. Mechanicsburg, PA: Executive Books, 1999.

Although it's fiction, in many ways, The Ultimate Gift *is very similar to my first book,* Navigating the Dark Side of Wealth: A Life Guide for Inheritors. *The novel format works well and reiterates many of the same points I make.*

Twist, Lynne. *The Soul of Money: Transforming Your Relationship with Money and Life*. New York: W. W. Norton & Company, 2003.

Many of my clients find this book to be inspiring, especially in the realm of philanthropy.

Ward, John. *Perpetuating the Family Business: 50 Lessons Learned from Long-Lasting, Successful Families in Business*. New York: Palgrave Macmillan, 2004.

Ward's book is an excellent and thought-provoking guide to the important work of creating sustainability in the family business.

Willis, Thayer Cheatham. *Navigating the Dark Side of Wealth: A Life Guide for Inheritors.* Portland: New Concord Press, 2003.
Within these pages lies the guidance that, if taken to heart, can lead troubled inheritors to a more balanced and fulfilling life.

Recommended Movies

Reaching, motivating, and inspiring young adults can be a challenge fraught with awkward questions and evasive answers. More than ever before, family members are immersed in electronics: computers, smartphones, iPods, anything with a screen. While many of us who are older have become proficient at visiting the electronic world and can even get around in it pretty well, our children and grandchildren are natives. They've grown up on short bits of information presented in intriguing ways. A powerful key to reaching them is to find ways to speak with them in their language.

Most teenagers and young adults love to watch movies, and I have found that they can be thoughtful and articulate in discussing them. So I have developed a repertoire of movies that are relevant to the principles I teach. I have my younger clients watch selected movies from my list, and we then discuss the pertinent issues and values. You can do this too. Here are my favorites.

Feature Films

A Good Woman (2004) PG
The dynamics of relationships that involve at least one of the partners being out of money are shown intensified in this film. This is a provocative movie that will have you reflecting on morals and wealth.

Greedy (Michael J. Fox) (1994) PG-13
Many very real attitudes and behaviors are portrayed in this classic depiction of greed. Though seemingly overstated in a dramatic movie, the familiar human impulses are well represented. Watching can be helpful in understanding family members who are behaving badly.

The Inheritance (Arven) (2003) NR
The theme of this movie is the clash of personal hope and sense of duty. This takes place in the realm of family business pressures at their most intense. It is a tough movie to watch, as we see the damage that this stress can cause.

The Philadelphia Story (1940) NR

The Philadelphia Story *is the classic tale of an heiress, her men, society expectations, and love's demands. It is fun to experience the great Katharine Hepburn, Cary Grant, and James Stewart at their best, and thought provoking to watch them in their element in 1940.*

Pride and Prejudice (Keira Knightly) (2005) PG

Jane Austen's writing is rich in understanding of human interactions and emotions. In this movie, we see Elizabeth Bennet and Mr. Darcy struggle with the pride and prejudice they have acquired growing up in different classes.

The Pursuit of Happyness (Will Smith) (2006) PG-13

This movie, featuring a bright and penniless man working to make a life for his young son, inspires us all to think about our own pursuits of happiness.

Sense and Sensibility (BBC) (2008) NR

Questions about sincerity, seduction, and abandonment arise as two sisters, who are as different as night and day, explore possibilities with their suitors in this Jane Austen classic. By the end of the movie, we have all formed our answers.

The Ultimate Gift (2006) PG

Like Stovall's book of the same name, in many ways, the messages of The Ultimate Gift *are very similar to those in my first book,* Navigating the Dark Side of Wealth: A Life Guide for Inheritors. *Stovall has crafted a masterful story, which comes to life on the screen.*

Wall Street (1987) R

Wall Street *explores the bad behaviors of investor greed. Full of intrigue, it is sick but fascinating to watch.*

Wall Street: Money Never Sleeps (2010) PG-13

The infamous Gordon Gekko, out of prison after all these years, gets a new run at bad attitudes and behaviors. This time he uses his future son-in-law to accomplish his destruction. It's a view of what some people are like, and inheritors are wise to be aware.

Documentaries

The Ascent of Money: A Financial History of the World (PBS) (2008) NR
Best viewed in segments, not all at once, this documentary is a fascinating study of how money in our world developed as it has. There are surprising and not-so-surprising facts that contribute to the context and effectiveness of our financial capital.

Born Rich (2003) NR
Born Rich *is a look at the insular world of some of the world's richest young adults. Their realities are useful perspectives on our own beliefs and priorities.*

The One Percent (2006) NR
This film is a thoughtful exploration of the wealth gap. The interviews in it, for instance with Milton Friedman, Steve Forbes, and James (Jay) Hughes Jr., are varied and add depth to the complexity of the wealth gap challenges. The One Percent *offers an unusual view of our world.*

Index

About the Author

AN INTERNATIONALLY ACCLAIMED AUTHOR, educator, speaker, and leading authority in the area of wealth counseling, Thayer Cheatham Willis has been a licensed, practicing psychotherapist since 1990. Her primary focus is on facilitating a national and international clientele of inheritors and their families as they cope with the psychological challenges of wealth. A child of wealth herself, born into the founding family of the multinational Georgia-Pacific Corporation, she brings to her increasingly important field a unique insider's perspective on contending with family dynamics as they relate to the mental and emotional challenges of wealth.

Accredited with an M.A. from the University of Oregon and an M.S.W. from Portland State University, Thayer is a licensed clinical social worker, LCSW, specializing in wealth-related issues. Thayer offers over twenty years of hard-earned experience in a field she helped pioneer and dominates as one of its most prominent, foremost authorities. Working privately with a global client-base, she has helped thousands of inheritors and their families in six countries and four continents resolve wealth-related family conflicts.

Noted for her eloquent yet down-to-earth, no-nonsense, practical approach, Thayer has earned an international reputation as a renowned expert, charismatic educator, motivating presenter and inspiring keynote speaker. Her interactive approach to her specialty of relationship dynamics among families of wealth is based on field-tested methods that clarify and facilitate understanding, problem-solving and action-planning. Particularly proficient in assisting clients to create pathways between generations, Thayer helps clients prioritize parenting tasks while instilling financial responsibility in younger family members.

Thayer is the author of Navigating the Dark Side of Wealth: A Life Guide for Inheritors. This invaluable handbook for families on the difficult journey to freedom beyond wealth serves, in her own words, "a largely invisible, often misrepresented, long underserved population that commonly struggles with the psychological challenges inherent in the stewardship of wealth." Thayer has wrtitten many articles for *Worth* magazine and writes a quarterly newsletter, available on her website. She also has been interviewed for top financial publications including *The New York Times*, *The Wall Street Journal*, *Financial Times*, *The Business Journal* and *Time* magazine.